Red in the Rainbow

Red in the Rainbow

THE LIFE AND TIMES OF FRED AND SARAH CARNESON

LYNN CARNESON

Published by Zebra Press
an imprint of Random House Struik (Pty) Ltd
Reg. No. 1966/003153/07
80 McKenzie Street, Cape Town, 8001
PO Box 1144, Cape Town, 8000 South Africa

www.zebrapress.co.za

First published 2010

1 3 5 7 9 10 8 6 4 2

Publication © Zebra Press 2010
Text © Lynn Carneson 2010

Cover image © Lynn Carneson

All rights reserved. No part of this publication may be reproduced, stored in a retrieval system or transmitted, in any form or by any means, electronic, mechanical, photocopying, recording or otherwise, without the prior written permission of the copyright owners.

PUBLISHER: Marlene Fryer
MANAGING EDITOR: Robert Plummer
EDITOR: Beth Housdon
PROOFREADER: Lisa Compton
COVER DESIGNER: Michiel Botha
TEXT DESIGNER: Monique Oberholzer
TYPESETTER: Monique van den Berg
INDEXER: Sanet le Roux
PRODUCTION MANAGER: Valerie Kömmer

Set in 10.5 pt on 14.1 pt Minion

Printed and bound by CTP Printers, Boompies Street, Parow 7500

ISBN 978 1 77022 085 0

Over 50 000 unique African images available to purchase from our image bank at www.imagesofafrica.co.za

*This book is dedicated to my parents,
Fred and Sarah Carneson, my brother John and my sister Ruth.
It is also dedicated to all the brave and noble comrades who
enriched the lives of the Carnesons and changed the course of history.*

Contents

Foreword ix
Preface xiii
Acknowledgements xix

PART ONE | BLOOD OF THE RAINBOW: 1965–1967 1
1 A Kind of Hell 3
2 The Cruelty of Torture 11
3 Isolation 20
4 Prison Letters 23
5 The Trial 39
6 Comrades 51
7 The Sentence Begins 54
8 Family Under Surveillance 59

PART TWO | BLACK, WHITE AND RED: 1916–1967 73
9 Sarah Rubin 75
10 Fred Carneson 82
11 Courtship and Marriage 94
12 Relatively Free 101
13 Lost and Found 107
14 The *Guardian* 111
15 Named 114
16 56 Barrack Street 121
17 Banned 127
18 Defiance 131
19 The Freedom Charter 135
20 Treason 138
21 State of Emergency 150
22 No Going Back 163

23 Umkhonto we Sizwe 167
24 Split in Half 173
25 Banned Again 178
26 Snipers 182
27 Underground 186

PART THREE | JOURNEY INTO EXILE: 1968–1991 191
28 Dislocated 193
29 My Stars Are Trapped 207
30 Freedom Is Not Always Easy 221
31 The Struggle Continues 228
32 Unsafe in a Safe Place 237
33 Time to Travel 245
34 Nearly There 252

PART FOUR | RAINBOW DAYS: 1991–2010 257
35 A Warm Welcome 259
36 Turning Point 269
37 The Dream Danced Awake 272
38 Reflections 275
39 Late Life Love 282
40 'Bella, Ciao' 289

Epilogue: Was It Worth It? 295

Appendix: South African 'Comrades' 301
Abbreviations 303
Index 305

Foreword

Should auld comrades, dads and moms be forgot ...

WE USED TO meet secretly in Newlands Forest on the slopes of Table Mountain, at different hours, usually on Sunday mornings. 'Welcome to the boardroom,' Fred Carneson would say with a laugh as we gathered under a large tree deep in the woods, sometimes as soft rain was falling. The early 1960s were particularly dangerous for the underground resistance in Cape Town. If we were spotted, it meant ten years or more in jail for all of us.

One by one our numbers were to diminish. Individuals left South Africa to carry on the struggle, usually with great distinction, from abroad. The first to go were Chris Hani and Archie Sibeko, followed by Alex La Guma, Reggie September, Ray Alexander and her husband Professor Jack Simons, and Brian Bunting. Many had already been imprisoned, and some, like Looksmart Ngudle and Elijah Loza, tortured to death. Only Fred was left.

We all knew that the security police were waiting to pounce on him. Eventually they did so, and interrogated him with a vengeance for five days and nights, virtually without sleep: he collapsed and required oxygen support. People he was suspected of having worked with were relentlessly rounded up. I was one of them and, like Fred, was subjected to sleep deprivation. The police were hoping to break my spirit and turn me into a witness against Fred. I felt huge indignation: we were being punished not for being bad, but for being good – for fighting for a decent South Africa where everybody would have the vote and be treated as equals. Yet the prospect of being held endlessly in solitary confinement was unbearable. Equally unendurable was the idea of gaining release by giving evidence against Fred. I felt crushed by the dilemma, by my lack of clear courage.

Yet Fred performed one more act of bravery: aided by some brilliant defence by his counsel, Sam Aaron, he took full personal responsibility for the underground work he had done. The result prevented us from being called to testify. Greater love hath no man than this, to give his liberty for the lives of his friends. Many of us were saved by his ultimate gesture: Amy Thornton, Simon Eggert, Gillian Jewell and Bernard Gosschalk are just some names that spring to mind. These people, together with many others, formed our generation, of which Fred was a steadfast and energetic member.

Some years into Fred's sentence, when I was living in exile in London, his daughter Lynn married Charles McGregor at the Quaker Meeting House in Hampstead. The undoubted high point of the ceremony was the reading out of a letter from Pretoria Central Prison in which Fred stated that he raised his tin mug to the bridal couple. Now, forty years later, in a heartfelt and vividly told story, Lynn lifts her tin mug to her dad. The gesture is also to her mom, Sarah, and all those who, without ever achieving office or fame, defied repression and taboo to give reality in their lives to their beliefs. This they did by joining the Communist Party, willing to give their lives in the fight led by the African National Congress for a non-racial, democratic and socially just South Africa. By imagining a different world, they led extraordinary lives, had remarkable stories to tell and contributed directly towards the massive transformation our country has undergone.

Fred's story, like that of countless South Africans, has never been fully told. He was by far the bravest and most resolute of us all. Yet, today, his name is barely known outside of his family and to those who worked closely with him. I read this book with pride and joy, knowing that at last he was being honoured, and in a most fitting fashion, too. And I was especially moved by the fact that the tribute to him was being conjoined with a sensitive eulogy to Sarah Carneson, a principled and committed activist herself, who, in addition to all her other contributions to the freedom struggle, bore the brunt of maintaining a home for the family and looking after the children in conditions of severe repression.

The story of Fred and Sarah is one of pain mixed with joy. Throughout, the reader follows the emotions of children who sought to understand the predicaments in which they found themselves and who wrestled with the question of why their lives were so different from those of other children their age. Many have questioned whether it was morally permissible for people like Fred and Sarah to volunteer for a cause which could result in their children growing up in circumstances of loss and insecurity. And, to further complicate the matter, the struggle for justice is not always just in its individual outcomes. For all his exceptional courage, Fred never recovered the extraordinary ebullience of his days of militancy. Nor was he to be elevated to positions of honour or senior responsibility.

Yet, far from railing against her parents for choosing the path of the liberation struggle, Lynn writes with pride at being the child born into a family of such calibre. What Fred and Sarah did was not for honour or material advantage; it was for their dignity, for their right to live as free people in a free country. Their huge gain was to feel the exaltation of living in a country where the basic rights for which they had fought were at last being acknowledged. In that sense they lost their personal security but profited by gaining a whole world, a world of justice that validated the idealism of their endeavours.

A feeling of elation shines through this narrative of terror and tribulation. The Red in the Rainbow was often hidden by clouds of repression and disinformation. And, many would say it besmirched itself by defending the indefensible. Yet there is a core crimson idealism that transcends ages and circumstances. This book captures the quintessentially honest energy of two brave individuals, Fred and Sarah, who, like millions of other South Africans, believed in and helped to achieve a country based on human dignity, equality and freedom. Thank you, Lynn, for writing it.

ALBIE SACHS
JANUARY 2010

Preface

ON THE EVENING of 16 June 2000, I was sitting in my London rooftop garden sipping a glass of white wine and enjoying the summer fragrance of bright pink and red roses when my mother, Sarah, phoned me from Cape Town. 'Dad is not well,' she said. 'How soon can you come back?' I knew it was serious.

I flew to Cape Town on the next plane so that I could go with them to the hospital to talk to the specialist. When I arrived, my parents were extremely anxious. They had been on a holiday to Avalon Springs and Fred had collapsed in the Montagu hotel. Our family doctor had suggested a brain scan, and the prognosis did not seem good.

We were all silent on the way to Groote Schuur Hospital. When we arrived, my father held our hands and said, 'I feel that this is not going to go well.' We were not surprised when the consultant told us that my father had a brain tumour but, when Fred asked, 'How much time do I have left?' we were utterly shocked by the doctor's response. My father had about two more months to live. Although we sensed that this was no false alarm, we knew that my father had such a love of life that he would fight for every second he had left.

While he could still walk, we went to the beach at St James to watch the waves crashing on the rocks. Fred asked me, 'Can you write our story?' He felt that he and my mother had gone through so much that their lives should not be forgotten.

The promise I made that day started my journey of discovery about Fred and Sarah. Children take their parents for granted, but I began to ask, who were they really, these parents of mine? Could I, together with my brother John and my sister Ruth, learn from the lives that they had led? Had the sacrifices they made for their country been worthwhile? I started to learn how a man who tenderly loved his family had ended up being tortured and imprisoned as an enemy of the state; how my mother had

PREFACE

quietly and steadily continued to work underground, even though she was banned and under twenty-four-hour surveillance; how, though frequently arrested, she had managed to make ends meet and keep the family together; and how their difficult lives had affected their marriage and, inevitably, their children.

Why was it so important to write this book? Historically and politically, my parents made a significant contribution to the liberation of South Africa from apartheid. Had it not been for them and their small group of white comrades who fought side by side with the African National Congress in tough times, South Africa might not have been as tolerant of different races as it is today. Because they were humble people who never acted in their own self-interests, they could easily be overlooked, but their input and sacrifices should not be forgotten.

Writing as a daughter, it wasn't possible to be objective about their lives. They and their comrades had a huge impact on me, although my own struggle and life path has been very different. It is not often that one has the opportunity to live with real heroes. My parents were very human, with their own personalities, strengths, sense of humour, faults and failings. They affected me both painfully and joyfully.

To be as true to them as possible and to tell the story as 'their story' rather than 'my story', I asked them to talk to me and write about their own lives, thoughts and feelings. I also interviewed other family members and comrades who knew them. Fred and Sarah worked underground, often separately and in secret, so this was the only way I could uncover what they were doing at certain times of their lives. Fortunately, before my father died, my son Simon, Wasima Fisher and Margaret Green spent hours recording my parents talking about their childhoods.

Because they were highly organised and had a strong sense of history, my parents left boxes and boxes of family archives, prison letters, newspaper clippings and pamphlets from different periods. I also managed to get hold of their police files. This book is based on all of these sources. Where relevant, I have quoted complete letters to give as accurate a picture of them as possible.

The story spans seventy-five years. It is not just a book about two political activists; it is also a love story about the long-lasting marriage of two very different, strong-minded people. Both were second-generation South Africans: my mother came from a cultured liberal, but puritanical, Jewish Russian–Lithuanian background with a deeply embedded commitment to communism, while my father was of poor, hard-drinking, working-class Catholic, Portuguese, Scottish, Irish and German descent. Their expectations, especially regarding the equality and roles of men and women, often conflicted. What drew them together was their belief and commitment to the struggle. The fact that they stayed together through many years of tension and separation is nothing short of a miracle. Testimony to the deep love that they felt for each other and for their family are their letters to each other, written when one or both of them were in prison or in hiding.

As I moved through their history, I felt that the quality and spirit of each time period was dancing in front of me. Many of these stories brought back memories of my own childhood, so where relevant I have shared some of my own and my siblings' experiences. It is my hope that this will provide a vivid sense of what it was like to survive years of oppression, to joyfully experience their end and then to live in a country with a new history and an uncharted future.

This book is called *Red in the Rainbow* for two reasons. The first is that my parents' lifelong dream was that South Africa would be a peaceful country in which all races could live in harmony with each other. The first democratic election in 1994, an event that they had fought so hard and sacrificed so much for, inspired the world. Nelson Mandela, at his inauguration as first black president of South Africa, called the country the 'Rainbow Nation':

> We have triumphed in the effort to implant hope in the breasts of the millions of our people. We enter into a covenant that we shall build the society in which all South Africans, both black and white, will be able to walk tall, without any fear in their hearts, assured of their inalienable right to human dignity – a rainbow nation at peace with itself and the world … We dedicate this day to all the heroes and heroines in this country and the rest of the world who sacrificed in many ways and surrendered their lives so that we could be free. Their dreams have become reality. Freedom is their reward … The sun shall never set on so glorious a human achievement!

The second reason for the name *Red in the Rainbow* is that my parents were dedicated communists. They, together with their comrades, were the 'Red' in South Africa's Rainbow. Jim Connell, political activist of the late nineteenth and early twentieth centuries, wrote the famous socialist anthem 'The Red Flag', which captures the spirit of communism as experienced by my parents in their youth:

> The people's flag is deepest red,
> It shrouded oft our martyred dead,
> And ere their limbs grew stiff and cold,
> Their hearts' blood dyed its every fold.
> Then raise the scarlet standard high.
> Within its shade we'll live and die,
> Though cowards flinch and traitors sneer,
> We'll keep the red flag flying here.

My parents came from a world in which bloody battles were the norm. Workers were beaten up, and they had to deal with the carnage of the First World War, the Holocaust and the Second World War. They were deeply concerned about the plight of the disadvantaged, and believed that communism was a viable alternative to the oppressive effects of colonialism, capitalism and fascism. International communism would unite the human race and build an equal, just and peaceful society for everyone. If it was necessary to sacrifice oneself for the greater cause, then so be it. In South Africa, the liberation of the country and its people from the oppression of apartheid needed to be achieved, followed by the development of democracy.

As a child, I experienced living in an environment where communists were hated and punished. I often questioned who the real terrorists were: The oppressive regime? Those that opposed it? Or both? We were treated like devils or lepers. But I knew that my parents were good people who were doing their best to make South Africa a better country for all. It was ironic that most of the white population practised the very behaviour they accused my parents and their comrades of enacting. Frequently I wonder whether I would have the courage to stand up to what I know is wrong in a repressive regime. It is difficult to predict what will happen when one's ability to endure an impossible situation is stretched beyond endurance.

My family was exposed to the effects of terrible cruelty in a hostile environment over a long period of time. What was hardest for me was the suffering of close family members and friends. It is difficult to know what is worse – those of us who witness our loved ones suffering or those that suffer first-hand. The horror, the fear and the grief are wounds that are deeply embedded in my soul. There were periods when I felt that my intense anxiety, anger and loneliness would destroy me, but my parents' courage and perseverance helped me through hard times. What I gained from my parents was more than an academic understanding of political theory: they gave me a sense of right and wrong, of justice and of compassion. They imparted their deep love of all human beings and showed me how important it is for people to have a vision, and to dance their dreams awake. They gave me faith in the goodness of people, including myself. My parents certainly had their weaknesses and faults, some of which I have inherited, but these were not important. As they grew older, more than anything else I benefited from their growing capacity for loving life and each other. They were highly political, but they were also parents, friends and comrades. There is something very special about the unity of a family that has been through hell and has emerged intact.

When I was small, I used to believe that I could climb up one side of a rainbow and slide down the other side. By exploring the Red of the Rainbow, I have discovered that there is much more than gold at rainbow's end.

Acknowledgements

I WOULD LIKE TO thank the following people, who helped me on this journey:

Lionel Snell, my constant companion, husband and support, who helped edit and compile the pictures.

Anne Schuster, Clare Gibbons, Mike Nicol and Ron Irwin, who guided me through my writing.

Members of the Carneson and Rubin families, who contributed greatly.

Sherry Woods, my PA.

Carol Opie, Wasima Fisher, Margaret Green, Simon McGregor, Sonya Niederhumer, Benita Loff and Busisiwe Carneson, who helped me with research or interviewed people on my behalf.

UWC–Robben Island Museum Mayibuye Archives, for permission to reproduce pages of the *Guardian*, *New Age* and *Spark*, as well as Eli Weinberg's Treason Trial photograph.

My editors, Beth Housdon and Robert Plummer, and the staff at Zebra Press.

I would also like to thank those who agreed to be interviewed or provided input for the book: Zuraya and Fuard Adhikarie, Kader and Louise Asmal, Hilda and Rusty Bernstein, Doug Brown, Brian Bunting, Jacques de Wet, Phillip Dexter, Peter Gabriel, Denis Goldberg, Bernie Gosschalk, Major Holloway, George Johannes, Wasima Fisher, Sadie Foreman, Zaahida Hartley, Willie Hofmeyr, Norma and Basil Jaffe, Kay and Mansoor Jaffer, Pallo Jordan, Ronnie Kasrils, Wolfie Kodesh, Blanche La Guma, Sheila Lapinski, Caroline Lassalle, Leon and Lorna Levy, Margaret Ling, Nontobeko and Dumisani Mafu, formerly Bongi and Mazolo, Phyllis Naidoo, Saru Naidoo, Lionel and Carol Opie, Michael Richman, Albie Sachs, Reggie September, Errol Shanley, Garth Strachan, Bubbles Thorn, Amy Thornton, Louis and Pamela Tsolekile, Ben and Mary Turok and many others.

LYNN CARNESON
MARCH 2010

PART ONE

Blood of
the Rainbow

1965–1967

1.

A Kind of Hell

WHEN I RUSHED from England to Cape Town in June 2000 because my father was dying, it was the second time that I had had to make an emergency trip across the oceans. The first was in 1965, when I was twenty. I was living in London, completing three glorious years of training at the Central School of Speech and Drama and looking forward to Christmas and New Year parties. My life would have been perfect, except for the deep anxiety gnawing at me like a constant bad toothache. My father, Fred Carneson, was in hiding in Cape Town. It was only a matter of time before the security police would arrest him. I knew that, when he was caught, he would be tortured as most of his other comrades who were in jail or dead had been.

On 8 December, I woke up after an all-night panic attack. Anne and David Hutton, with whom I was staying, knocked on the door, saying softly, 'Can we come in?' As they entered I said, 'You don't need to tell me. It's bad news.'

'Your mother has just phoned to say that your father was arrested at eight this morning under the 180-day detention law. She's not allowed to leave the house, so she wants you to go home as soon as possible. She doesn't know where he is or what is happening and there is no one else around to help.'

'I'll find out flight times,' I said.

'We've seen to that. We have already booked your flight.'

I arrived on 19 December 1965. It was sad not to be greeted at Cape Town airport, but I knew that neither my mother nor her friends were allowed to meet me. Under house arrest for their political activity, they were confined to the areas around their homes and were banned from venturing further afield. I took a taxi and arrived home half an hour later. I walked up the steps lined with my much-loved cycad trees, the flower beds around the lawns blazing with purple, yellow and red dahlias and *vygies*. The familiar sound of water from the fountain welcomed me back. I had left over two and a half years earlier, in 1963, and it was good to return to Mount Pleasant, my old home at 49 Belmont Avenue, Oranjezicht. I had forgotten how beautiful the house and garden were.

My mother opened the door and we hugged. She put her finger to my lips to remind me that the house was bugged. I went up the stairs to my bedroom on the first floor. I loved that room with its green shutters opening onto the balcony, which was bordered by a delicately carved dark-green wrought-iron railing. The sea shimmered below and tranquil Table Bay was full of yachts and ships. I could see across to Robben Island, where so many of my parents' black comrades were imprisoned. As I walked to the other end of the balcony and turned the corner, I saw the woods behind the house and, above them, Table Mountain, magnificent against a clear blue sky. After having been away for two years, I felt the same, and yet different. My home was familiar; I belonged here. But I had tasted other countries and cultures and gained new perspectives, which made what was happening all the more shocking and painful. How could there be so much misery in all that beauty?

I already knew that this period would be one of the worst times of our lives.

While my father was indeed being tortured in prison, the rest of my family also suffered. Not only did we not know what was happening to him or where he was being held, but my forty-eight-year-old mother, an ordinarily cheerful, cuddly, generous person, was coping with extreme financial hardship and anxiety. The Nationalist government had frozen my parents' bank accounts. Although banned, Sarah had obtained special permission to run a guest house and to do administrative work for the Cape Town Eisteddfod, but only as long as she was not in the presence of more than two people at a time. Restricted to a small area around Oranjezicht, she was permitted to go to the nearest shop and to take a short bus ride once a week, when she had to report to the police station. If she wanted to go anywhere else by bus, she would have to ask permission – which, she knew, would be denied, as the police believed her to be too dangerous for the company of the general public. She didn't drive and her friends were not allowed to contact her. Most, in fact, were in the same boat. If she breached her banning orders she risked being arrested and jailed, a threat that was meant: she and my father, before his final arrest, had been thrown into jail on a number of occasions for breaking their banning orders. The house and garden were bugged and the house was under twenty-four-hour surveillance.

When I arrived home that December, my brother John, who was fifteen at the time, was recovering from aches and bruises caused by trying to warn Fred that the security police were there to arrest him. Eight policemen had piled out of three cars. 'Dad was out when they came so they stood inside the front door waiting for him,' John told me. 'I tried to warn him by jumping out of the window from the upper balcony, but a policeman got there first. Dad yelled at me, "Don't you ever jump from the first floor. It is too dangerous. What were you playing at?"' Then John, his friend Maurice, who was with him that day, my younger sister Ruth and my mother looked on as the police clamped handcuffs on Fred and pushed him roughly into a car. They watched the police car drive away until they could see it no more.

John was constantly anxious and had nightmares every night for years after this. He was accident prone and repeatedly stubbed his toes. But he braved things out, cracked jokes and spent as much time as possible diving for fish or mountain climbing with his friends.

My sister Ruth was a physically well-developed, pretty thirteen-year-old with long black hair and green eyes. My mother, said Ruth later, did her best to keep their spirits up: 'One day there was a man on the opposite side of the road reading a newspaper. He was holding it in front of his face. We knew he was Special Branch. It got dark and he was sitting there in the dark reading the paper. So Mom crossed the road and said, "Would you like a torch to help you?" Another time Ma and I went for a walk. A "tail" was sitting on a bench just in front of us. He hurriedly put the newspaper in front of his face. It was upside down. Mom went up to him and said, "Excuse me. Your newspaper is upside down."

'The Special Branch used to follow me to school and back and scared off most of my friends. They also asked the guests to spy on Mom. There was a fat man who would sit all day and night outside Mom's bedroom door. When we went past in the corridor, the dog used to growl. Some of the other guests thought that the man was having an affair with Mom!'

Ruth also had nightmares every night and my mother would often have to calm her down. Sometimes, late at night, my mother would check to see if Ruth was all right and find her bed empty. Ruth used to climb out of the window in the middle of the night and not say where she had been. She later told me that she often snuck out to join a group of young boys who drank their parents' alcohol and smoked dagga. My mother, who was worried about Ruth's safety, was also concerned because she thought that some of these boys were police informers.

Both John and Ruth were very confused. Neither understood what was happening or why my father had been away from the house for long periods of time before he was arrested. In London, so far away from my family, I felt helpless. Every day I would wake up with a knot in my stomach. I went frequently to South Africa House, the South African embassy, to read the newspapers for reports on my parents and our friends. There was very little news. Everything was secretive. We knew only that my parents' comrades were being taken in for interrogation and that people were being tortured and dying in jail. Old family friends were being arrested as state witnesses to testify against my father and other members of the Communist Party. We were terrified about what would happen to them. When I arrived in Cape Town after my father's arrest, my mother, brother and sister were tense and bewildered. A diary entry of mine from the time, titled 'Mount Unpleasant, Cape Town', describes the atmosphere:

> We could not speak freely in the house on the day I arrived. Mom insisted on talking on the pavement two blocks down because she said there were electronic bugs everywhere. I asked, 'What, even in the garden?' She told me, 'Yes, even in the garden and in the hedges around the garden.' Days after arriving from the safety of London, there I was, searching for bugs. So far I've found three: one on the branch of a tree, another in a hedge and one in an urn with roses in it. Inside the house I've found bugs in books – they even hollowed out my favourite poetry book! I've also found bugs in vases and on the tops of the kitchen and bedroom doors. The microphones were picking up our conversation everywhere. Because the phones were tapped and we were surrounded by security police, it was impossible to find any privacy. As we walked, so did two security men at a discreet distance behind us.
>
> Mom managed to say that the day before I arrived six security men had brought my father to the house to do another search for incriminating evidence. She was relieved that he was still alive and able to walk. Three came from Cape Town and three probably came from Pretoria. My father was handcuffed. My mother said, 'He did not look too good. I had baked a Christmas cake ready for Christmas and took it out of its tin. I cut it

into slices and offered it to the security police because I could not just offer it to Fred. Van Wyk [senior member of the Security Branch] from Cape Town refused a slice, saying, "I don't know whether it is poisoned."' But one of the men from Pretoria accepted a piece. 'We hear that your wife is a good cook,' he said to my father. After he took a piece, the others helped themselves and my mother was able to let my father have a slice.

My mother was busy running the house, cooking and looking after guests, but I knew she was struggling. One morning after breakfast I asked her whether she would like an apple or a pear. It took her half an hour of agonising to decide which to choose. In the end, she asked me to decide for her. She never mentioned what she thought might be happening to my father. I tried to be calm and practical and to give her strength, but could not help worrying about what might happen to John and Ruth if she were also arrested.

In spite of the lovely weather and the city's unspeakable natural beauty, pain was everywhere: rivers of suffering flowed through the whole country. Fear was so deeply entrenched in the apartheid system that I knew we would need all our human strength and more. We did not want to give the security police the satisfaction of breaking us down past resistance point. All we could do was focus on small everyday tasks and try to immerse ourselves in them. I found solace in pruning roses and dead-heading huge pink and yellow daisy bushes.

Every day the news was worse. Too many suicides in prisons were being reported, and we knew what that meant. You just don't throw yourself out of a multi-storey police building when you are shackled and handcuffed. I would sit on the veranda and look over the bay and wish that I could wave a wand to stop it all from happening. Fortunately Lionel Opie, a South African friend I had met in England – a Rhodes Scholar from Oxford University – had returned home to visit his family, who lived in Cape Town. He came to see me and we went to Muizenberg beach for a walk. Later on he took me walking in the Cederberg for a few days. We did not talk politics or difficulties, but I sensed that he knew what was going on. His normality covered me like a comforting blanket. I told him that it was dangerous to visit us, and he replied, 'Why should that stop me?' Later, I asked him to park his car around the block. I didn't want the security police to be able to trace him.

For days I had tried, without success, to find out where my father was being held. I sent letters to the authorities and I phoned almost every prison in South Africa. Then, on 13 January, my father's birthday, I had an intuitive hunch to phone Caledon Square Police Station in Cape Town.

The phone was continuously engaged, but after six attempts I got through. 'I am trying to find out about my father, Fred Carneson, who has been detained without trial. Who can I speak to?' I waited for an eternity. Then an abrupt voice said, 'You can see him tomorrow. He is being charged.'

'What for?'

'Sabotage. And that, lady, carries the death sentence.' The phone went dead.

I arrived at Caledon Square Police Station, my heart pounding like a loud drumbeat. My mouth was dry. At the dark-brown-painted reception desk there were two policemen dressed in khaki. I asked where my father was, and one pointed up the stairs: 'Second floor. Room 201.' I entered a dirty-cream room. There were two more khaki-uniformed policemen behind another cheap wooden counter.

'I'm Lynn Carneson. I've an appointment to see my father.' They ignored me. 'Excuse me, do I wait here?' One policeman pointed to the side of the room. I stood waiting, feeling nauseous.

My father appeared in a doorway in a corner of the room. He was so thin he looked as if he had come out of a concentration camp. He was having difficulty walking and held on to the counter for support. We embraced, and I felt the fragility of his bones. He looked so much older. I have never seen a look of such total exhaustion and bewildered desolation. He said very quickly, before he could be stopped, 'Let them know the methods made it impossible not to crack. Other people must be prepared for this.' One of the policemen said that we were to stand apart and that we had only ten minutes. My father asked me about Mom, John, Ruth and the house.

'They are fine. All bearing up well.' He leant forward to listen, and I realised that he was having difficulty hearing me. I raised my voice a little. 'My hearing is damaged,' he said in response.

'If you talk again about your condition, she will have to go,' barked the policeman.

I told him about the latest play I had seen in London – *Macbeth*. I talked about the production and the acting, using the play to try to communicate what was happening in the country. I used fictitious names of uncles and aunts to tell him who had been arrested and who had got away. I also told him that I had gone especially to the Royal Festival Hall in London to listen to Beethoven's 'Pastoral' for him, as it was his favourite music. I was relieved to see the glimmer of a smile. But he was also crying, tears streaming down his cheeks. He wiped his face with his sleeves. He seemed stunned and I was not sure how much of what I was saying he understood. What I did know was that he was pleased to see me.

In the middle of a sentence they stopped me: 'You have to go now.' With the ghost of a smile of the dad I used to know, my father said, 'It's wonderful to see you, Lynn. They won't keep me down long.' In no time at all, the visit was over.

I went down the stairs feeling numb. 'I must stay calm,' I told myself, 'no matter what. Close down – have no feelings, or I won't be able to cope. I have to cope.'

A little way down the street was a bench under a palm tree. I sat down and stared into space for a long time. Then a wagtail hopped onto the bench and looked at me with its head to one side. I decided it was time to go home and tell my mother about the visit. At least I could let her know that Dad was alive and on his own two feet – just.

The morning after my visit to my father, the papers were full of news about him. He was accused of sabotage, being a member of the South African Communist Party (SACP) and being in possession of illegal literature. If found guilty of the first two charges, he could be sentenced to death or, at the very least, be given a life sentence. We were not enthusiastic about either prospect.

Having located my father, the next challenge would be to find lawyers who would defend him, particularly as we did not have the R25 000 or more that we would need for the legal fees. My first step was to go to our old friend and family lawyer, Himie Bernadt, but when I arrived at his office, he was shaking. He looked up at the ceiling to indicate that we were being bugged and said loudly, 'I can't help you. They have just been here and say I will lose my licence.' At the same time he wrote down a number on a piece of paper and slid it over the desk. 'I can't help you any more. Get out.' I walked past his desk and slipped the note into my pocket. It was the number of Defence and Aid, an organisation that would shortly be banned. Desperate for help in any form, I found a phone booth and phoned the number.

'Defence and Aid? Hello, who's speaking?'

'My name's Lynn Carneson. My father's in prison for political purposes. We need some help.' Silence. Then, 'Where are you? Someone will meet you outside Stuttafords in half an hour. He has dark-brown hair, wears glasses and has a green shirt.' The phone went dead. I felt that I was in some kind of Kafka-like nightmare of shadows, doubts and paranoia – but this was for real, not a novel or a film.

The man wearing the dark-green shirt was already there when I arrived, taking quick puffs from his cigarette. He did not introduce himself. I explained the situation, and he replied that Defence and Aid was under threat and extremely stretched for funds. He suggested that I try Christian Action in London.

I had a problem, however, because I couldn't phone from the tapped home phone but to phone from a call box would take more money than I had on me. I managed to dial collect to David and Anne in London. They said they would see what they could do. I knew that there would be no help from anyone in South Africa; it was simply too dangerous for them. The only hope lay outside the country.

I had to go to different phone booths with lots of change three times before David had an answer: 'They have agreed to pay for the lawyers' fees. Arrangements will be made to pay Mr Sam Aaron, who has agreed to defend your father.'

When I put the phone down, my hands were trembling and I was in tears. 'There are people out there in the world who care about us after all,' I thought. 'They really care.' I travelled home so quickly to tell my mother that I was not even aware of how I got there. At least I could go back to London feeling that one important thing had been accomplished.

London was cold, damp and bleak. My anxiety attacks returned. It was difficult to concentrate. Every minute was spent worrying about my mother, John and Ruth, and imagining how my father was. Would he survive? What had they done to him? How had they managed to reduce him to a shadow of his former self?

2

The Cruelty of Torture

WE FOUND OUT what had happened to my father in detention a long five months later, on 15 May 1966, when he was permitted to read out a statement in court before he was sentenced. Even then, his statement did not include everything that the security police had inflicted on him.

On Wednesday 8 December 1965 I was taken into detention under the 180-day clause. I was told that I was being held as a state witness in the trial against [Bram] Fischer.

As I turned in from the street I saw my son John jump through his bedroom window, a drop of some two metres. Before I could reprimand him, two men rushed from behind the corner of the garage. One yanked open the door of the car and said, 'You are under arrest; it's no good trying to get away.'

I realised then that Johnny's leap through the window had been a desperate attempt to warn me, to give me time to escape. Two Special Branch men had kept him and a playmate penned in his bedroom to make sure he did not slip out of the house. When Johnny had heard the familiar sound of my car he had dashed to the window and, before they could grab him, flung it open and made his jump.

Later, while taking me to Caledon Square, Major Rousseau, head of the Special Branch in Cape Town, said to me, *'Jou seuntjie is 'n baie dapper mannetjie'* [Your son is a very brave little man].

I only hoped that I would prove as brave as he had been.

The men, one in front and one behind, led John and me through the kitchen door into the lounge, where Major Rousseau was waiting with another three or four men. He told me that I was being held under the 180-day law. Sarah stood with her arms around Ruthie's shoulders. Ruth was wide-eyed, apprehensive. They came forward to embrace me, watched closely by the Special Branch men.

Sarah turned to Rousseau and said, her voice strained, 'Don't you let anything happen to him.'

'Don't worry, Mrs Carneson,' he replied, 'nothing will happen to him as long as he is in my care.' In the event, I was not to remain in his care for very long.

They took me off clutching a small suitcase containing a toothbrush, a safety razor, a shirt and a change of underwear. Sarah, Ruth and John followed us to the gate, where we embraced once more.

We waved to each other as the car pulled off. It would be a long time before I next had a chance to embrace my family.

On the way to Caledon Square, Rousseau stopped in Adderley Street for five minutes. Crowds were beginning to go home, and sitting there between two hefty Special Branch men I was suddenly very acutely aware of being a captive and just how isolated I was. I already felt cut off from normal life. The people who were passing by in the street were no longer part of my community; I was cut off from them completely. It was a very sharp, painful feeling.

They then took me to Caledon Square and left me in the charge office, with a policeman guarding me, of course. I waited there for twenty/thirty minutes and then two men came in, two Special Branch men – one a hefty florid-faced man, the other thinner, but equally mean-looking, and they said, 'Come!'

There's not much politeness in police stations. They took me upstairs, and as we were going upstairs, Swanepoel – he was a major at that time – said, 'We are the two men you said killed your comrade and fellow freedom fighter, Looksmart Ngudle.'

When I heard of Looksmart's death I had asked others, who were under interrogation at that time in Pretoria, who had killed Looksmart. They had named Swanepoel and, I think, Ferreira. They had been part of the team, with Swanepoel heading it, that was responsible for Looksmart's death. I had put this information in a report somewhere or other. I don't know how they got hold of it. They knew that I had reported them as being responsible. That wasn't a very good start.

They took me into a room. It was a small room with a simple deal table and four or five chairs. The walls of the room were lined with soundproofing, probably to facilitate the tape-recording of questions and answers and some other things too. They sat me on the one chair and they sat on the other side. Swanepoel asked if I wanted to make a statement. I said, 'No, I don't want to make a statement.' Swanepoel replied, 'They all start off like that …' and we sat in silence. I was quite determined at that stage not to make any statement whatsoever.

We had discussed in the Party what tactics we should use when under interrogation, and various ideas were put forward. One was that we should have a cover-up story, tell the story and stick to it. But after long discussion, it was decided that the best tactic would be not to answer any questions. Hold out for as long as you could, but don't talk. So they looked at me and I looked at them, and that was it. We just sat there, looking at each other. At around about seven or eight that evening, they said, 'Come, we want something to eat.' They put me in a motor car and took me down to the Grand Parade, where there was a 'café-de-move-on'. They ordered some food for themselves and asked me if I would like something to eat. I declined. So they ate and when they were finished took me back to the interrogation room.

I thought that this was a funny business. Normally you would be banged into a cell and that would be that. There were a number of suitcases in the room. I looked at them but didn't say anything. Swanepoel said, 'You are going off to Pretoria tomorrow, by military plane. You would be surprised how many people have ended up on the ground in the Karoo, slipping out of the plane.'

I didn't say anything. If it was going to happen it was going to happen, but I didn't think it likely. I felt that they were just trying to put the wind up me.

They kept me up the whole night and would not let me sleep during the day. This went on and on for days. Sometimes one of them would go off for a spell, and come back, and the other would go off. They kept me up all night asking questions, or banging the table, or rustling papers – that sort of thing. Your nerves are so much on edge that it would have been difficult to sleep even under much more comfortable conditions.

One morning, they took me down to the police mess and gave me a bit of breakfast, then took me to the airport – I think it was Youngsfield Military Airport – and we flew up to Pretoria. I noticed that when they filled in details for the passenger list they entered me under a false name, Constable Somebody-or-other. I thought to myself, 'I'm going to have a tough time up there; I'm going to try to get some sleep on the plane.' But they were much too wily to allow that to happen. Swanepoel sat in front of me and every now and then would turn around and tap me on the shoulder, or call me by name, or make some remark or other, like, 'How are you, Carneson?' or 'Don't go to sleep, we'll soon be there.'

When we got to the other end there was a group of five Special Branch men waiting for us. They put me in a car and took me off to the Kompol building in Pretoria. That was one of the first prisons-cum-police-stations built in the old Transvaal Republic. It was a massive, forbidding building with red-brick-faced frontage. They took me right to the back of the building to a big empty hall with some wires sticking out of the walls. Not a very inviting place to be taken to. There was a little partitioned-off room in one corner of the hall. The outside walls were very thick and the one window casting some light into the room was heavily barred. I was told to sit down on one side of the desk and they all filed into the room. At this stage there must have been about six of them there, and they all stood around and started to bombard me with questions, boasting how much they already knew.

They then said, 'Stand up.' I said, 'No, I'm not going to stand up.' There had been a court case just the other day where a judge said that the police did not have the right to make anyone stand up during interrogation. Their reply was, 'Fuck the judges! You stand up!' I said, 'I'm not standing up.' Two of them came round to my side of the desk and forcibly lifted me off the chair. The one pulled the chair away and then they pushed the desk against my stomach so that I was pinned like a fly against the wall. And they kept me there for hour after hour after hour for days at a time.

From time to time they would badger me to make a statement, saying 'Why won't you make a statement? Everybody's talking. We already know about this, that and the other ...' I tried to listen as best I could, trying to discover how much they did in fact already know. My stock reply was, 'I'm not making any statement. I'm not talking.' They kept hammering away at me. Sometimes Swanepoel would go off and come back. 'Oh, yes,' he'd say. 'We've got some more information. Someone we're interrogating in Cape Town has told us this.'

I was feeling very tired. The lack of sleep and the tension were obviously taking their toll on me. My stamina – and I've got quite a bit of stamina – was wearing out. They had kept me without sleep and standing for days. I stuck it out; I stuck it out. How I stuck it out I don't know.

Towards the end of Thursday night they would take turns, two or three of them in the room at a time. The group of them was actually sleeping in an adjacent room. They had their Primus stoves to make themselves coffee and keep their food warm, and camp beds. So the whole interrogation team was keeping together. There were never less than two of them in the interrogation room keeping me awake. I was all this time standing pinned against the wall. Every now and then they would seemingly relent, pull the desk forward and give me a chair: 'You can have a rest now.' But at odd intervals, without any warning, they would say, 'Stand up again!' Or they would let me doze off, go to sleep, and then they would give the desk such a bang it seemed like the whole building was coming down. Or else they would wait until I'd dozed off again and then they would scratch on the surface of the desk, *grrrh, grrrh, grrrh*, to bring me out of my sleep. I'd start up to find this man staring at me – a nightmarish sight.

I held out and held out, determined not to yield. On Friday they kept me standing the whole day, and that, combined with the lack of sleep, was really weakening. I could feel myself weakening all the time. And once – inevitably they speak to you and you speak to them – I said to Rousseau, 'You chaps know what you're about here.' And he said, 'Yes, we're policemen, we're well-trained policemen and we've been trained by bloody good psychologists.' He himself told me that he'd been to Algiers to see what the French were doing there during the Algerian War – and the French were pretty rough with their prisoners, so he boasted.

On one occasion he said, 'You visited a woman called Felicity in the Northern Transvaal.' We used to go and collect money from her, for the newspaper. 'We had her sitting in this same room, interrogating her,' Rousseau said. I knew her – Felicity was her name, Felicia – and from the time we visited her to the time we left, she never ever stopped talking – you couldn't get a word in edgeways. So I laughed and said to Rousseau, 'I bet your problem was to stop her talking, not to get her talking,' and he burst into laughter. Then I knew I had asked the right question in order to find out whether she had given anything away. I'm sure she wouldn't have given them an opportunity to talk. There weren't many humorous points like that in my interrogation, I can tell you.

The whole of Friday they kept me standing. And, round about when I got up and when they let me go to the toilet, I felt like an old, old man. It was a physical, not just a mental and psychological, strain. It was physically exhausting standing all that time. When I walked down the corridors to the toilet, I walked like an old man. I was stiff; I could hardly walk, because my limbs had all gummed up. On three occasions during that walk I physically collapsed and they threw water over me and gave me stimulants to revive me.

They took me in a military passenger plane and continued to question me. They continued to force me to stand up. I cannot remember how many days I had been without sleep and food. During that flight down, the Special Branch pressed me to give information I was not prepared to give. They threatened to throw me out of the plane. I was then forced to stand up in the aisle with my hands on the backs of two seats. I went into spasm. My legs lifted horizontally in the air; I lost control of my limbs.

I don't know at what stage when – I feel terrible whenever I think of it – I knew that they'd defeated me. I knew that I couldn't go on. I thought I was going mad; I felt as if my eyes were popping out of my head.

I can't remember the exact thing that triggered it off, but I thought, 'Right, I can't go on now. Finished now, absolutely finished. I can't go through it any more.' And one of the things that happens to you at the end is that they don't need to keep you awake or going; you're fighting against yourself all the time. You say to yourself, another half an hour, another quarter of an hour, another hour, stick it out, stick it out – until somewhere along that line I'd reached the end of my tether. Quite literally finished.

I said, 'All right, I'll make a statement.' They said, 'Will you write it down?' I said, 'No, you take it down.' I wasn't going to do any writing. So they started off. What they got from me was confirmation of things that they already knew. There were a lot of things they didn't know and I was also withholding a lot from them. I was telling them only what I thought they already knew. And they were saying, 'Yeah, but we know that already; we know that already.'

One of the things they were saying to me during the run-up to my crack was, 'You know, Carneson, you can start talking now. The people you've been protecting, they've already left the country. You've given them a chance already; there's no point in you holding out like this. You're just harming yourself; your fate is in your own hands.'

One of the things they wanted me to do was to give information about, or give evidence against, Bram Fischer, another communist, because it was his arrest and the subsequent interrogation and arrest of others that led directly to me. Not that they were not already watching me all the time. But they said, 'Look, you give evidence against Bram, and we'll set you up with a new identity in another country, any country at all.' There was one thing I was absolutely certain about: they might force a statement out of me, but there was never, ever going to be an occasion when I'd stand up and give evidence against any comrades in the court – Bram or anybody else.

So I made a statement and they wrote it down. I was feeling absolutely terrible. I felt as if I was betraying everything that I'd fought for all my life. It was a terrible defeat, a personal defeat. I felt humiliated. I had hoped and hoped and hoped that I would withstand anything they could throw at me, and I hadn't measured up to it. So, it was a terrible moment for me, and whenever I think of it I feel bad. So they took down the statement and said, 'Right, you can have a couple of hours' sleep. We're taking you down to Cape Town.' While we were waiting to leave, my constant thoughts were, 'If I can get down to Cape Town there might be a chance of my giving them the slip.' During the plane journey down from Pretoria, I again lost control of my limbs.

In his court testimony Fred described much of what had happened to him. However, according to what he told his fellow political prisoners when he eventually joined them in Pretoria Local Prison, his interrogation was a great deal worse. It included hanging him in mid-air in total darkness, making sporadic noises to keep him awake and giving him no food or drink for up to five days at a time. They fed him stimulants, and we found pills for treating a heart attack hidden in the seams of his clothes. We heard that, at one stage, they had to put him in an oxygen tent to revive him. The security police also used psychological torture, saying that my mother had been unfaithful to him and that she had had an affair with another woman. They told my father that certain named comrades had betrayed him. Although we later found out that some people had indeed been disloyal to him, none of the comrades mentioned during his interrogation had said anything. It was common knowledge among the other political prisoners that my father had been given the worst treatment of any other white prisoner.

When I eventually found out what had happened to him, I wondered whether the security police had wanted to humiliate him because he was defiant and cocky and often outwitted them. Yet no amount of provocation from his side could justify their systematic and extreme cruelty. I often think that they may have kept him alive at the time only for the sake of extorting information from him.

Knowing how my father had been treated had a profound effect on me. I knew that there was no limit to the brutality the security police would inflict if they could. They had perfected the art not only of physical torture, but – even worse – of breaking the human spirit. I was horrified at what human beings can do to each other. The constant pain of it in my gut was so intense that it was impossible to relieve the feeling by crying. I could see from my mother's dry and worried eyes that she was experiencing similar emotions. I struggled between feeling so angry that I wanted to hit out and punish them, and knowing that this behaviour would not achieve anything. My atheistic communist parents had influenced me in the past by saying, 'Christ was right. Many of these people "know not what they do". You can hate their actions but it is more important to put things right than to waste time on revenge.' The knowledge that I was capable of such rage was frightening. What if I was no different from the security police? I felt that the only thing I needed to do was to hold on to my capacity to love. However, trying to feel love for my enemies at that time was extremely difficult.

It had been easier to cope when I was in Cape Town with my mother, Johnny and Ruthie. At least there I could provide some practical help and some comfort. My mother survived by going into mechanical overdrive, trying to focus on domestic chores like cooking meals for us. She would tell me, 'The children and Freddie need me, so I have to keep going.'

One day my mother and I discussed what to do about Johnny and Ruthie if something happened to her. She looked so desperate that I hugged her. When I put my arms around her she shook for about five minutes. I tried to reassure her that I would ensure that Johnny and Ruthie were fine but that nothing would happen to her. Privately I hoped that relatives and friends would be able to help, although at that time I felt that we were completely isolated and without support. The thought that my mother might not be around to look after my brother and sister was too terrible for her, so I ended the discussion swiftly.

John and Ruth had grown into teenagers during my two years in Britain and, on my return, they were almost – but not quite – strangers to me. They were trying hard to be brave. John used humour and bad puns to try to lessen the tension. Ruth would voice loud, defiant opinions about such things as allowing teenagers to drink if they wanted to. I felt guilty about having left them to go to study in England, and I sensed that Ruth was very angry with me. But she was honest and open enough to be able to ask me why I had left and to share with me that she was having difficulty sleeping at night. With John it was more difficult. I knew from the dark shadows under his eyes that he was not sleeping either. He told me that he had terrible nightmares every night, but that he could handle them: 'They are just bad dreams.' I tried to stay awake to be with them if they needed me in the still, dark hours of the night, but felt helpless because I knew that I was going to leave again.

    I was extremely worried, not only about my father's physical condition, but also about his mental state. How was he coping? What was he thinking? Would he ever be the same as he had been before? All this was a constant, gnawing stream at the back of my mind. While waiting for the verdict, however, I was totally fixated on one thing: Was he going to be handed the death sentence or not? And, if he was given a life sentence, would he ever come out alive? Nothing else seemed important at the time.

3

Isolation

*I landed in a prison cell
where introspection gnawed at my heart
like a rat on a chunk of cheese.*
— OSWALD JOSEPH MTSHALI

F RED SPENT HIS first thirteen months in prison in solitary confinement. The first month, during which the security police did everything they could to force from him a statement against his comrades, was the most intense. Although he told them nothing that they did not already know, he was unable to withstand the pressure, and he cracked. As far as he was concerned, to break down was a complete betrayal of everything he stood for. Fred had always believed that he was strong enough to withstand anything. After all, he had survived fighting in the Second World War and had continued the struggle in South Africa long after others had left or been arrested. Because his mental and physical strength had failed, he felt that he had let the movement down, particularly as it was Party policy not to crack under torture. Fred and other members of the Communist Party were deeply influenced by a book that they had read and discussed in the fifties, when the security police had started to employ methods of torture. Written by Julius Fučik, a Czech communist, the book was called *Notes from the Gallows*. Just before he was executed by the Nazis, Fučik wrote, 'It is better to have the courage to die than to crack.' For the South African comrades it was unforgivable to break down before their interrogators, regardless of the intensity of the torture – something Fred fervently believed. He was haunted by the terrible deaths of some of his comrades and felt that, instead of bowing to the pressure, he should have died. He had compromised his standards; he was fallible.

My father never forgave himself, even though by the late sixties it was known to be impossible for anyone to withstand certain methods of torture, especially sleep deprivation. He was deeply ashamed: he was not the person he thought he was. Not only did he feel that he no longer deserved the reputation of a good leader, but he felt responsible for the fates of many close friends who had been arrested and tortured as a result of having worked with him. He believed that he had ruined their lives and the lives of their families.

His capitulation had come after weeks of interrogation and sleep deprivation. The security police had done what they had set out to do. They had nearly destroyed his spirit and almost totally undermined his self-confidence.

When he was not being interrogated, my father spent the first four months in Cape Town's Pollsmoor Prison in a tiny eight-by-seven-foot isolation cell. With nothing but a thin mat and four blankets, he was forced to sleep on the concrete floor. Since the cell had no table or chair, he had to sit on the hard concrete or squat on his haunches while a bright light was kept burning twenty-four hours a day. He had little to do but think about his life, his weaknesses, what he had done wrong and the damage he had inflicted both on his family and on others. His thoughts went round and round in his head like a broken record that he could not switch off. There was no one to persuade him that he was being too hard on himself.

Even after he was charged with sabotage on 12 January 1966 and became a prisoner awaiting trial, my father was continually interrogated both in Cape Town and in Pretoria, the security police persisting in their hope that he would testify against his comrades. The relentless, repetitive interrogations further sapped his energy and his fast-diminishing morale.

After he was charged, Fred, at the mercy of the security police and prison warders, was forbidden to talk to any other prisoner. While awaiting the trial, however, he was provided with paper, a pencil and the Bible, and he was allowed to read two books a week. He was permitted to see Sarah once a week and to write and receive letters limited to 500 words. During that time he was also given permission to see me twice.

Sarah received only two of the many letters Fred wrote to her before his sentencing. I received two letters and John and Ruth received one, at the end of the trial, written to say goodbye to them. All the unsent letters were returned to my father by the prison officials when he was finally released from prison eight years later.

Nine years after my father died, when I was going through the family archives to find material for this book, I stumbled across the letters he had written. They were still tied up in a bundle, the unsent letters all unopened. I was the first to read the letters that we never received. I felt that I was opening up a treasure chest revealing an integral part of my family's history, yet my excitement was paired with anxiety about revisiting past, painful times. At two o'clock that afternoon, I put the letters in chronological order on my desk. At four the next morning, I finished reading them. I spent the rest of the day weeping.

Before reading the unsent, long-unopened letters, I had known my father as a busy, committed person dedicated to saving the world. He did not find it easy to express his emotions – especially love – but I knew that he loved us deeply. Reading his letters introduced me to a more intimate and vulnerable side of my father and enabled me to understand the pain that he had experienced in prison so many years before. Just before he died, he told me that his time in solitary confinement was one of the worst periods of his life. Through the letters, I shared the terrible ordeal of a man, my father, struggling to maintain his sanity and to retrieve his sense of dignity and self-confidence after breaking down under interrogation. His naturally social, gregarious and optimistic character had been crushed. I wished and wished that he could have been there with me as I was reading the letters, so that we could have talked about what he had endured.

My father's words from so long ago stretched across time to reopen the still-raw pain of old memories. As long as the 'roots' of grief remained, I realised, it will be continuously 'reborn':

> The grass may wither, but its roots die not,
> And when Spring comes it renews its full life;
> Only grief, so long as its roots remain,
> Even without Spring, is of itself reborn.
> – Ch'ên Shan-Min (mid-thirteenth century)

4

Prison Letters

WHEN I ASKED my mother what she felt during my father's interrogation and subsequent imprisonment, she said, 'I didn't feel. I was stunned. I felt confused and very frightened. We didn't know where he was or whether he was alive or dead. I didn't know if I would ever see him again or if he had survived the interrogation.'

I was still in Cape Town when my mother received one of the two letters she was sent while my father was awaiting trial. It arrived on Christmas Eve. For Sarah, 'it was the best Christmas present I could have received.'

He wrote from Pretoria Central Prison. After I had visited him at Caledon Square Police Station, he had been taken back to Pretoria for further questioning. Sarah had not seen him since he was brought to Mount Pleasant by the security police in early December, just before I arrived in Cape Town. I was still reeling with shock at his condition, so I was relieved that he was able to write a reasonably normal letter. John and Ruth were in a state of confusion about what had happened to Fred, and were also pleased to see the letter – John even joked about Fred's request that they work hard rather than enjoy the school holidays. Even so, there was an empty place at the table on Christmas day. Fred's letter held pride of place on the mantelpiece.

Prisoner No. 322/66
Isolation Cell
Pretoria Local Prison
21 December 1965

Sarah darling
When Sunday came and went I had given up all thoughts of a visit from Lynn after they told me she had arrived in Cape Town. You can imagine my surprise, pleasure and excitement, when, on Monday afternoon, I was

told she was there to see me. It was good to see her again, although of course I wished it were under different circumstances.

On Monday night I whiled away the time imagining the excitement of her arrival home, and none of you have been out of my thoughts all day. I wish I were with you! There will be lots for you to tell me about in your letters, which I hope to start receiving soon. Apart from Lynn, I have not received any visits or letters. While I am in Pretoria, please ask Ida [Sarah's sister] to apply for a visit. Lynn should also apply for a further visit before she leaves.

Bram's case is not likely to be heard in the Supreme Court much before March and I have applied to the Attorney-General to be detained in Cape Town pending my hearing, so as to be able to receive visits from you and Lynn. It's too early for a reply, so I suppose we'll just have to exercise some patience – not much else to do, is there?

I want to know all about the garden when next you write and how the various plants are coming on. Please be sure that the indoor plants are watered regularly. They always seem to be lost sight of somehow.

I've not yet received any books, though there is a good chance that they will start coming through soon. I have some money in the kitty here – about R14 if I remember correctly – and that should last me at least a month, smokes and all. You would not like the smell of my cell! I'm smoking like the Hout Bay snoekeries!

Before I forget: see that you don't infringe any of your banning orders. One of us in jail is enough, and Ruth and John need all the love and care they can get, particularly at this difficult stage of their lives. Please tell them I expect them to study hard and well right from the beginning of [the school] year, and to give you all the assistance they can – without moaning, groaning or dodging! How are things going with Mount Pleasant? Full? If I remember correctly Farm Fresh delivers, so you can try that if you're stuck for transport. Please don't forget to see that the car doesn't stand idle for too long ...

I was amused by my father's tendency to lecture, but knew it was his way of showing that he cared. He was a heavy smoker, so in spite of his mental and physical condition he must have charmed one of the warders to get him cigarettes – precious currency in prison. I wondered what it was like for him, locked in a bare prison cell all day. What must it have been like without newspapers, letters or anything else to read, especially as a journalist? At least he knew that, as an awaiting-trial prisoner, he should soon be allowed letters, books, newspapers and visits once a week. When he was eventually granted these privileges, Sarah had to make sure that he had enough money to buy cigarettes, soap, chewing gum and other small things, and to find out if he was permitted fresh clothing, food and photos of the family.

Fred must have been desperate for news not only of his family, but also of the people who had been arrested as state witnesses against him. Although he really did love his garden, we knew that he was also using it in his letters as a metaphor for what was happening to the others. His reference to 'indoor plants' in the letter below concerned those already in jail, with a plea to help them. In this way – through the garden metaphor – we wrote back with what news we had of comrades, their families and the state of affairs outside the confining prison walls.

As an 'indoor plant' himself, Fred was having a tough time, particularly as he continued to spend much of his time criticising himself. In his isolation, he shared his deepest thoughts with Sarah. The following letter is one of the ones that she never received.

Pollsmoor Prison [*Not received*]
27 January 1966

The bell has rung; the cheering chatter has died away. All is quiet, save for the occasional cough or faint rustle from one of the cells. The chirping of the crickets emphasises the silence of the night.

And, as always at this time, my thoughts have turned to you and the children and all the warmth that home means. At this hour, more than at any other hour of the day, one's heart slips through the bars and goes winging to where the loved ones are. A sad yet tender hour it is, filled with yearning, vibrant with memory; a precious hour. Another day has passed down the slipway of time. Tomorrow waits its turn.

Prison has its compensations, not least the opportunity for meditation, for self-analysis. One looks at one's past as from a great height, as one does on a landscape from a mountain top, strangely detached, seeking out the known landmarks and surprised to see how different they look. Weaknesses and mistakes all there, as graphic and as matter-of-fact as lines drawn on a map. The sunshine is there, too, but it is the shadows that one examines most closely. And when one returns from the heights, what then? Does one trip over the same weaknesses, make the same mistakes all over again? Some do, others draw new strength and wisdom from the long view.

My! My! My! What a lot of philosophising! But I'll let it stand. It's helped bring bedtime and blessed sleep a little closer. What did Shakespeare have to say? Something like: 'And sleep hath knitted up the ravelled sleeve of care.'

Is there any human emotion that that man didn't know and capture in vivid phrase? Had he lived in our time, he would no doubt have become a great psychologist – and the world would have lost all the singing of him.

Damn it! There I go again, letting my thoughts and my pen run away with me. But you'll forgive me, I'm sure, for I have no one to talk to and you know, in any case, my weakness for the monologue! In your letters – and I hope that they start coming through regularly and promptly now – do give me all the little details for which there is not time during your visits. They help to bring you and the children that much the closer.

Have a look at the fish pond for me, count the babies that have survived and tell me if they've changed colour yet. Tell me about the sunflowers I planted at the back, near the washing lines. Have they also flourished? If you want them again next year you will have to buy the seed, for I doubt if you will be able to get them as seedlings, except if you raise them yourself.

Heavens! There are so many 'tell me's' that I could put down. But I'd best leave time for a note to Ruth and John before I grow weary of writing.

I love you – Fred

The mention of fish and sunflowers in the above letter masks a request from Fred, who was always concerned about how many people had been arrested and had survived – especially the younger ones – and which ones had turned state witness. The sunflowers are a specific reference to Umkhonto we Sizwe (MK), the armed wing of the ANC, whose members frequently met at the back of our house near the washing lines. Fred was concerned about how MK could continue with so many of its members in prison or dead. We continued to invent many relatives to talk about. However, it was impossible to establish the extent to which Fred really understood what we were trying to say and, by the same token, to determine how many of his cryptic messages we decoded correctly in the letters we did receive. Many years later, we discovered that some references were understood and some completely missed.

We lived in a state of constant anxiety and deep stress, in an atmosphere where nothing felt secure or real. It was like walking in a minefield, where catastrophe could strike at any moment. We had been existing like this for some time when Sarah was finally allowed to see Fred. Even though I had warned her, she had not expected him to be in such a bad state. 'When they brought him back to Cape Town, he was a completely different person,' she said later, continuing:

> He had lost an enormous amount of weight and he looked dreadfully ill. When I visited him I wanted to hug him, but we could not touch each other. He was always in the presence of at least four security police. We were not allowed to talk about prison conditions or news of our comrades; we couldn't say anything except talk about the children. I spent all my spare time working on how I could get permission to see him more often – even if only to ask Fred if I could take John to the dentist. Any books he was allowed had to go through Juta's book shop and were heavily screened. As I couldn't go to the book shop [due to banning orders], I was frequently on the phone to them. I tried to do whatever I could to make his isolation less difficult.

Knowing what Fred was entitled to and having something concrete to fight for was a small comfort to Sarah, if only for the distraction it brought. She also frequently wrote letters to him in the full knowledge that not all would reach him. Sarah was very careful to describe the garden and the flowers, and to try to reassure Fred that the children were all right. She wrote that she missed him and reminded him of good times that they had had together, saying how much she hoped they would have such times again.

On 27 January 1966, I was allowed to visit my father once more before I went back to London. I hated leaving my mother and John and Ruth; I felt as if I were abandoning them. But I had to return to the UK to earn a living and to organise the money for Fred's defence. I also needed to help raise consciousness overseas about what was happening in South Africa.

At the time of my scheduled visit, Fred was in Pretoria. I was nervous that the police might arrest me, as I had been donating money to the ANC, an illegal action with severe consequences if found out. I stayed with my Aunt Ida in Johannesburg and she drove me to the prison. On arrival, I was led through a series of gates that were systematically unlocked, armed guards watching my every move. When I saw my father, we were in separate cubicles and divided by mesh. Two security men stood between us so that we had to crane our necks to see each other. I was relieved that he looked better than he had on my first visit. He had put on a little weight, looked smart in khaki and was standing tall. The meeting was half an hour and conversation was stilted. As usual, we were not allowed to discuss anything except family and personal affairs. Neither of us knew when or if we would see each other again. We both pretended to be cheerful to deprive the security police of the pleasure of our suffering, but the grief I felt when he was taken away was as acute and intolerable as an incapacitating migraine. The only compensation was that my father told me he was returning to Cape Town, which meant that Sarah would be able to visit him.

Back in the snow in London, I tried to throw myself into my teaching job. The children helped to distract me, although I woke up every morning with a feeling of dread and exhaustion. It was difficult to explain what my trip home had been like to friends in safe England, and, although they were supportive, I sat obsessive and alone in my room. What more could I do to change things? There was nothing.

Meanwhile we all waited for the trial to begin at the end of March. Fred, in his isolation, continued writing to Sarah, even though she did not receive his letters. Keeping to his daily letter-writing routine, he wrote to her the day before he was due to see her. As I read the following letter years later, I could sense clearly his love for her and his yearning for freedom.

6 February 1966 [*Not received*]

I know I'll be seeing you tomorrow, but it's now that I'm feeling lonely and in the need to write, even if only a few paragraphs.

    Our lunch was over and done with two hours past; yours is just beginning. I'm following your movements as you go along: ladling the soup, carving the chicken, setting out the sweets, all to the accompaniment of clattering plates and the warmth of the stove. Then you'll sit down to your own meal and, afterwards, a quick snooze. It's a good day for a Sunday-afternoon nap – a small nip in the air and the wind strong enough to make indoors desirable. Right now I'd swop the indoors for the outdoors even if it were blowing a hurricane!

After writing all that about your afternoon nap I was overcome by sleepiness myself and succumbed. Then came exercise, a very early Sunday supper, some reading and some chess, and an unexpected visit from Swersky, the lawyer. He picked an awkward time, just as the day-shift warders were due to go home. I don't think he was very popular, eating into their leisure hours.

I've been looking through the first batch of family snaps again. What memories they evoke! They make me feel sad, though that's not the reason I'll return them to you tomorrow. I don't want them lost in any moving around I may have to do.

I, too, sit and dream of all the things we enjoyed doing together. The walks along the beachfront; the stroll through the garden, seeking out the new-growing plants; tea at Stuttafords on a Monday morning; your affectionate amusement at my cooking efforts. The memories weave through my thoughts like the golden threads through a dark tapestry; warm sunny memories, lighting up the dull hours and taking some of the ache of loneliness away.

One day, perhaps, we shall be able to lead an ordinary, normal life, with no fears in the background to nag at our simple joys, no danger to cast its shadow on our pleasures. The 'perhaps' is personal, for there is no 'perhaps' about the new world being built about us, a world in which loneliness, estrangement and hatred will be all but unknown.

What a contradictory time we live in! A man-made machine on the moon, exploring new wonders for mankind – and man-made machines in Vietnam, spreading death and destruction in a cruel and bitter struggle. The contrast is too great to endure for long. The volcanoes are rumbling, the earth trembling under our feet. One way or another, mankind is getting ready for another big jump forward, either into the unimaginable horror of an atomic war or into a better world. If the former, our personal problems won't count for a tinker's damn; if the latter, they will be eased so much the quicker.

1966? 1967? 1968? 1969? 1970? Five years, and each one carrying a big question mark. Only a fool or a lunatic can believe that what is today will remain unchanged tomorrow.

Continuation

One of the warders came to work today with a three-day-old headache and called it a Blue Monday. Perhaps some of his mood rubbed off on me. Maybe it's just fatigue, or delayed shock or something, but all in all not one of my best days.

If the newspapers are correct, my case won't be heard until the end of next month. For myself I don't mind so much, but the thought of the others having to sit in prison as well makes me feel miserable. I think of them constantly. Knowing that it had to happen sooner or later doesn't help my feeling of self-reproach. The basic, though inevitable, error was to push too many burdens on too few people for too long. When that happens, somewhere along the line something is going to break. Pity we all have to learn our lessons the hard way!

To get away from that subject, let's talk about coffee. I hear you are allowed to visit me on Wednesday, so could you bring some? While I am awaiting trial and during the trial, I am allowed two visits a week. I'm completely out of stock, and there's no chance of getting any from the canteen until next Monday. To fill the gap this evening I used Vegemite. Enjoyed it too, but there's a limit to how much vitamin B I can absorb.

You looked tired and harassed in court today my love. I hope you are seeing to it that you get enough rest. Don't allow anyone to eat into too much of the few hours of leisure Mount Pleasant allows you. I wish I were there to help you.

I'm too tired to write more tonight.

I love you.

Fred

In retrospect, it was highly probable that Fred was struggling not to succumb to clinical depression. I was impressed by his efforts to think about the world outside and by how concerned he was for Sarah. I don't think, if it had been me, that I would have coped.

11 February 1966 [*Not received*]

I have a good copy of the Bible here, with fairly good print. I started reading it at much too fast a pace, but am taking it in small doses now, a chapter at a time. Anyway, this forces me to think a bit more concisely, which helps to keep my mental processes from running flat, from sheer inertia and lack of anyone to share them with.

A line, a sentence, a thought which, in normal times, one merely slides over, suddenly jumps to life with a thought-provoking, personal significance. 'By heavens,' you say to yourself, 'that man's got me taped! He knows what he's writing about.' It makes reading a lot richer, if somewhat disturbing. Seeing one's blemishes in a literary mirror isn't the most comforting of pastimes. However, there is always the consolation of knowing that there are only a few hundred million other people just as bad or as good as yourself! Anyway, I now have a deeper understanding of why Dracula screamed and went mad with rage each time he saw a mirror, poor fellow.

As the months went on, my father continued to berate himself for his fallibility, although his letters did display occasional glimpses of humour. I was struck by the fact that his way of dealing with deep emotional pain through reading was similar to my own reliance on books in times of emotional struggle. It was not something that he had actively taught me. I realised that I had been influenced unconsciously by my parents' love of literature. I wondered how much else I had absorbed from them without knowing it.

While my father and I were comforting ourselves through literature, my mother, who knew how fragile Fred really was, would lie awake at night and worry about whether he was coping with the interminable solitude. At the same time, I was anxious about how *she* was coping on her own under house arrest, under surveillance, with financial worries and the responsibility of caring for John and Ruth. I also never stopped worrying about how my brother and sister were doing. They told me later that one of the worst things of that time was the social isolation. It was a deeply lonely time for all of us.

With these thoughts in mind, Sarah wrote to Fred asking him if he felt alone and if she could do more to help him. He tried to reassure her.

14 February 1966 [*Not received*]

Don't worry love, I do not feel alone. My faith in what we believe is too deep-rooted for that, though my faith in myself suffered a blow. That, too, I feel, will be restored, at least in part, once I have the opportunity of meeting others who have gone through the same mill. Solitude has made me my own severest critic, and I hope I'm being too harsh!

I would give a great deal to be able to discuss this freely, standing alone with you at the edge of the sea, with the surge of the waves coming out of the darkness and the stars bright overhead, making one feel small and humble yet at the same time at one with all that moves and breathes on our earth, good or evil. I would feel better then, for you would give me strength, help rebuild the ramparts with the cement of love and understanding.

Strength and weakness; opposite poles in the dialectics of human living, yet inescapably bound together, constantly interchanging. Only the one who knows and acknowledges his own weaknesses can give another true strength to overcome, in turn, his weaknesses. That is why the never-done-wrong preachers seldom convert anybody to anything; no one really believes in perfection and instinctively treats as counterfeit he who claims it.

Which all boils down to this: I'm longing to get together with some other fellow sinners!

Waiting like this brings to mind what Fučik had to say: 'Every man has some gold of humanity in him.' It's our duty to dig for it, bring it to the light of day. With such an approach one can never feel alone, whether surrounded by friend or foe; rich man, poor man; beggar man or thief.

The essence of loneliness lies in this: the inability, or lack of opportunity, to love and be loved, for there is an elemental need for both in every normal human being. Think of some of the unfortunates we know, who are more alone at liberty than many a prisoner in solitary confinement.

So here am I, alone yet (as you say) not alone, for I know that I am loved, and loving too. Loving you and the children, and through and because of that love, loving all humanity – inside or outside of jail, in all the four corners of the world. So, how can I feel alone?

<u>Wednesday</u>
You looked very fresh and desirable in your green candy-striped dress today. I could have gobbled you up! It's so strange to be able to see you so clearly, and yet not be able to touch you. Like some precious object lying at the bottom of a deep, crystal pool, looking tantalisingly close, yet unattainable.

On another topic. Thank you for bringing the Soma cube mind game of constructing different shapes from different sized squares on paper. It looks fascinating and should be a wonderful pastime, which is what I need – something to kill time. One becomes tired of reading, and chess also has its limitations. This game has the advantage of making one use one's hands, even if only to a limited extent.

The silence is making me sleepy.

Goodnight, my love. A warm hug for you and John and Ruth.

Both Fred and Sarah looked forward to their visits immensely. They wanted to see as much of each other as possible in the event that contact was made impossible after the trial. Fred later told me that he counted the hours and then the minutes to each visit, and that he memorised and contemplated everything Sarah said. My mother, by contrast, had to fit her extremely busy life around visits: they took place amid her political activity, looking after her children, her petitioning for Fred, running the guest house, and the constant fear that she would forget to report to the police station and face arrest. Yet their visits were vitally important to both of them. Having to say goodbye at the end of each visit was extraordinarily painful. Fred later said to me: 'Seeing her go felt like a part of me was being amputated.'

As time went on, my father found his solitude more and more intolerable.

23 February 1966

Earlier today I remarked to one of the security chaps that I normally feel like a hen in a battery coop – except that I don't lay eggs!

It really is cold tonight. The chill has crept through the concrete into my mood, leaving me feeling flat and stale, with little inclination to do anything except sit and stare vacantly at the walls, vague thoughts slowly tumbling through an almost vacant mind. Just one of those days, I guess, with the weather playing as large a part as any other factor.

Time to warm myself up with some exercise then wrap my blankets round me and try to sleep. I'll feel and sound more cheerful tomorrow.

Goodnight, my love.

<u>Thursday</u>
A better day altogether, perhaps because the skies were clearer and the cell a little warmer. I didn't do much: read some poetry, studied

some Xhosa and that's about all. And now the last bell has just rung, accompanied by the usual final yells, as if the prisoners were youngsters welcoming the ice-cream cart. Part of the tradition, it seems, for the same thing happens in Pretoria.

I have just received the new collection of poems by Louis MacNeice. Many thanks. There are some lovely poems, including one entitled 'Sunday Morning', which begins like this:

> Down the road someone is practising scales,
> The notes like little fishes vanish with a wink of tails

The election drums are already beating fervently, with Nationalists and United Party trying to outdo each other in reactionary propaganda, and the Progressives piping thinly but bravely in the background. Not much good will come out of this infernal racket. Reaction will emerge triumphant, but underneath inexorable economic and social forces are developing which will soon wipe the smug smile of satisfaction from their faces. One can't govern at odds with reality for ever. What happens when there's not enough sugar on hand to sweeten the poison pill?

Time for bed again, not that I ever wander far from it! It's the one bit of furniture I have, though it lies flat on the floor.

Fred was lucky to have got away with the reference to sleeping on the floor. As soon as Sarah realised what he was saying, she phoned the prison, pointing out that it was against prison regulations. They told her that there was nothing that they could do, so she phoned Swersky, the lawyer, who said he would see if he could help.

In the meantime, Fred was waiting to receive another visit from the lawyers. They, in turn, were waiting to hear whether people who had been arrested as state witnesses against him had produced any more incriminating evidence before deciding what approach to take. All Fred could do was wait, read the papers and think about the forthcoming elections.

10 March 1966 [*Not received*]

In this country we are forced to rely on scanty newspaper reports and the occasional press photograph, sandwiched in between murder cases and the even more dreary and depressing reports of political speeches. We are being denied one of the most valuable of modern mass media – television – because our present rulers fear anything that might enlighten the people of our country and break their isolation from the rest of humanity. Smith, in Rhodesia, with his draconic censorship, has carried that fear to its logical conclusion.

    See nothing, say nothing and hear nothing. A truly monkey philosophy, fit only for the timid and the cowardly, and for those who profit from ignorance. Anyway, enough of that; I'm not fighting an election.

    I've not been doing much reading lately, except for the daily press. I can't concentrate on any one thing for long. My thoughts flit around like a butterfly, alighting now here, now there, never settling down for more than a few seconds. Not quite as bad as that, for since penning that paragraph, I read almost three-quarters of the Steinbeck novel …

    I've still not had a visit from the lawyers. They are no doubt waiting for further particulars from the Attorney-General before discussing the matter with me. The indictment was served on me today, by a messenger from the deputy sheriff's office. It had first been sent to Roeland Street Prison. After all these months they still don't seem to know where I am!

The lawyers arrived four days later. Fred's subsequent letters, one to me and one to John and Ruth, were farewell letters: it had become clear to him that he would be spending many years in prison. Bram Fischer and others were being handed life sentences. While the death sentence was still possible if they found Fred guilty of sabotage, I now expected that after the trial he would probably be sentenced to life imprisonment. My father tried to prepare us for the likelihood of bad news:

14 March 1966

Lynn darling
This will probably be the last letter you receive from me for a long time to come.

    I had a lengthy consultation with the lawyers today and it is almost certain that I shall be found guilty on at least two of the five charges, one of which could carry a fairly heavy sentence.

    I am in no way despondent, although, of course, I am not exactly filled with pleasure at the thought of the years ahead. Life in prison can be hard, even harsh, but I've no doubt that I can take it. I shall in any case be in excellent company! …

My contribution to the cause in which I believe is small in comparison with what others have made. I have only one regret: that I did not prove strong enough to resist pressure, did not hold out for as long as I would have liked and suffered temporary defeat. Too many years of unremitting stress and strain had sapped my strength too much. This is a case for regret and also for shame ...

On 31 March we shall have been married for 23 years. For all the odd spots of bother, it gave us you, and John and Ruth, and a steadily growing love and understanding.

You will be in my thoughts every day.

Lots and lots of love from your Dad.

Many hours have slipped by since I wrote the above paragraph, yet if you ask me what I have been doing, I can only reply: reading, thinking, eating and sleeping. To some it may sound an ideal existence, but its dullness, unrelieved by stimulus of human contact, often becomes excruciating. My eyes grow tired of reading and my sensibilities blunted by lack of things to see and feel.

I have just had my first dance since my arrest – alone of course. One of the men across the courtyard began singing an Africanised version of 'Amigo' and the rhythm proved too strong for me to resist; I jived merrily. Had the warder looked in while I was doing my solo performance he would have undoubtedly called in the 'trick-cyclist' and had me certified. I haven't had so much fun in ages.

I wept when I read the above letter. Similarly, neither John nor Ruth were overjoyed when they received the letter that he had sent to them and, through them, also to Sarah.

24 March 1966

Dear Ruth and John

My trial starts in a few days' time. I saw my lawyers today and, as I have known all along, it seems certain that I shall be found guilty on at least two of the five charges, one of which is that of being a member of the South African Communist Party.

Whatever the sentence is it will mean that I shall have to spend several years in prison, and I am writing to you now because I may not have the opportunity of doing so for some time once the sentence is passed.

Don't be unduly upset, my children. Many men and women have been imprisoned before now for their political beliefs and activities, and, as you know, there is no shame attached to them. On the contrary, there are millions who admire them for having the courage of their convictions, for not bowing the knee to their political adversaries and for refusing to count the cost of personal sacrifice. I do not for one moment regret the course of action I took. What I did, I did believing it to be in the best interests of our country and its people, the South Africa we love so much.

Be good children to your mother while I am away. Do nothing which will cause her heartache or grief. Help her as much as you can. Work hard at school, for knowledge is a precious thing and without it you will not be able to give of your best to society, or do justice to your own abilities. Play hard too, for life is meant to be enjoyed, to be made bright and interesting.

I've run out of dos and don'ts now, and that's as well: sermons can become terribly boring.

I shall miss you, and I know that you will miss me. But time passes quickly and we shall be together again, all older and a little wiser no doubt, but with lots of life and happiness ahead of us.

Keep smiling. My fondest love and a big kiss and a hug to both of you.

Dad

When I asked Ruth about her memories of those times, she struggled to recall any details or what she felt: 'I don't remember any of it. It is as if I blanked everything out. It all seemed unreal to me. The only thing that I do remember was the difficulty of writing letters, as I had to be careful of what I said, cancel words and talk only about films and books. I felt disconnected.' It was only when Ruth read the letters recently that she was able once again to feel the poignancy and sadness of the time.

John remembers some of his feelings from that period:

My overwhelming feeling then was one of fear for Dad and violent anger against the regime and its white South African supporters. My being active later in the anti-apartheid movement and the ANC, and my involvement in progressive causes generally, was in part driven by these emotions. However, my commitment to the struggle was much broader than this, and was based on a deeper understanding of the conditions of the people and what was being fought for.

I saw Dad largely in iconic terms or as a victim. I only gradually learnt about his actual life in prison later, partly through books about the prison, such as Hugh Lewin's; through meeting fellow prisoners such as Marius Schoon and Denis Goldberg; and through Dad's stories when he came to London. The letters are amazing. They make Dad's human response and humanity come alive. Prison letters are usually very special, as every precious word is weighed carefully. Dad's character and especially his concern for us shines through in his letters.

5

The Trial

M Y FATHER'S TRIAL lasted from 28 March to 26 May 1966. A number of charges had been laid against him under the General Law Amendment Act (Sabotage Act) and the Suppression of Communism Act, including unlawful possession of explosives; being an office bearer of the Communist Party; serving on the Communist Party's Central Committee; planning the activities of Umkhonto we Sizwe; and acts of violence against government installations. He was also charged for having five copies of the *African Communist* unlawfully in his possession.

As part of the accusations concerning sabotage, the prosecutor, Mr Lategan, linked Fred to known communists and Central Committee members Bram Fischer, Walter Sisulu and Duma Nokwe. He alleged that 'Carneson, with others, planned certain acts of violence during and just before the election in the Transkei. These acts were against the public in the Transkei and against the whole Republic.' Fred, along with other 'terrorists', was also accused of 'planning guerrilla warfare against the White population whereby Africans hiding in the mountains of the Western Cape would come down and kill indiscriminately', and he was said to have been in possession of several cartons 'containing a powder, plastic bags containing potassium permanganate, sacks containing white crystals and bottles of liquid'.

I knew that the accusation about planning to kill whites 'indiscriminately' was untrue and ridiculous. At that time, however, people were being convicted for all sorts of things. Given the unpredictability of the judicial system, even if they dropped that particular charge some of the accusations were extremely serious.

Shortly after my father's arrest, a number of comrades were detained as state witnesses against him. These included Albie Sachs, Amy Reitstein, Rowley Arenstein, Bernard Gosschalk, Sylvia Neame, Zolli Malindi, Simon Eggert, Gillian Jewell, Alex La Guma and Caroline de Crespigny. Others, who were already in prison, were brought to the court to give testimony against him. These included Alan Brooks and Bartholomew Hlapane. We were all sure that the security police would use whatever interrogation methods they could to obtain evidence against Fred and other comrades. Those brought to court to testify against Fred faced a one-year sentence if they refused to give evidence.

Back in London, where pure white snowdrops and yellow and mauve crocuses marked the beginning of spring, my life seemed to consist of rushing to work as a drama teacher at Clissold Park School, located in a rough area in London's East End, and then speeding to South Africa House before it closed to read the news. I still desperately wanted to be there to give support, but it was not financially viable to return to South Africa. Cape Town seemed such a long way away. I worried about Johnny and Ruthie, but felt helpless. I tried to imagine my father in prison and my parents in court and looked forward to the conclusion of the trial, when there would be an end to the waiting for the worst to happen: I still feared that my father would receive the death sentence or, if not, a life sentence.

My concern over my father's well-being intensified when, after reading an article in the *Cape Argus*, I learnt that his prison cell had no bed. I was shocked. Although I knew that he had been tortured and placed in solitary confinement, I could not believe the extent to which the security police could continue to be so vindictive.

CARNESON: 'NO BED IN CELL' SAYS COUNSEL

A complaint that Fred Carneson (45), who is on trial at the Criminal Sessions, Cape Town, had no bed to sleep on or anything to sit on in his 8ft. by 7ft. cell at Pollsmoor jail was made by Mr. Sam Aaron, S.C., today.

Mr. Aaron said that in terms of prison regulations a prisoner was entitled to one single bed and Carneson had been detained since December, first as a detainee and now as an awaiting trial prisoner. He had been given two mats and four blankets.

There was no chair or table in his cell and he either had to sit on the floor or squat on his haunches while the light was kept burning 24 hours a day, Mr. Aaron said.

The matter had been taken up with the authorities who agreed that Carneson was entitled to a bed but said that the cell was too small to accommodate one.

'My argument is that if the cell is too small, Carneson should be given a bigger one,' Mr. Aaron said. – *Cape Argus*, 31 March 1966

While Fred was squatting alone and uncomfortably in his tiny cell, Sarah was obsessed with trying to make his life easier. She asked the prison warder if she could bring Fred freshly baked bread. The warder said that Fred would not be permitted a whole loaf, but that he would arrange for him to have a slice every breakfast time. Sarah described that warder as 'very human … In fact, when they had Sunday lunch, the warder's wife would prepare an extra portion and the warder would bring it to Fred for his Sunday lunch. We never found out the warder's name to thank him.' Sarah believed that the warder's humanity stemmed from the fact that 'he was so used to real criminals that he found Fred very different'.

Although Sarah was working hard on administration for the Cape Town Eisteddfod at the time, she worked nights so that she could be at the trial every day, in full view of Fred. In addition to her two visits a week, she was allowed special visits when she could think up an excuse to see him. 'I used to take special care how I dressed,' she told me, referring to her trial sessions and her visits to Fred. 'I dressed as if I was going on a very important date. My hair looked good. I would wear bright flowers on my clothes so that Fred could see them.' On one occasion, she remembered, 'I was late for some reason and Fred spent the whole time agonising about where I was. Those were very confusing times.' Because anything could be used against them, they were very careful about what they said: 'Even if it was gossip, we said nothing.'

How my mother found time to write to me in London, I have no idea. I was deeply grateful that she kept me informed and gave me some idea of how she, John and Ruth were coping.

Mount Pleasant
29 March 1966

Dearest Lynn
I am enclosing news reports of Dad's and Bram's cases. Although Dad's case is only two days old, it seems to be going on for years. Yesterday the court was packed with Security Branch cops and members of the legal profession.

The first witness was Alan Brooks, who is serving a two-year sentence for unlawful organisation. At first he refused to give evidence. However, he did give evidence after Dad's counsel asked him to. My heart broke into a thousand pieces seeing him stand there so young (he is twenty-five) and so sure of what is right and what is wrong.

John and Ruth had a visit with Dad today – and as are all visits, it was very tense and brittle. Apart from the normal tension, Dad is in fine spirits – the first thing he did when he came into the dock was to give me a great big wink, and I heard someone say: 'It's the same old Fred!' The wink was not for the Special Branch.

The prosecutors had produced evidence that Fred had stored a parcel containing explosives in Pickford's storage depot in Epping. Fred's lawyers had tried to persuade Alan to tell the court that Fred had no idea what the parcel was about, but Alan had absolutely refused to give evidence. Only after Sarah begged him to provide this evidence, explaining that it would exonerate Fred, was he prepared to say anything. Alan had been willing to risk an extra year in prison for not giving evidence. Fred knew that Sarah had been instrumental in getting Alan to change his mind; when he saw her in court he was delighted and blew her a kiss.

1 April 1966 [*Not received*]

Sarah darling
It was wonderful to see you in court each day, to know that all I had to do was turn around and there you'd be. Now, for a while, it's back to the bi-weekly visits and the letters.
    I was given a bed today, and it makes an enormous difference, both to my comfort and to the appearance of the cell. From being a cold, alien box the latter has been magically transformed into human habitation. I seldom sleep during the 12–2 pause, but simply couldn't resist it today. It was the most restful snooze I've had during the last four months. I can see difficulty arising in the morning – I won't want to get out of bed!
    Though I had a good sleep this afternoon, I'm already feeling tired, not having yet recovered fully from the court proceedings, which I found somewhat of a strain, in spite of, or perhaps because of, all the stimulating peeks at you, which are now absent. In the meantime I shall use my new comfort to fall asleep dreaming of you and the children.

The court was adjourned from 1 April to 7 April. On the one hand, the adjournment gave my parents a rest from the trial, and Fred could sleep comfortably on a bed – which the security police had been forced to provide on account of the publicity of the trial. On the other, there was a question mark over how the other detainees had been treated and whether they had cracked or not. My father was beginning to suspect that the case would drag on longer than expected. The break, however, produced the opportunity to write to the family, including me. He wrote me two letters, on the second and sixth of April.

2 April 1966

Lynn darling
My lawyers – eternal optimists – had led me to believe that the trial would have been over and done with by now. As soon as the prosecutor started on outlining the State case I knew they were hopelessly out in their estimate.

The prosecution started off by accusing me, inter alia, of planning to organise groups of Africans in the Western Province mountains and then have them swoop down and kill white people indiscriminately! Some charge that. Although the prosecutor did not say so, my own logic leads me to believe that my own wife and children, my numerous relatives and friends would all have been among the potential victims of the slaughter. So far, of course, there's been no evidence to substantiate this charge, nor can there be either! My counsel correctly described it in court as a hair-raising bit of fiction. But this technique of mud-slinging turns my stomach; I had to listen to enough of it during the Treason Trial in 1956 even though all 156 of us were acquitted.

Anyway, let's get away from that nauseating subject. There are pleasanter things to talk about. I saw Mum every day in the courtroom and we always managed to exchange a few quick kisses. We had longer together on the Monday and the Wednesday, which would normally have been our visiting days. Mum saw to it that I had plenty of good things to eat during the lunch break – there was a delicious chicken curry on our wedding anniversary, and a big slice of her excellent fruitcake.

Then, to make my cup of joy spill over, I was allowed to see Ruth and John for a few precious but all too short minutes. We met before court began for the day, in a little entrance hall. John was, as usual, far more tense and emotionally charged than Ruth, who was quite at her ease. Although John didn't show anything, I could guess what state he was in by the fact that he had forgotten to take his hat off – the unforgivable crime at his school! During the period I've been absent his voice has deepened and now bears no trace of his childish treble. Ruth told me that she would be attending an audition for a big part in a play today. She would do well on stage.

What do you know? Mum did in fact forget to report last Monday. Very natural oversight under the circumstances, but there is a threat to prosecute her, even though she was under the eyes of the Special Branch all day long! Another little worry to add to all those already there.

I forgot to tell you at the commencement that I've pleaded guilty to being a member of the Communist Party and to being in possession of banned publications. I did so in the hope that some of the detained as witnesses in my case would be released, and to spare others the painful dilemma of either giving evidence against me or going to jail for a year.

I had a lot of difficulty in getting to the polling booth to cast my own vote. I won a minor battle to do so virtually at the last moment. First I was told that I had no right to vote; then that I had already voted (at Sea Point, where I am not registered); then, finally, someone 'forgot' to tell my SB escort that I should be taken to the polling booth. A hell of a lot of unnecessary trouble over one solitary vote I had wanted to cast quietly and without any fuss or bother. I thought I had seen some 'passing the buck' in my army days, but that little performance beats anything I've ever experienced before ...

I had read about the evidence that was given against Fred. I felt sick at the thought that people had turned state witness, but I also knew that I had to take into account that some people were unable to withstand interrogation. When I next saw her, I asked Sarah how she felt about those who had given evidence against Fred. She said that her feelings towards Bartholomew Hlapane differed from her feelings towards another man who had turned state witness and become an informer, Piet Beyleveld: 'When [Beyleveld] came to Cape Town from Pretoria, he used to stay with us. Then I heard that he had turned state witness against Fred. In court I saw him chatting and laughing with the security police and, as far as I was concerned, as a person he no longer existed for me. To me he is no longer a man – he sold his manhood to become a Special Branch paper doll. For him one can only feel sick. I felt completely different about Bartholomew Hlapane, who had been under severe and lengthy interrogation. He was the one who said that Fred had organised for Africans to come down and kill whites. When Aaron cross-examined Hlapane, I saw his eyes getting crazier and crazier and more and more desperate. I thought, "This man has been destroyed." I felt nothing but pity for him.'

My father, who had so little, was able to appreciate little treats – the home-made lunches during the trial and the chicken curry on my parents' wedding anniversary. He savoured the times that he saw my mother. We all knew that once he was sentenced his conditions would be harsher and it might be a long time before he saw her and the children again. For all of them, however, the visits were excruciating. In spite of this, my father managed to be cheerful.

In London, I was particularly anxious that my mother would again forget to report to the police. I wondered whether I should borrow money to be ready to fly out if she was detained, worried about who would look after John and Ruth. I was slightly reassured by the fact that my aunt Ida in Johannesburg had promised to take care of them if they were stranded.

Four days later, on 6 April, I was overjoyed to receive another letter from Fred, whose descriptions of the way in which he spent his days brought me closer to him.

6 April 1966

Lynn darling
You ask about my day: it begins just before dawn, when a bell is rung. I seldom hear it, being wakened usually by the cheerful sound of singing from the African prisoners across the courtyard. There is one chap who whistles one of those never-ending, always-the-same-yet-always-different tunes I remember the herd boys whistling in the veld when I was a child. Once awake I give the cell a good clean-out, then wait for breakfast. Sometimes our head warder (a credit to any prison service anywhere in the world) brings me the previous night's *Argus* when he 'opens up', and I glance through it while waiting for my chow. Then there is shaving and a bit of reading till exercise time and a shower if I feel like it. Then more reading or studying, broken perhaps by an early-afternoon nap, till just after 4.00 p.m., when the chessboard comes out. Then more reading or writing until I'm tired enough for bed. Not very exciting, but it gets me through my day adequately enough. I sleep very well, on the whole, and my health remains good.

The court is adjourned at the moment, but when the trial is on I'm taken to court at about 9.00 a.m. and am brought back when the proceedings end at about 4.15 p.m. By then I'm quite pleased to get back to my cell. Seems like home, somehow!

Please let all our friends know that I sincerely appreciate their good wishes and their assistance. You can assure them that my morale is high and my confidence in the future is completely unshaken.

I was not sure how high my father's morale really was, but I was comforted by the fact that he was starting to sound a little like the old fighting father I used to know. At that time it looked as if there were no real case for finding him guilty of sabotage, which must have been one reason for his good mood when he next wrote to my mother, on the day that the court proceedings recommenced.

7 April 1966

Darling Sarah
You looked very attractive and most desirable yesterday and I came back to my cell head over heels in love with you! I've been in a cheerful mood ever since.

What has also helped is the fact that we have had a succession of really pleasant officials on duty this last week. There are some fine men among them and one cannot help but feel good about it. The personality of the men on duty makes a tremendous difference to the general atmosphere. An ounce of kindness and understanding on the part of officials is worth more than a ton of handcuffs or leg irons. Providing, of course, that their humanity is well laced with firmness, for there are plenty of tough and altogether unscrupulous characters in their charge. There are few angels in a prison!

I'm enjoying the two books you brought me. I've also been enjoying the bread, cheese and boiled eggs. I do hope you can get some more of that meal. My lunches would not be the same without it. All these luxuries will, of course, vanish like the snow in summer once I'm 'settled' [in Pretoria Local Prison], but it's nice to enjoy them in the meantime. Anyway, there will be compensation in the way of work, company and greater freedom of movement, so I'm not worried at the prospect of the Spartan life.

Fred's love for Sarah shone through in his letters. When I asked my mother how she felt forty years later, when she read many of the letters for the first time, she said that 'Fred was normally too frightened to be emotional. I think that it was because he was always on the edge of danger. Maybe he couldn't think too closely about how he felt when he was in danger. I know that he was always worried about the security of his family. It was mainly through his letters that he expressed the warmth of how he felt about me.'

My mother's constant love and support of Fred helped cushion his experiences in his cell to some extent, but not enough to divert him from the suffering of other prisoners. When I found the following unopened letter in the bundle, I found it so sad that I was unable to read any more letters for a few days.

23 April 1966 [*Not received*]

Lynn dear
Sitting among people again, seeing Mum every day, had reawakened and sharpened my longing for human company. My cell seems smaller and lonelier than ever. It will be good when the trial is over and done.

Down the passage, not ten paces from where I sit on my bed, are five condemned men waiting to be taken to Pretoria. Each is in a separate cell with the outer door open. They talk to each other and frequently sing in harmony. One has a fine, true tenor. Their songs are sad to hear. Some are mournful, some sentimental and others decidedly gay. They are surprisingly young, these men, yet each guilty of callous, cold-blooded murders. They seem indifferent to their fate and often laugh and joke with the warders, who keep twenty-four-hour watch over them. At the moment they are singing a song to the tune of 'Old Ireland'. I cannot catch all the words, but the refrain goes something like this:

> *Have you ever been across to Robben Island?...*
> *You can sit and see the moon rise over Cape Town*
> *And see the sun go down on Table Mountain.*

A prisoner's song this, and very moving. I find it hard to keep the tears from my eyes. When I think of those young men, I peel back the short years and see them as children and curse the things that turned them from the path of life.

Fortunately the trial was able to distract him from overly gloomy thoughts, and Fred was delighted that the ten people who had been detained to testify against him had been released. His decision to plead guilty to being a member of the Communist Party had worked!

29 April 1966 [*Not received*]

Sarah darling

You looked absolutely lovely today; the temptation to ruffle your hair proved almost irresistible. It's meant a lot to me, seeing you in court each day, although I've felt a little guilty whenever I've thought of the extra burden attending places on you.

Anyway, it won't be long now before it's all over and we can both get down to some sort of normality. For my part I've become enthusiastic at the prospect of systematic study again.

<u>Sunday</u>

I had a pleasant surprise today – a letter from Lynn; a surprise because I did not expect to hear from her until tomorrow at the earliest. Her letter and the glorious weather outside have made my day for me. I've showered, shaved and changed into fresh clothes. I feel so good I feel tempted to kiss the Chief when he comes round. Just to see the surprised look on his face would be worth it! I don't think he would accept the explanation that it's just exuberance and an unbounded love for all mankind. I'd probably get sixteen days' spare diet at the best, and the loony bin at the worst.

Lynn tells me the boys at Pretoria Local are awaiting my arrival with eagerness. A fresh face in prison is like a newborn babe in a home. It helps cement the family. It's comforting to have company in adversity – the more the merrier.

I've just heard the good news about the ten who have been released, and I'm overjoyed about it. They must have spent a wonderful weekend breathing free air again. If they've any sense they would all have been basking on the beach today, watching the waves sparkling in the sun and the bikinis wiggling by. To those with whom you are allowed to communicate, my best wishes for a long spell of liberty. I'm afraid the news has driven just about everything else out of mind, not that there was much there to begin with. I'm no expert at drawing inspiration from concrete vistas.

Kiss the children for me, and give the dog a pat on the head.

All my love, darling,

Fred

During the trial, many people from all over the world wrote to my parents expressing their support and solidarity. Among the African National Congress exiles to the United Kingdom was Thabo Mbeki, destined to become president of South Africa. He was studying economics at Sussex University at the time. On 26 May 1966 he wrote to my father.

Dear Fred
I should have written to you some time ago. Please accept my apologies. I trust you are well and as comfortable as can be expected. Lynn was down in Brighton two days ago. She is well. Perhaps she told you I am her grandfather. She says I am and therefore have the task to watch out for her welfare. The extent of my success is a debatable question.

If you do get sentenced Fred, I trust you will write something. From afar one has heard quite a lot about you – has sometimes searched there for inspiration and strength. This is why I am hoping you will write – even to have the manuscript destroyed. It does not matter. Few people, perhaps, have had the peace … to sit down, without being encumbered by everyday detail and think seriously about anything more universal (rather, abstruse) than the struggle at home.

There are great problems which I believe will in the future engage us more than they have done other people, because of our peculiar history. That is, engage us from the very start. For instance, the problem of Art and Society, Consciousness and History (this latter has been discussed provocatively by a British philosopher called Peter Winch. I can't remember the title of the book). One may think further about such questions as the Press and Society. One of the tragic things for us young people from there is that we have rubbed shoulders with men of outstanding stature without being able to collect even a quarter of their more fundamental thoughts, ways of working and so on. That denied to the bulk of the country by peculiar circumstances adds to the tragedy.

I trust Fred you are indeed well. I am just about to sit for my M.A. exams and I have to do pots of work. It should not be very difficult really. The perpetual question one asks oneself is how valuable is the knowledge when not tempered with experience. But we are all cramming it down at a marvellous pace and hoping for the best. Sometimes it is very exciting when you think you have alighted on a bright idea – but then it fizzles out again soon after.

> We are all hoping that soon we shall be writing to you under normal conditions. It should be marvellous.
> Good luck Fred and love.
> Thabo Mbeki

That same day, 26 May, I received the crucial telegram about my father's sentence: *Not guilty of sabotage. Verdict 5 years 9 months.* Anne and David Hutton, with whom I was staying, presented me with it when I arrived home from work. I was so delighted that I rushed to the off-licence and brought back a bottle of champagne for us to share. The sentence was so much shorter than I had expected. I was deeply grateful for Sam Aaron's brilliant defence. I was also grateful that the judge, Justice Michael Corbett, had acted with complete integrity, had understood what was going on and had given a sound judgment based on evidence. Here was one judge who was not bowing to the pressures of the system, I thought. Justice Corbett restored my faith in humanity ... some of it, at least.

Fred was found guilty on three charges under the Suppression of Communism Act. The judge sentenced him to eighteen months in prison for having been a member of the Communist Party and to four years for taking part in the activities of the Party (which was the most serious of the three offences, particularly his 'encouraging [of] other people, some of them young students, to join an illegal organisation'). He was also sentenced to three months for having in his possession certain banned literature.

Justice Corbett acknowledged that 'Carneson was sincere in his political beliefs, however dangerous or misguided they might appear to the court and society generally'. He also said that indications were that 'Carneson did not actively advocate violence'.

In the statement that Fred gave at the end of the trial, he – true to character – stood tall and proud: 'When it comes to love of South Africa and patriotism,' he declared, 'I stand aside for nobody.'

It was only when I lay awake the following night that the full impact of the sentence hit me. Five years and nine months is not as long as a life sentence, but it is still a long time, especially as Fred had been in prison for over five months already.

6

Comrades

A NEW LIFE IN prison awaited Fred. His years of relative freedom and political activity were over. He would be deeply missed but not forgotten by his family, nor by those comrades who were arrested to give evidence against him and then released. Years later, when I interviewed some of the people who had been detained, I was impressed by how vividly they remembered their experiences. Their views on Fred contrasted with Fred's own harsh judgement of his own weaknesses.

Bernie Gosschalk was one of those detained under the 180-day law as state witness against Fred. 'In December 1965, when Fred was arrested, I was a young architect,' he told me. 'I knew that I too was in big trouble when I heard from Sarah that Fred had been questioned and broken at the terrible interrogation centre in Pretoria.'

Bernie was arrested and put in solitary confinement for four months. His little cell was completely empty: it had nothing, not even water. He had nothing to do but examine the walls and door. On the day of his arrest, he noticed something scratched on the cell door: it was a note from Albie Sachs. It said that Albie had been interrogated the previous day for many hours.

The same senior Special Branch detective who had interrogated Fred questioned Bernie. Theuns Swanepoel and his team were totally and utterly ruthless. They questioned him relentlessly. What saved Bernie was that one of the Special Branch men told him that Fred had been training Africans in the Paarl mountains to come out and slaughter whites. Bernie replied, 'That is something that Fred would never have done.' On the third day, the detective and his team asked Bernie about certain people, and he knew his time had come.

'I was cut off from the world, sealed in a thermos flask. No way can you turn,' he said afterwards. Then the questioning stopped suddenly. He couldn't understand why. Bernie later discovered that Fred had admitted he was a member of the Communist Party 'so that people like me would not have to stand and give testimony'.

Amy Reitstein, a young teacher and activist, was also arrested and then freed. 'Fred saved me from being charged because he admitted to being a communist,' she stated. 'It meant that no one else had to give evidence. I saw Fred the day they took him to court. When I saw what had happened to him, I felt that it was heroic of him to admit what he did. I was grateful for that.'

When Alex La Guma, fellow comrade and writer who had worked closely with Fred on *New Age*, was in prison, his wife, Blanche, was allowed to visit him at Woodstock Police Station. She informed him that Fred had told her it was all right for him to give evidence against Fred. 'I won't give evidence,' Alex replied.

'But Fred said that it was all right.'

'This visit is over,' declared Alex. 'I will not be a roaming traitor. What will Sarah think of me?'

Albie Sachs, a young lawyer and son of well-known trade unionists, was also arrested. He suffered badly from sleep deprivation: his food was laced with certain substances to prevent him from sleeping, and the Special Branch forced him to stay awake by physically propping his eyes open. After being awake for twenty-four hours, Albie knew he could not stop himself from collapsing. He decided he would control his collapse, so he made a statement but emphasised that it was made under duress.

Albie's saving grace was that Bernie Gosschalk had whispered to his wife, Ruth, during a short visit, that Albie was being subjected to sleep deprivation. Ruth Gosschalk immediately started proceedings in the High Court, sleep deprivation being an internationally forbidden form of interrogation. Albie managed to smuggle a note out of prison verifying that he was being denied sleep. After the High Court judgment, the Special Branch was restrained from continuing with sleep-deprivation practices.

Albie would walk up and down his tiny cell in Roeland Street Prison, wondering if he had the strength to refuse to testify against Fred. The thought of the interrogation continuing unrelentingly was overwhelming. Fred, said Albie, acknowledged his guilt 'to save us from that dilemma'. In admitting that he was a member of the Communist Party, Fred was also working with his skilful lawyers to try to prevent a lengthy sentence for himself.

Even though Fred never forgave himself for cracking, Albie had the highest regard for him: 'Fred went through an absolutely agonising experience. He held out for a long time. The longer he lasted, the less resistance he had at the end. He gave them information only about people who had left or information they already had. Fred was never the same again. He fought hard and kept going under the most difficult circumstances. I think that his sleep deprivation and making a statement hurt his soul. He never recovered. I suppose history doesn't have much to do with fairness. But if there was a straight link between courage, perseverance and tenacity, and ultimate recognition, Fred would have received the highest acknowledgement.'

During the trial, those comrades who could attend the court proceedings did, to support Fred. When the trial was over, my father did not see his friends or close family as a free man for nearly six years. Following his sentencing he was taken back to his isolation cell in Pollsmoor Prison, where he was kept in solitary confinement for another seven months before being transferred to an isolation cell in Pretoria. He was permitted to join the other political prisoners on 31 January 1967.

Solitary confinement for a gregarious man like my father must have been the closest to purgatory that he could get, particularly as he was his own worst self-critic. It is amazing to me that he went through the long dark night of the soul and emerged at the end without a trace of bitterness.

7

The Sentence Begins

THE TRIAL WAS the last time Fred saw people from the outside world for almost a year. The only people he was allowed to speak to were the prison warders, and he could receive a visit and a letter only every six months. Just after the trial, my father was permitted to send one more letter to Sarah and receive a letter and a visit in return before going back into total isolation.

After about a month in his isolation cell at Pollsmoor Prison, where he had been moved after his sentencing, he discovered that he could communicate with the person in the next cell by tapping Morse code on the pipes. He and the other prisoner spent hours constructing chess sets out of paper and anything else they could find in their barren cells. They would then play chess by tapping on the water pipes – when they had the energy and when the warders were not around.

During this time, Fred was deprived of some of the visits allocated to him. Sarah refused to give up nagging the authorities that this was his right. Eventually she was allowed a special visit on 17 June, her birthday. After the visit, he started writing letters again to Sarah, even though he knew she would get only one every six months.

18 June 1966 [*Not received*]

Sarah darling
It was great seeing you again, even though it made my heart ache for home and family. I'm sure I'll dream of all of you tonight, and of sitting around a warm fire, listening to the record the children bought for your birthday, watching Tinky trying to crawl onto your lap ...

My days crawl by much as usual, though now each one seems to be suspended in an icicle, with me shivering in the middle. I sleep warm as toast, however, wrapped in my blankets, head and all, like an Arab.

Whatever the day is like, the night is my own, and I crawl into my bed with the same certainty of comfort as a babe into its mother's arms.

I've almost finished the Latin grammar book and I shall soon start some intensive revision. I should have a good basis for the more advanced lectures, when they eventually arrive ...

My transfer should come through soon and then I'll be able to start working my way up to where we shall be allowed three letters a month. Won't that be wonderful! In the meantime, letters or no letters, my love goes out to you and the children each day and all day. My thoughts are with you always.

I love you, my dear.

Fred

Sarah also obtained permission to write to Fred, knowing how hard it would be for him after her birthday visit. I felt terribly sorry for John and Ruth because I knew how difficult it was to write letters of any interest when restricted to only 500 words. The details of everyday life were vitally important to Fred. But for me, the routine of daily life was dull; I could not understand how teaching in a tough school each day could be interesting to Fred, but I was forbidden from telling him about my evening talks to groups of people about torture going on in South Africa. The discipline of 500 words meant that we had to write what we called 'telegraphese'. Letters were stilted and often unintelligible to the recipient. However, after a lot of careful consideration, Sarah managed to write fluently. Her June letter must have given Fred a great deal of joy.

20 June 1966

Fred my darling

It was wonderful seeing you on Saturday. You looked well and more relaxed than I have seen you in the last six months. The best birthday present I could have had.

I received a delightful and long letter from Lynn. After a long struggle she received a letter from the university saying that her qualifications were considered sufficient, so she has applied to do a BA Honours degree in psychology at Birkbeck College. Should she be successful she would continue teaching at the old school for four days a week, study one day a week and go to night classes. It will be wonderful if it works out. She still takes French lessons with Marcus who is busy knitting for his friends [code referring to a comrade who was campaigning for political prisoners]. She spent a week holidaying in Norfolk, sailing on the Broads – she says they are like fifty of our own lakes, joined together by little rivers, sprinkled with windmills. Her visits to Norfolk always make her feel nostalgic.

The concert that they allowed me to organise is all fixed up and ready to go on Wednesday. I was given a smart pair of earrings and a box of chocs for a 'job well done'. I don't think anyone expected me to pull it off – I have just come to, and wonder where I have been over the last few months. Maybe some good fairy did it for me.

Did I tell you that the Tea Bushes are in full flower and looking very lovely, and we have green peppers – only they are red. From the first of the month I am going to plan for the spring and the summer. At the moment we have a lot of red in the garden and I am trying to think of some red for later in the year.

John and Ruth send their love; they say as they have not done anything but swot over the last month they can't think of any news to tell you, but that you will hear all about their holiday in their next bit of news to you.

The weather is quite fantastic but I am sorry that I have not the time to enjoy it more, and to have you enjoy it with me.

I must get back to the million-and-one jobs I always have waiting for me and never give me a minute's peace, or for that matter too much time to brood.

I love you so very much.
Sarah

The above letter was the only letter my father was permitted to receive for six months. On his own for such lengthy periods, he had a great deal of time to think about many things, including the family. Apart from imprisonment, his greatest heartache was the loss of my brother John to England. He had agreed that Johnny should go to a boarding school in the UK to escape the draft, as he was nearing sixteen – the age of conscription into the South African Defence Force. He desperately wanted to see John before he left on 9 January, but did not know whether this would be permitted. Extracts from the next letter do not adequately express the pain he was feeling about saying goodbye to Johnny. Years later he told me that he felt he had failed to be there for his children.

7 December 1966

My darling Sarah
The colonel has written to Pretoria about my request to study and about my transfer to Pretoria Central Prison. I have been in isolation for exactly one year now. I am heartily sick of it, as you can imagine, and I'm holding thumbs for favourable developments soon.

The books have been a wonderful tonic and I look forward to their arrival each week …

Yevtushenko's autobiography, brief though it be, is stimulating and thought-provoking. It will be interesting to see how his poetry develops …

I sleep well and often and always fall asleep thinking of you and all my loved ones. Sometimes nature is kind and I see you in my dreams and then, when I awake, I lie very quietly, letting the dream 'linger into the dawn' for as long as possible. My golden hours!

I keep in good spirits, though there are, naturally, the inevitable moments of depression, never deep or long lasting, thank heavens. What I miss most is some real human warmth and affection, the kind only a family can provide. How wonderful our first meeting in freedom will be! And just imagine how joyful our first all-together reunion!

John, my son, just in case I have no opportunity of seeing you before you leave, let me say *au revoir* now. I am confident that you will bring credit to us and our country. Later, when I am permitted to write more frequently, I shall keep in touch with you regularly.

I love you all so very much.

For Fred, solitary confinement was intolerable. Sarah and I were worried about his mental and emotional state; both of us had written on a number of occasions to the Commissioner of Prisons to ask whether Fred could join the other prisoners, even though it meant that my mother, under house arrest, would probably not be able to visit him in Pretoria.

16 January 1967

Dear Sir
On 8 December 1965, my husband Fred Carneson was arrested as a witness in the 'Fischer Trial'. Early in January he was himself charged and

brought to trial. On 25 May he was sentenced to five years and nine months. In November 1966 he was once more brought before the court and this time found not guilty. During this period he has been kept in the isolation block at Pollsmoor Prison, where he has spent all of his time in isolation. In addition to this, although he applied for permission to study as soon as he was sentenced, permission for study facilities has not come through from Pretoria. From reports that appear from time to time in our daily press, I have been led to believe that prisoners are encouraged to study, and that prisoners are not kept in isolation for such lengthy periods. I would therefore be glad if you could inform me as to the reason why my husband is being kept in isolation and not allowed study facilities.

As I am deeply concerned about my husband's welfare, I would be glad if you could let me have an immediate reply.

I am yours faithfully,

Sarah Carneson

Her letter crossed with the commissioner's letter to her, which said that Fred had been transferred on the same day to an isolation cell in Pretoria. She, John and Ruth had not been allowed to visit him to say goodbye.

8

Family Under Surveillance

WHILE FRED WAS coming to terms with his sentence, Sarah was trying to deal with problems at home. I was concerned: I knew that she was struggling to make ends meet. The government had frozen my parents' bank account and Sarah was earning very little from the work she did for the Cape Town Eisteddfod. She was still restricted to a small area around her neighbourhood and, because she didn't drive, transport was a problem. These difficulties were compounded by her financial situation. Over the weekends she would have to decide how best to spend what little she had on transport: 'There was only so much for transport. We would choose where we wanted to go – after that we couldn't go anywhere else. We had to economise.' Although the area she was permitted to operate within was very limited, even that cost money.

The police kept on harassing John and Ruth and looked for any excuse to arrest Sarah, who had to report twice a week to the police station. The children would wake up at night terrified that Sarah would be arrested. By then they were almost totally socially isolated and surrounded by police twenty-four hours a day. Every room and every bush in the garden were bugged and all conversations were recorded – even to joke was dangerous. My mother, Ruth and John were followed by security police wherever they went, unless they were able to give their shadows the slip.

One day they were at Caroline de Crespigny's house, talking about the mushrooms they had picked in the woods. Caroline was a fellow member of the Communist Party who had not yet been named or banned. My mother later told me, 'Caroline made a joke about feeding poisonous mushrooms to Verwoerd, the prime minister. She said that she would invite him to dinner and feed him with poisonous mushrooms. We found this very funny, but the Special Branch treated the joke extremely seriously.'

It was hardly surprising that Sarah was suspicious when she received an invitation from an African woman called Joan whom she did not know well, but who used to do some driving for her. 'I thought it was a ploy to get me arrested,' Sarah said, 'so I kept on saying no, I would not go.' Then Joan came with a further message: 'The women want to see you now. It is very urgent.'

'So against my will, I asked Joan to take me where they wanted. She took me to a place in Nyanga.'

When Joan arrived with Sarah, there was a crowd of women in the room. For most of them it was illegal. Sarah knew all of them – a combination of ANC and SACP members, including Mrs Huna and Mrs Malindi, comrades and friends whose husbands had worked closely with Fred on *New Age*. Sarah said, 'I can only be here for a couple of minutes', to which they replied, 'We have each other for support, but you have no one. So we just wanted you to know that we think of you. We feel strongly about you and you have our support and love.' The women wanted to know how the children were doing. Sarah just burst into tears and had to walk out, profoundly affected by their kindness. 'It meant so much to me,' she said.

One of our concerns was that Johnny was nearing the age where he would be conscripted into the South African army to fight 'terrorists' on the South African borders. I persuaded my mother that it would be dangerous for John to go – we were hearing horror stories of how sons of activists were being badly treated. Among other atrocities, I heard that such boys were being beaten up and their arms and legs deliberately broken.

I shared my worry about John with Evelyn Cadbury. Evelyn was a Quaker who lived in Worcestershire and had come over from England to South Africa in the early fifties to do social work, through which she had worked with my mother. When I first arrived in England as a student, she adopted me, and her home in Worcestershire became a welcome and regular retreat for me. I explained the problem to her over a cup of tea in her rose garden. She said that she would see what she could do.

Evelyn came back to me a week later saying that the reports about what was going on in the South African army were grave, and that the Quakers had agreed to pay John's school fees at a Quaker school in England. What's more, she would be going back to Cape Town in a few weeks' time and could visit my mother. We used to call Evelyn my 'fairy godmother' – she could always almost magically solve problems. But I knew that my mother would be distraught at the prospect of losing John, even to the relative safety of England. My mother expressed these fears to me in the following letter.

27 October 1966

Your fairy godmother was in to discuss John. She is very keen that he should leave as soon as possible, but it is not quite so simple – he is still a little boy and as long as I am around it is important that he should be with me – and I agree with you that it would be quite wrong for him to leave me before he has grown up a bit more – thinking it over, perhaps going into the army would be a lesser evil than leaving me too soon. He is fifteen in Standard 8. The thinking is that if needs be, one can always make a snap decision. He is madly keen on science, but the field must be the ocean. We'll see what happens when he leaves school. I think it is a good idea to have a plan in mind in case it is needed, but only to use it if necessary. So if you make any plans, do so on the understanding that they might not be necessary ...

Something strange is going on – large numbers of people are being taken off the banned list, while others are being added to it – it looks as though they are trying to isolate listed communists by imposing stricter restrictions on them and lifting the ban on fringe people ...

One day the security police came to visit my mother. Van Wyk looked at her and smiled.

'Mrs Carneson. We are here to do you a favour. If you give up communism and make a public statement, we can take you off the list and stop making life difficult for you.'

'Thank you for your offer,' she replied, 'but I will never give up my beliefs and values.'

'Mrs Carneson, you are making a big mistake. You will hear from us.'

The police files reporting that meeting said that 'she refused to change her colours' and that it would be 'necessary to clamp down harder on her'.

A couple of months later, my mother changed her mind about John and wrote to me that she thought it would be better for him to leave the country. She told John that I had arranged for him to go to school in England.

During that period John felt extremely isolated. He experienced both immense relief and a sense of loss at the thought of leaving the country. Even before he knew he was going, he had had a premonition that we would be forced to lose our beautiful home. With his father's arrest, he had a strong sense that the family was breaking up; its existence was so fragile. There was an ongoing feeling of uncertainty about the future and he could not shake off a deep sense of grief and loss.

Sarah wrote to tell me that she had booked a passage on a boat for John.

21 December 1966

I have booked John on the *Edinburgh Castle*, which sails on 28 December and gets to England on the ninth ...

You must get a letter from the school saying that John is a pupil of theirs and you will get a 10 per cent reduction. What is more important is that John must have a statement from the school saying that he is a pupil of theirs and a statement from you saying that you are his guardian and accept responsibility for him, otherwise he will not be allowed to land. John is very excited and has promised to work very hard, but of course he does not understand how homesick he will be and what it means to be away from home. You will have to help him there. As we are in the middle of summer, no one has winter-weight underwear in stock, so you will have to get him some in London and let me know how much it is.

I have received a mass of Xmas greetings from all over England and some from other parts of the world – can you think of any way of letting people know how much this has meant to me – please tell my friends that I send love, greetings etc., and to forgive me for not sending personal messages. All these messages have been rather overwhelming and rather wonderful ...

My mother later wrote that John had had a farewell party and had asked a lot of people to come. As she was banned, she thought it best not to be in the house, so she sat at the front gate. At that time young adolescents were notorious for gatecrashing and smashing up parties, so Sarah was on the lookout. When a group of hoodlums arrived, she said to them, 'Have you been invited?'

'Stand aside,' they said to her haughtily. Sarah pointed behind them: 'You see that car outside the gate? It's full of police.' They took off hurriedly, not realising that the police were there to watch her!

Leaving Cape Town was a terrible experience for John. 'The sense of loss reached its height when the *Edinburgh Castle* passed Robben Island – the last bit of land I could see,' he later told me. He felt that, as well as losing his parents and his sister, he was losing his country and his roots.

In England, I couldn't wait to see my little brother again, but at the same time I was heartbroken that he had had to leave. My mother and sister, alone at home, were even more isolated and vulnerable. Ruth was already showing signs of deep distress and disturbance, a condition that was made worse when Sarah was arrested again for breaking her banning orders at a New Year's Eve party on 31 December 1966.

That day, Ruth said that she wanted to go to the New Year's Eve party. Sarah was torn, knowing that she could be arrested if she went. 'You're being hysterical,' her friends told her. 'It's nonsense.'

Sarah wanted to make sure that Ruth would be all right, so eventually she decided to go along. At the party she was careful to sit in a corner on her own – but it made no difference. Six burly Security Branch officers turned up to arrest her. Sarah asked them, 'Do you really need six great big men to arrest me?'

'Yes,' they said, 'because we need to protect ourselves.'

'What, against me?' she replied incredulously. 'I'm only five-foot tall!' Two of them walked in front of her, two at the back and two at the side as they escorted her out of the house.

When Sarah was arrested, Ruth was also taken to Caledon Square Police Station. One Special Branch man grabbed hold of Ruth, saying, 'This woman is coming with me.'

'Let go of her!' shouted Sarah fiercely at him. 'Don't you dare touch her; she is only a child.'

He released his grip on Ruth and took Sarah to a cell, leaving Ruth alone in the police station at midnight on New Year's Eve. A woman called Flora, whom Ruth did not know, arrived at the police station saying that she had been asked by the hostess of the party to collect Ruth and that my sister could stay with her until things were settled. It suddenly hit Ruth that her father was in jail, her mother had been arrested, and her sister and brother were in England. She was all on her own.

Sarah, meanwhile, was locked in a holding cell. She wanted to phone a lawyer, but the security police wouldn't allow her access to the phone. It was only after the man in charge of the police station – an ordinary policeman – asked her, 'Have you got any complaints?' and she replied, 'Yes, I want to use the telephone', that she was able to use the phone to contact the office of our family lawyer, Himie Bernadt. 'I just sat there in this smelly holding cell thinking to myself, "Well, how long am I going to be here for?" I sat waiting and got very bored and anxious.'

Sarah was let out on bail pending her trial, which was in March. Himie

Bernadt explained that he could no longer defend her, so a young lawyer named Michael Richman offered to take on her case. The Anti-Apartheid Movement in England agreed to pay.

Sarah was in prison for about four days, but it was enough to make life very difficult for Ruth. There was no Fred to help – contact with him had almost completely dried up. After his trial he was back in solitary confinement and placed in the worst possible D Category. All privileges were denied, a terrible infringement of his rights. By then he had been in solitary confinement for thirteen months. We were all very worried about the long-term effects of complete isolation.

Sarah's trial did not turn out to be as disastrous as it could have been. In fact, it provided some comic relief.

21 March 1967

Lynn darling
After yesterday I feel more like Alice in Wonderland than ever. Our old Special Branch friend Van Wyk gave evidence. I personally think the chap should be locked up – he seems to see me everywhere, even if I am not there. He has a very personal hatred of communists and would like to see all people he considers communist dead. Poor chap sat up in a fig tree most of New Year's Eve watching the house I was in. His evidence that he was there was a felt hat totally covered in fig drippings! The fig tree was in the house next door so I don't suppose he had a very clear view – anyway, I hope he got a lot of fig juice in his eyes. In his evidence he said he sent for reinforcements (the number of SB there consisted of 10 per cent of the force in Cape Town) because he feared for their own personal security. What he thought I would do to them I don't know.

The lady of the house, who has never given the situation in this country a thought, and always thought of cops as chaps who should look after her property, simply could not make out what was what. She was too funny for words in the witness box – when the magistrate asked her where she came from, she said, 'Glasgow! Where do you come from?' When she was asked if she kept a guard outside her house, she replied, 'You mean the security police?'

My counsel then told her what the security police had said, and she lost her temper and said, 'How dare you ask me such stupid questions in a witness box?' She wanted to know if they thought she was James Bond.

When she had asked me to come to the house I told her I was not allowed to be with other people, so she told me that no one ever visited her and that she had no friends. When she was asked this in court, she said it was true – she had no friends and did not expect anyone to come into the room where I was. Then she went on to say, 'I asked Mrs Carneson to come to my house, and see what happens to me. I end up in court.' After this experience she will probably think it better she does not have any friends.

It seems hard to believe an entire day of the court's time was taken up to determine if I was on my own in the house or not, or if I talked to anyone or not. A GREAT BIG CRIME. The case has been adjourned to 20 April. The magistrate will then decide if the case should be thrown out – if not we go on from there. It looks as though it will be a long, drawn-out affair.

All this has affected Ruth rather badly. She is sleeping very badly, and if I go out at night she will not go to sleep until I return. She does not mind going out, leaving me on my own all weekend, but gets into a dreadful state if I go out. She is very friendly with a number of young students, but there are so many informers among the students that as soon as anyone becomes friendly, you wonder why. The students themselves have become very tense and distrustful of everyone. In addition to this, the Special Branch follows Ruth around and she is aware of it, and of course you know how unnerving that can be. When I tick the Special Branch off about it, they of course don't know anything about it.

Am having difficulty getting permission to see Dad and am very short of cash. Until my case is over I am not in a good position to do much about this. I mean putting up a fight about this sort of nonsense.

Enjoy your holiday in Paris.

Love from Ruth and myself

It was almost impossible for Ruth to cope with the situation. She became increasingly wild and was behaving rebelliously at her new school, Westerford. Sarah was forbidden to go to the school to discuss the problem. It got worse and Ruth was expelled for insubordination and being unruly. Much later, Ruth provided this account of the period. (Taylor was her headmaster.)

I was expelled from Westerford High School when I was fourteen. I wrote all over the windows:

VORSTER IS A FASCIST
TAYLOR IS A HYPOCRITE
MAKE LOVE NOT WAR
THIS IS THE HENDRIK VERWOERD MEMORIAL WINDOW

I was quite wild. I got up to drinking, smoking and smoking dagga, and going to parties. I used to climb out of the bedroom window at night and come home only in the morning. I stayed up all night with friends in Sea Point – nice Jewish boys. We used to drink their dads' beers when their parents were asleep.

I was overwhelmed by my feelings. I didn't know what to do with them. I was watched and followed. I was scared to go out. I was falling apart. Everything scared me. The buildings scared me, but I couldn't understand why. I was feeling so awful. I knew I was very privileged: I had a nice house and food to eat – not like children in the townships. I couldn't find a reason for feeling like this.

I would go somewhere familiar and feel completely disorientated. I was so disorientated that I didn't know whether I lived up the road or down the road. The tension and the constant fear just took its toll.

We lived all the time in terror. If Mom was in a room with one other person and we heard a knock on the door, everyone would run away and hide. There was very little money. It was difficult to run the boarding house because the security police threatened people, scaring them off. Some of our guests were very unfriendly and supported the security police.

When Mom was on trial, her friend Joan Shchedrin went with her and happened to see a friend of mine who was behaving as if she were a paid informer. Joan said to me, 'That friend is not to be trusted. Stay away from her.' That was the last straw; I fell apart. It was the turning point. My sense of reality went haywire. I felt a deep sense of betrayal, and I couldn't keep it together any more.

It was nerve-wracking to be watched all the time. A car would always follow me. I became very depressed and suicidal. 'I can't go on with this any more,' I thought. 'I must kill myself.'

After I was expelled from school, I took an overdose. I couldn't see any other way out. I went into Groote Schuur Hospital, had a stomach pump and was sent home again. I had already seen this psychiatrist, Dr Van Zyl, and had told him what was happening. He said to Mom that I was suffering from paranoid delusions, was psychotic and that nothing could be done for me. Mom said, 'They are not paranoid delusions. It is real and it's true.'

After they sent me home from hospital, I took another overdose. Things were not getting better. I went to hospital and stayed in hospital. I loved it there; I felt safe. It was wonderful. At least I had company, and it was such a relief to feel safe.

The Special Branch came to the hospital and wanted to question me. That was when the psychiatrist finally realised what was happening and that we were telling the truth. He got scared and decided to go on a long holiday. Before he went, he said to Mom that I mustn't go home and must leave the country as soon as possible.

At that time, the only school that would have me was a Steiner school. I enjoyed being there and stayed with a schoolfriend called Tessa who lived near the school until I left for England. I never went back home to Mount Pleasant.

From my mother's letters and phone calls, it became increasingly obvious that life for her and Ruth was impossible. We had to wait for my mother's appeal, but in the long run it would not make much of a difference. If she got off, there would be more arrests. I started exploring whether they could come to England as political refugees. I wrote a letter to the UK government requesting refugee status for them both. I was optimistic because both John and I were in England and the UK government welcomed South African refugees.

Sarah had to get permission from my father to leave the country. He and Sarah had sworn that they would never escape from South Africa, but she felt that she now had no choice. The authorities would not permit her to leave Cape Town to visit him and, knowing his fragility and his temper, she was nervous about how he would cope with the news. Fortunately, Father Magennis, a Catholic priest who saw Fred on a regular basis, agreed to tell him about Ruth's breakdown and to argue that my mother and Ruth should leave the country.

By then my father was in Pretoria with the other political prisoners. Denis Goldberg, one of his fellow inmates, knew something was wrong: 'There we were in prison, freezing cold, standing on our stools to get our heads in the sun and sewing mailbags at the same time. Fred was called out. After a time he came back, swearing and weeping. He was in a most terrible state about what they had done to his Ruthie. He was in terrible distress.

He was inconsolable. He told me that the chaplain had been given permission to tell him that Ruthie had had a breakdown. Fred was outraged about the pressure put on the family. Sarah was being constantly harassed and arrested. Ruthie couldn't take it any more. There is terrible anguish when you are in prison and unable to help.'

At that time political prisoners weren't allowed to talk to each other. Fred was so distressed that Denis jumped down from his chair. He felt that it was important to give Fred support regardless of the consequences. He walked and talked with Fred, letting him vent his rage. 'Don't give the Boers the victory they want by showing how much you are hurt,' Denis urged him.

Fred wrote to the commanding officer at Pretoria Local Prison, asking to be promoted to B from C Group so that he would be permitted a meeting with Sarah and Ruth, or at least could write a letter to them:

5 June 1967

Dear Sir

Monsignor Magennis informed me on Saturday that my youngest daughter Ruth had a breakdown and was in hospital undergoing treatment, and that the specialists were of the opinion that both she and my wife should leave the country almost immediately. As this involves an unexpected and serious crisis in our family affairs I should appreciate it if you would grant me permission to write a special letter to my wife, and also a brief letter of encouragement to my daughter.

Denying family men adequate contact with those for whom they feel a keen sense of responsibility and anxiety not only imposes a punishment on them but, more important, inflicts an unwarranted punishment on their wives and children as well.

In my own case the altogether inadequate contact with my family, limited at the time to one letter every three months, has had catastrophic consequences; it has been a definite contributory factor in causing my fourteen-year-old daughter to have a very serious mental breakdown.

The Department has consistently turned a deaf ear to all representations made in regard to this aspect of my imprisonment.

With concern for the welfare of my family ever uppermost in my mind, I urge you, Sir, to promote me to at least 'B' Category immediately.

Yours sincerely
Fred Carneson

This letter was ignored, as were many others. Sarah also sent several letters to ask whether she could go to Pretoria to see Fred. She was granted permission only once, but it was impossible for her to go: she was told that she would have to fly to Johannesburg, drive to Pretoria and back, see Fred, and then visit a police station in the middle of Pretoria. On return, she would have to visit a police station in Cape Town in the middle of the afternoon. It was just not possible to do this, and Sarah felt that they were 'taking a sadistic pleasure' in playing with her.

Outside Mount Pleasant, the Special Branch men were openly threatening my mother with violence. 'If you and your lovely daughter stay here any longer, your daughter won't be lovely any more. We know where she is,' they would say. Sarah realised that Ruth needed to leave the country as soon as possible. Because she could not accompany her, Ruth would have to go on her own as soon as Fred's permission came through.

The loneliness without both of her younger children would be unbearable. I knew just how hard it would be for my mother and wished I could be with her in Cape Town to support her.

Ruth arrived on 15 July. I was with Charles McGregor, with whom I was going out, and John. We waited for two hours after the plane landed, but no Ruth. Eventually the intercom requested us to go to the information desk. We were told that Ruth would soon be with us. She arrived dressed in a bright-pink dress with a pink hat, holding a teddy bear. She had refused to answer the immigration officer's questions and, had she not had all the letters allowing her into the country, they might have deported her. When we drove her back into London, she hung out of the window for the whole journey, shouting, 'Hello, London!'

Ruth stayed with me at the beginning, but as I had only one bedroom and was teaching full-time, I could not give her as much attention as I wanted. I had to find a family who could look after her better and get her into a school. I felt dreadful that she could not stay with me, and wished I could take time off teaching, but I was not able to find a replacement.

I took some comfort in the fact that John was fairly well installed at Leighton Park, the Quaker school in the country in Reading. I used to visit him on Sundays in my 1935 Ford Popular and take him and his friends out to lunch. I also attended Parent–Teacher Association meetings, where I heard parents saying that I looked 'much too young to be a mother'!

In London, I scanned the papers to find news of my mother's appeal. She finally got off with a suspended sentence. Van Wyk warned her: 'Mrs

Carneson, we are telling you, if you break your banning order again, it will automatically mean a ten-year sentence.'

Faced with this, Sarah decided that it would be better to keep what was left of the family together in England. She was told that she would have to leave South Africa as a stateless citizen on a one-way ticket. But no aeroplane or boat would take her without having a visa or some sort of documentation. Eventually I managed to obtain a United Nations document granting her permission as a stateless citizen to travel. I also received a letter from the British government saying that she could land in England as a political refugee so that she could be with her children.

Before leaving, Sarah was determined to see my father one more time to say goodbye to him. On her second attempt, she was given permission to see him. She was allowed to stay with her sister Ida in Johannesburg on condition that she reported to various police stations six times a day in Johannesburg and Pretoria.

As she approached the prison, a priest came up to her and said, 'Are you Mrs Carneson? I'm Father Magennis. I see your husband regularly. Would you like me to write to you to let you know how he is?' It was good to see a friendly face. Sarah thanked him for all he had done for Fred and for the family, telling him that she would never forget him. They agreed to keep in contact with each other so that he could pass on news of Fred and she could inform him about the children.

The twenty-minute visit was supposed to be a 'contact' visit, where my parents would be able to sit next to each other. This, however, was not permitted: they were allowed only to hug each other when they said goodbye, and that had to be brief. During the interview they were separated by a glass window, with one security guard behind Sarah and one behind Fred. It was impossible to say everything in twenty minutes, and they could talk about personal matters only.

After the visit, the warden showed Sarah to the main door of the prison and shut her out. She was so upset that she stood outside the door trembling. As she started walking towards the gate, a man came up to her and said, 'Would you like a cigarette?' She was as white as a sheet and, although she never smoked, she took one. The man introduced himself as Joel Joffe, a lawyer who was doing some work for other political prisoners in the jail. Sarah's mother, Grandma Anna, was waiting for her at the exit and was shocked when she saw Sarah smoking. 'You're smoking,' she said accusingly.

Sarah felt completely drained. Her atypical behaviour reflected her turbulent emotional state. 'Fred and I both seemed very calm during the visit,' she said, 'but that was a surface thing. We were too emotional even to say goodbye properly.'

Sarah returned to Cape Town, visited the police station, packed and walked out of the front door of the home she would never see again. She didn't look back.

She was escorted to the Cape Town docks by the security police and boarded the SS *Vaal* to England on 6 September 1967. Like John and Ruth before her, the last piece of land she saw was Robben Island, where many of her black comrades were in prison.

Fred was beside himself with grief. He swore, ranted and raved at the government until the authorities reluctantly agreed to send a telegram on his behalf to Sarah's ship: *To Carneson. SS Vaal. Docks. Cape Town. Bon Voyage darling. All my love you and children. Fred.* This was followed by a letter to me with a message for my mother: 'The heart travels faster than boat, aeroplane or spaceship. Mine will be at Southampton to welcome Mum. Please give it to her wrapped in a big hug, sealed with a loving kiss from me.'

The Nationalist government had succeeded in splitting our family apart. It was a painful, confused and troubled time for all of us. Fred was suffering in prison, and Sarah had had to break a promise to herself and Fred that she would never leave South Africa. She was on her way to another country, with no work and an uncertain future, and she was worried about Ruth, who was feeling like a displaced stranger in a foreign land. John had been putting on a brave face but was missing his parents terribly. Like me, he felt helpless. I felt extremely guilty that I could not spend more time with John and Ruth or support the family more financially. We were separated from each other physically, and each of us was emotionally drained, exhausted and in a state of shock. Separately we had to cope as best we could.

After so many years of fighting the oppression of the apartheid regime, this was an exceptionally tough time.

One has to ask why the Nationalist government and the security police of the apartheid regime feared and hated my parents and their comrades so much. The simple answer is that they were active communists and staunchly supported the then banned ANC. My parents believed that the apartheid regime was an oppressive form of fascism, and they fought the injustices of apartheid with unwavering commitment. This was perceived as even more heinous because, as whites, they were regarded as betraying their own race.

The more complex answer lies in who they were and where they came from: the seeds of their ultimate fates were planted in their childhoods.

PART TWO

Black, White and Red

1916–1967

9

Sarah Rubin

My mother, Sarah Carneson, née Rubin, was born on 17 June 1916 in Johannesburg. Her father, Zelic, came from Lithuania and her mother, Anna, from Russia. Both were Jewish and had had to embark on long, difficult boat journeys to Cape Town to escape the then prevalent anti-Semitism in their home countries. Zelic arrived in South Africa with his father and brother in 1901; Anna and her mother landed a year later, in 1902. Zelic and Anna met in Johannesburg and found that they were both committed Marxists and trade unionists; both would be inspired by the Russian Revolution. They brought their European beliefs and visions with them and loved to read literature and discuss Marx and Lenin. In the photograph I have of them, they are good-looking, well fed and seem full of energy. My grandmother Anna, with her high Slavic cheekbones, shiny black hair, flashing brown eyes and tiny waist, was beautiful. Zelic was handsome in a quiet way, with fair skin, blue eyes and a warm smile. In the same photograph are my oldest aunt, Katie (about six), my uncle Solly (about eight), my mother (about three) and Ida, who was still a toddler. My great-uncle Eli is also in the photograph, wearing a light linen suit and a straw boater.

When Anna and Zelic married, they had little money and, at first, life was tough. They started out in a small terraced house in Foxbury, Johannesburg. It was very basic, and had no bathroom. Sarah remembered that bath times were never pleasant: 'We used to have to heat the bath water on the kitchen stove. My mother, who could stand a lot of heat, used to dump us in scalding-hot water. We would make a terrible fuss about this but my mother was never sensitive to our physical and emotional needs. She could sometimes be quite violent. Perhaps that was because she was so hardworking and had only one kidney, so she never had the time or patience to bother about how we felt.

'My parents were the opposite of each other, which was the saving grace for us. My father was kind, gentle, loving and very generous. He was always there to smooth things over and come to our rescue when my mother lost her temper. When we saw that Anna was angry and about to hit us, we would run to our dad for protection. He smacked me only twice in my life, and I was shocked. That was enough to keep me in line.'

Zelic came from a long line of radical thinkers. His grandfather was a freethinker in the Fabian Society. Both of his parents were dominant members of the Communist Party in Lithuania until anti-Semitism made life impossible for them.

Anna, whose parents were Orthodox Jews, came with her mother, brother and sister to South Africa. Her father (my great-grandfather) was a corporal in the Tsarist army and had been 'lent' to the British army to fight in the Anglo-Boer War. He was seldom at home and when he did return he was a fanatical religious tyrant. Anna hated him: he would punish her physically and verbally if she broke any religious laws. As a result, my grandmother became extremely anti-religious. Instead, she was interested in left-wing politics and was passionately in favour of the Russian Revolution. As a young girl, she used to throw marbles under the hooves of the Tsarist army's horses in Moscow to stop the people being trampled.

My grandparents were a strong and hard-working couple, and firm comrades: they worked closely together for the same communist ideals. They started life as tailors, saved their money and, after a few years, my grandmother became a shrewd businesswoman, successfully buying, renovating and selling properties. This meant that the family could move to the large house at 297 Bree Street, near the End Street Common in Johannesburg. Zelic had his own factory at the back of the garden. He employed black, coloured, Indian and white people, and they worked together as equals – something that was unheard of in those days.

Sarah recalled the house with great enjoyment:

> In our home, people who needed help were never turned away. The house was always open to people of all races including blacks, coloureds and Indians, which of course was taboo back then. In the 1930s, because of the Depression, many people went hungry. Both of my parents gave us a good understanding of the misery created by poverty in South Africa.
>
> Every day there would be about fifteen of us at the dinner table. This would include comrades of my parents, students, artists and those who were unemployed. The house was always full of writers and artists having constant discussions. My parents knew almost everyone who had left-wing

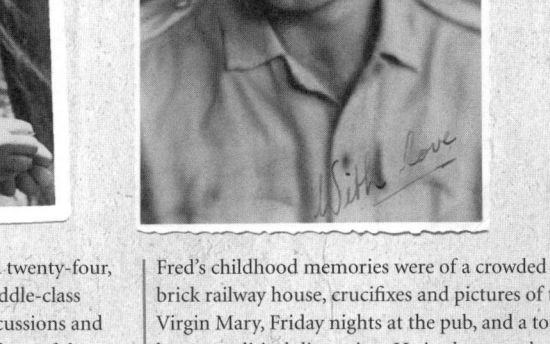

Sarah, pictured here in 1940, aged twenty-four, looked back on a comfortable middle-class Jewish family life, intellectual discussions and her parents' role as founder members of the Communist Party of South Africa

Fred's childhood memories were of a crowded brick railway house, crucifixes and pictures of the Virgin Mary, Friday nights at the pub, and a total ban on political discussion. He is photographed here in 1941, aged twenty-one

Young and independent, Sarah (right) saved money from her first wages to go on holiday to Madagascar with a friend, 1935

One of the leaflets used by Sarah, Fred and their comrades to campaign against the exploitation of black labour, c. 1940

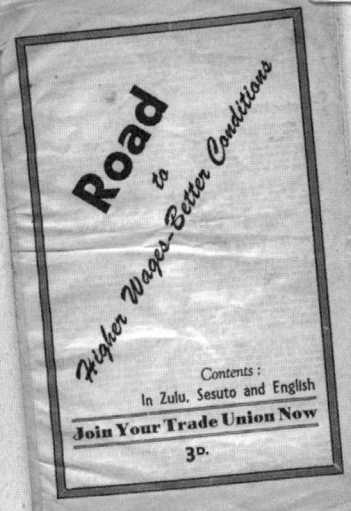

Sarah (bottom row, far right) and Pauline Podbury (centre) entertaining Egyptian visitors, who supported the South African Trade Union Movement, 1937

Signalman Fred, aged nineteen, in the desert during World War II, ready to fight in the battle of Tobruk, during which he escaped across the lines as one of five in his platoon to survive, 1939

Fred (second from right) and comrades in Italy before the Monte Sole massacre in 1944. The South African brigade was instrumental in liberating Italy for the Allies to come through

Fred in the *Guardian* newspaper office, 1947. He knew that if the National Party won the elections in 1948, not only would it mean the oppression of blacks, but also the eventual banning of the Communist Party of South Africa

The *Guardian* was a mouthpiece for anti-apartheid and pro-communist sentiment, and objected to the draconian measures that were being imposed on communists, 1946

Lynn winning first prize as *Guardian* angel at the *Guardian*'s annual fund-raising bazaar, 1952

One of the pamphlets educating people about the extreme-right-wing white group, the Broederbond, c. 1947

MEET YOUR ENEMIES!

AN EXPOSURE OF THE "BROEDERBOND"—THE ORGANISATION WHICH CONTROLS AND CO-ORDINATES THE ACTIVITIES OF ALL FASCIST MOVEMENTS THROUGHOUT SOUTH AFRICA.

Fred with members of the Communist Party, ready to tackle the Nationalists. From left to right: Zolli Malindi, Fred, Moses Kotane and Sam Kahn, c. 1947

Fred speaking at an Athlone rally, 1949, with Yusuf Dadoo (far left), John Morley-Turner (bottom row, second from left) and Chris Hani (sitting below Fred on right). The security police reported that Fred was 'an especially good speaker and easily [swept] his listeners to a high'

Fred and Lynn, 1948. When Fred and Sarah were reunited after being separated, Lynn, aged four, insisted on going everywhere with Fred

Fred and Yusuf Dadoo, who both belonged to the Central Committee of the Communist Party, 1950

'In excellent company': This picture of the accused in the Treason Trial amused Fred, who said that the trial gave the opposition leaders of South Africa the opportunity to plan future strategies together, 1956

The much-loved family home, Mount Pleasant, 49 Belmont Avenue, Oranjezicht, Cape Town. Even when life became difficult, the views of sea and mountain were a comfort

Lynn, John and Ruth at St James beach on a sunny day, 1956

John and Ruth were inseparable and loved walking in the Tokai forest, where the family picked mushrooms, 1958

Letter from Fred to Lynn on her first day of high school, 1957, while he was an awaiting-trial prisoner during the Treason Trial. His admission card indicates that he was charged with 'High Treason'

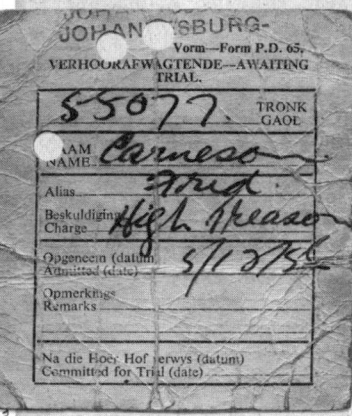

Fred with Chief Luthuli and Sonia Bunting, 1957, when Fred was asked to act as host and bodyguard to Luthuli during his Cape Town visit

'Strijdom, you have struck a rock': Women's March, 9 August 1956. Sarah worked hard underground to help organise the march and publicise the campaign, but she could not take part in the demonstration as she was banned at the time

Lynn, John and Ruth pretending to be happy for photographer Eli Weinberg after Sarah had been jailed for six months and Fred was in hiding, 1960

John was deeply affected by the temporary loss of his parents and used to compensate by being physically active, including climbing trees, c. 1960

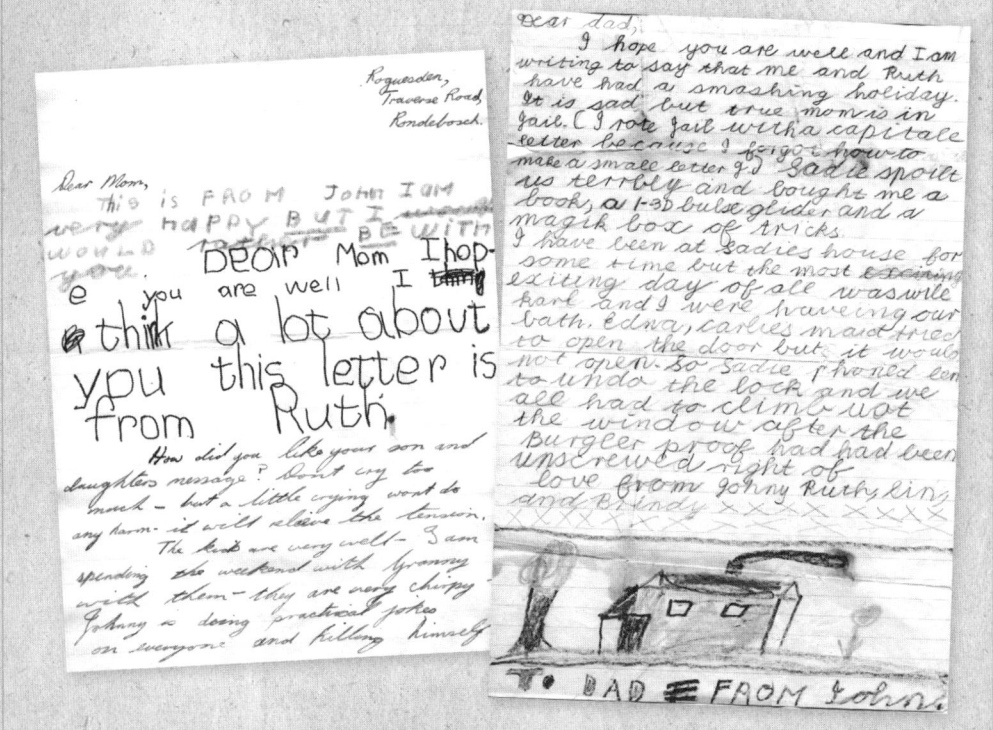

Letters from the children to Fred and Sarah. Lynn found it hard work persuading John and Ruth to write letters. When John wrote to Fred (right), he had no idea whether Fred knew that Sarah was in prison, 1960

tendencies. My mother managed to feed all of us and did not grumble about it; she did not mind cooking enormous amounts of food every day. Because she was a farmer's daughter, she knew how to make food go far. During the Depression she used to buy the head of a cow, boil it down and use the marrow. That's how she could feed so many people.

Our schoolfriends would look at us with wide eyes when they saw all these people sitting around the same table, saying "How could you?" At school we had one set of rules and at home another. There were times in my life when I wished that my parents were like other parents, that we were ordinary. Later, I was very proud of the fact that they were different.

My grandparents' hospitality extended to their relatives too. Sarah's cousin Alex Goldberg remembered that, when he was nine, he took extremely ill:

In my home town, Ermelo, I was operated on by a local doctor. The operation went wrong, and my parents decided that, since I was so ill, they should try Johannesburg. So we came to the Rubins' at Bree Street. When we arrived at Park Station after an overnight train journey, Sarah's brother Solly wrapped me in a blanket, lifted me through the window of the compartment, put me into his car and brought me to the Rubin house. I was lucky because my aunt Anna happened to be friends with the leading surgeon in Johannesburg, Lee McGregor. Unusually for a specialist, he came to the house to examine me. I had to be admitted to the hospital immediately. Solly took my mother, my father and me to the hospital and, after the operation, I stayed with them for months. Katie, Sarah's older sister, used to take me by tram to the end of Twist Street for therapy. I remember many happy hours playing with Sarah even though she was older than me.

Sarah was very sociable and loved playing with other children, but she had a heart murmur that forced her to stay inside the house while other children went out to play. She spent a lot of time alone, reading. Her father spent many hours with her explaining his theories and views. A well-read man, he was a dedicated Marxist who told Sarah that if it ever meant that he had to go against his principles, he would rather starve and have his children starve. But, as Sarah commented, 'We never starved and we had a comfortable, well-maintained home.' Zelic also explained to her that he and Anna had started off in South Africa as members of the Labour Party.

When the First World War broke out, they disagreed with the leadership of the Labour Party, who supported the war. 'It is a war that we should not be involved in,' Zelic said. 'If we go and fight, we could kill other workers. They don't know us, we don't know them and we have nothing against them.' They broke away from the Labour Party and, because of his views on the war, Zelic could not find work. He decided to be independent; to become his own boss. In 1921, Anna and Zelic were founder members of the Communist Party of South Africa (CPSA). They helped the miners who went on strike in 1922 by distributing leaflets and organising demonstrations for better wages and working conditions.

My grandparents used to have regular Communist Party meetings at the Trades Hall in Kerk Street, a few streets away from their home in Bree Street. Calling themselves the 'Liberal Studies Group' for protection, they would meet with people who shared similar ideologies. They would attend meetings or demonstrations every Tuesday and Thursday, where they were habitually beaten up by the police and right-wingers. Although they came back bruised and bleeding, they were never deterred. Sarah did not find this daunting, remarking, 'I was never too worried about this. It was a way of life.'

As a young girl, Sarah loved listening to her father. When she was ten, she tried to read *Das Kapital* by Marx, to impress him, but couldn't understand it. Her father was very amused. As she grew up, she found books and intellect less entertaining, especially as she saw her sisters go out with boyfriends. Katie, her oldest sister, was very fashionable, and Ida, the youngest, was pretty, a good tennis player and popular. Sarah made a life-changing decision: 'In my teens I had had enough of sitting on my own being careful about my health. One day I was at home watching my two sisters dress up to go to a party and I made the decision that I would rather die young and live a full life. So I "borrowed" one of Kay's dresses and went out with a friend. I had a really good time. The problem was that Kay and I came in at the same time and she was furious that I had taken her dress without asking.'

When Sarah was still at school, she joined the youth wing of the CPSA, but it took her a long time to decide to become a communist. She was not sure that she wanted to be totally committed, especially as she wanted to explore what life had to offer. She explained, 'It was a difficult decision to make. You couldn't take it lightly. You had to prove you were doing worthwhile political work; you couldn't just be a member. If you joined, it would determine your lifestyle.' At eighteen, she joined the Communist Party, accepting that it was a decision that would steer the course of her life.

When Sarah left school she worked full-time, performing administrative tasks for the Party. When the Party ran out of funds, she started working for an organisation that offered correspondence courses. They told her that she was one of the best administrators they had ever encountered, but after a few months she discovered that the people working there were underpaid. She decided to organise them into a trade union. 'I was sacked immediately,' she laughed. 'I came home that evening and told my parents that I had been sacked because I wanted to organise the workers. They saw this as a very healthy sign and congratulated me.'

Before determining her next step, Sarah went to Durban to help Ida, her youngest sister, who had married at eighteen and already had a baby. 'Jasper was the first baby between us,' said Sarah, 'and neither of us knew much about babies, but he survived our parenting.' Although Sarah worked part-time while helping Ida, she found it difficult to find decent work and missed her friends in Johannesburg. Once Ida was coping, she returned to Johannesburg to look for work and to help look after a black comrade called Josie, who also had a new baby and who, as a single mother with a missing husband, was finding it hard to manage with four other young children in addition to the baby.

Josie lived in Sophiatown. Her shack was made out of corrugated iron and the walls were lined with newspapers to try to shield the family from the intense heat in summer and winter's biting cold. It had one room with a table, some chairs, a bed and a mattress, where the children slept. The baby was lovingly deposited in a cardboard box.

When Sarah turned up, Josie was not well. Sarah paid to take her to the doctor. She was worried, and said to me many years later, 'I went to see her doctor, who told me that he was not happy with her pulse, and asked if I could take it every half-hour. Well, I did not know anything about taking pulses, having no nursing experience, but I was the only one there and I had to do what I could. While Josie was in bed feeling rather ill, she asked me to make lunch for her children. I asked her, "What have you got that I can cook for them?" She replied, "Oh, there's half a loaf of white bread and an onion that you could cook up. They love that." I was shocked. This incident convinced me that we had to get people away from poverty and that I had to commit my life to working towards bringing about change in the country. I felt that the trade unions were the best place for me to start.'

Sarah found work helping to organise the non-white branch of the

Railway and Harbour Workers' Union. She loved the job because the people were so interesting, and was particularly influenced by a man who 'was old enough to be my grandfather'. 'He worked in the laundry,' she recounted. 'He told me that until I could get myself involved in political work my life was meaningless. When I received a message from his family to say that he was very ill in hospital, I rushed to see him, but he had already died. I was extremely sad, and at his funeral I thought to myself, "Here is Tommy Ryan, who gave me so much courage. Surely his memory should go on." Whenever I got tired and fed up, I would think of Tommy, who with very little education helped to inspire the Railway and Harbour workers.'

Sarah became General Secretary of the union and started helping to set up other trade unions, including the Tobacco Workers' Union and the National Union of Distributive Workers, which represented white shop assistants.

When she helped the shop assistants, she was shocked by the plight of the poor whites. After the First World War, Afrikaans farmers who owned smallholdings were starving. They came to the cities with their families where, thin and undernourished, they lived in drainpipes. The English would not give jobs to those who had an Afrikaans accent or an Afrikaans name. Their daughters found work as shop assistants but were paid such low wages and were treated so badly that, if their families were not so desperately in need, the work would not have been worth their while.

Sarah was asked to go to Durban where she worked with H.A. Naidoo and the sugar-cane workers. She found the work inspirational, and said, 'We went to the sugar-cane fields and talked to the people about joining a union. People would meet us with a jug of coffee and sandwiches. We knew that they needed this more than we did. Membership consisted of people who were descendants of indentured labour. They lived in the most appalling conditions. Large families would live in one room, so if one member of the family contracted TB or cholera, the whole family would get it. Disease became a very serious problem when I was there. Many people died.'

The majority of workers were Indian. They were influenced by the Indian national struggle for independence. Young, fiery and intelligent people would get up and speak about the importance of standing together. Sarah found Indian men easy to talk to, politically educated and extremely attractive. She loved the people and the work: 'We worked hard and played hard. We had wild parties and, yes, I had some boyfriends. I had an affair with the president of the Indian Congress, Yusuf Dadoo, who was very good-looking and passionate. But that wasn't very important because he had affairs with many other young women. There were lots of other interesting men around. The times when I was working full-time were some of the best times of my life.'

In 1938, just before the outbreak of the Second World War, Sarah was twenty-two. There was a strong anti-war sentiment among the comrades because of the capitalist South African government's support for the war. Later on, Sarah and her comrades realised not only that the war had to be opposed on imperialist grounds, but that fascism had to be defeated too. Fighting fascism strengthened their solidarity with workers overseas; as Internationalists, they believed that they could change the world.

One incident in Johannesburg amused Sarah. Immediately after war was declared in 1939, many members of the police force supported Hitler. When South Africa joined the Allied Forces on 6 September 1939, the police went on strike. As a result, my mother and her comrades were able to hold successful demonstrations without trouble from the police, who had been imprisoned.

Not only did Sarah work closely with Indians in Natal, but she also maintained links with her black comrades. She was lucky to work closely with Moses Kotane, the impressive General Secretary of the Communist Party, who was instrumental in forming the ANC Youth League. As a boy he had started out herding cattle in the Transvaal, before moving to the city to look for employment. He worked in a bakery while educating himself with the help of some of the members of the Communist Party. Like many other black people, he was also an active member of the ANC. Initially an elite organisation for African intellectuals, the ANC was against white membership and felt that the Party was dominated by whites. Most of the black people who joined the Party did so because they believed that South Africa should belong to all races. Under the leadership of Kotane, the Communist Party fostered solid relations with the ANC, and when the ANC became more of a mass organisation, the Party always supported and worked closely with it.

Sarah's political life was closely intertwined with her family history. Yet while she had followed in the ideological footsteps of her parents, she was very much her own person with her own beliefs and attitudes.

Fred came from another world entirely.

10

Fred Carneson

THE BACKGROUND AND childhood of my father, Fred Carneson, could not have been more different from my mother's. He was born on 13 January 1920 in a wood-and-iron house in Goodwood, Cape Town. His parents were both second-generation South Africans. They had nine children, one of whom died soon after birth. The Goodwood roads at that stage were sandy with no pavements, and there was no electricity. The family's water was drawn from a well and they used a bucket sanitary system. Fred's parents were both almost illiterate, although his father did learn to read enough to enjoy simple books and to qualify as a house painter and decorator. Of the eight surviving children, there were six sons and two daughters. Steady and reliable, the oldest son, Albert, was interested in Morse code and was a radio amateur, while Mattie was more happy-go-lucky. Joe was quiet and struggled with partial deafness. Alfie, a collector, was proud of his collection of ties, while the youngest son, Anthony – named after his father – was physically active and enjoyed making and building things. Fred was the sixth child, born after his father's return from the First World War. The sons took up a variety of occupations: one was a painter, one a plumber, one a brickie, one a ticket checker on the railway and one a labourer, later a messenger for the bank. Both of Fred's sisters married early. His older sister, Aggie, had eleven children, ten of whom survived, while his younger sister, Hilda, was mother to four children. When her husband died, Hilda first worked as a shop assistant and then for the post office, servicing telephones. Fred's siblings were always full of fun, enjoyed jokes and puns and loved practical jokes.

Fred's father, Anthony, was born in Woodstock, Cape Town. When his family had come to South Africa from Portugal, they had anglicised their name from Encarnação to Carneson. He worked for the railways as a coach painter at Salt River until he was transferred to the Pietermaritzburg railway workshops in 1924, when Fred was four. Fred always remembered

Cape Town with immense affection. In Pietermaritzburg, they lived in one of the 'railway houses' that were provided by the railway company for its white workers. The house was a small, white, single-storey cottage with four bedrooms and a small living room, which was used only on special occasions. A kitchen led into the backyard, where the family spent most of their time. The outside toilet was also in the backyard, and there was a small garden at the front of the house. Because there was so little space, the children shared beds, sleeping one at each end. Fred slept in the same bed as his younger brother Anthony. Books were extremely uncommon in my father's household because, most of the time, the family's reading was limited to comics and racing forms – they often bet on the horses.

Fred's father was extremely hard-working but never recovered from the First World War, where he had seen two of his own brothers killed. He suffered from continual ill health when he returned to civilian life, and was bitter because, although he had risked his life for his country, he received no support from the government after the war. In spite of this, he had a huge capacity for enjoying life, and his children remembered him as being a fundamentally happy and affectionate person.

Anthony Senior was musical and enjoyed playing his banjo in the backyard, having sing-songs with his family. Although sociable, he was authoritarian and a very strict parent. He hated politics and forbade the teenage Fred to talk about it in the house after he had become a communist and an atheist. Fred used to irritate his father by saying grace: 'Thank you God for the food we make. *Ons skoene maak onsself* [Our shoes we make ourselves].' Then Freddie, as his family called him, would giggle while his father frowned furiously.

Fred's mother, Annie, was born in Salt River, Cape Town. Her family came from Scotland, Ireland and Germany. Before her marriage she worked as a domestic for the Catholic bishop of Cape Town and then, as a devout Catholic herself, spent the rest of her life living for her family. She was a kind person, obedient to her husband and sons. According to Fred's sister Hilda, 'Mommy was quiet; I'd say reserved. She gave good advice and was very hard-working. Although she was quiet, she had a sense of humour which we often did not expect. She loved to sing during the day while doing her chores. I remember one song in particular: "Close down the curtains, I can't sing tonight." She had a lovely voice.

'We used to joke that she was the worst cook in the world, which is why we hated eating fish on Fridays. She used to cook a huge roast on Sundays and we ate the remainders of the roast during the week.

'We never had much, but we had a lot of love and laughter. We were always teasing each other in a good-natured way. We were never hungry and we always had clothes and shoes.'

When they were small, the Carneson children loved chasing each other in and out of the house, playing a variety of games and joking and laughing hilariously at anything they thought was funny. Freddie enjoyed playing practical jokes and would tease his sisters mercilessly. He had an infectious laugh that set everyone off, often for no reason at all. The children also had free rein of the neighbours' houses. Hilda remembered the Colburns and the Osbornes, saying, 'We always helped each other out if someone was in trouble or needed anything.'

Friday nights saw the family parading in Church Street, doing their weekly shopping. Known as the 'monkey parade', the people would fill the streets: while their parents were intent on shopping, the young would eye each other. Later on, when they were old enough, the boys would join their father and go round the corner to the bar, The Thistle – called 'many a wife's nightmare'. When they were drunk enough, they loved a good fight and would often stagger noisily home with bruises and bloody noses. All the boys, including Freddie, swore like troopers, sometimes competing with each other to come up with the filthiest swear word they could find.

On Saturdays the children went to the bioscope, The Grand, to watch the matinee. For a penny they would buy peanuts in cone-shaped packets made from newspaper. Their favourite movies were the first 'talkies' – *Syncopation*, *King of Jazz*, and *Rio Rita*, with the actor John Boles.

Like the other children, Freddie was brought up as a strict Catholic, serving as an altar boy at the Catholic church in Pietermaritzburg. His family was deeply religious and went to church every Sunday.

Fred was extremely bright, curious and eager to learn. Although he was naughty, his teachers at his small local school were fond of his high spirits. In Standard 6 (Grade 8), when he was ten, they encouraged him to sit examinations for the most prestigious college of Natal, Maritzburg College. He won a bursary to attend the school, and was the first member of his family to be educated beyond Standard 6.

Going to Maritzburg College was a major culture shock for Fred. The school aspired to be the South African equivalent of such famous British public schools as Eton and Harrow. It was set in huge grounds, surrounded by woods, and the school building was a large red-brick Victorian house with imposing columns. The gym and sanatorium were housed in separate buildings, and there were tennis courts, sports grounds and a sizeable swimming pool. Fred had mixed feelings about the school. On the one hand he was passionate about Maritzburg College's core values, as they reflected those that had been instilled in him at home – honesty, courage, integrity, self-discipline, commitment and respect. He was deeply influenced by Alan Paton, author of *Cry, the Beloved Country* and Fred's teacher, who took Fred under his wing and encouraged him and the other boys to be critical of the racist system in which they lived. Fred's ambivalence towards his new environment derived both from the fact that he came from a less privileged background than the majority of the boys, and from his new awareness and questioning of racism. Fred said,

> I lapped up everything that I could learn and developed an enjoyment of culture – literature, music, philosophy and the arts. But I not only learnt how to develop my thinking; I also developed my ability to fight. Most of the other boys were wealthy. Because I was poor and smaller than most, I was mercilessly teased and goaded. I fought my corner – I was better at insults and swearing – but did not enjoy being there. I made a promise to myself that I would never ever disrespect anyone for being poor. I was also very aware that when we went to church, on one side sat the whites and on the other side, the Indians. I thought that that was wrong.
>
> I gained a first-class Junior Certificate at the college, but unfortunately my father could not afford to keep me at school. It was the height of the Depression and he was working only three or four days a week. I had to leave school to start working when I was fourteen. Having had a taste of education I was unhappy to leave so soon, but I swore to myself that I would never stop learning.

While Fred was looking for work, his father used to send him to the library to fetch the detective books that he liked to read. While the librarian was looking for the books, Fred would browse among the bookshelves, picking up books at random. One day he found a book called *The Lives of the Great Philosophers*. He started reading it, found it fascinating and borrowed it. Then he looked up the references in all the footnotes, a project that took him a couple of years. 'That is when I first came across Karl Marx and started to be proud that I was working class,' he explained.

Freddie first worked as a messenger at the post office for a basic three pounds, seventeen shillings and sixpence a month plus a bicycle allowance of seven shillings and sixpence. During this time he also had his first girlfriend, Edith. She told me that 'Freddie was always communistic – even as early as fourteen. When he earned his first salary, he gave most of his money to his mother, kept a little for himself and then wanted to give some to the poor blacks who had nothing to eat. So he changed the rest into very small change and we went into the middle of the beer hall. You can imagine how frightened I felt. Then he threw all the money into the middle of the hall and ran out.'

When Fred was old enough, he trained as a post and telegraph assistant and worked in post offices in Durban, Pietermaritzburg and Port Shepstone. During that period he shared lodgings with students who were communists, and he decided to join the Communist Party. Whether his decision to become a communist resulted from the influence of a young woman named Sarah Rubin, whom he met briefly during that time, or from interactions with communist housemates was a matter my father would never say with certainty.

Not long after this, Fred joined the army to fight in the Second World War. 'I lied about my age to get into the army to fight fascism and to meet up with other Internationalists,' he told me. 'We believed that if workers of the world united, it would be possible to have a better world where workers were not exploited by greedy capitalists because they owned the means of production. We really believed that if we enabled workers to develop consciousness, to be politicised and to mobilise the masses, we could change the world.'

When my father was dying, he said to me, 'Two times were the worst times of my life: when I was tortured and when I was a soldier in the Second World War. That had a terrible effect on me.' But when I asked him about it, he said, 'I don't want to talk about it.' When I had done some research and established more about his war experiences, I could understand why.

When I was trying to find material about the war and my father's involvement, out of the blue I had a lucky break. After an article about Fred appeared in the local newspaper in 2007, the phone rang. 'Are you the daughter of Fred Carneson?' a voice said. 'My name is Major Holloway. Fred was under my command when we escaped through the enemy lines in Tobruk. Would you like me to talk to you about it?'

Major Holloway was a tall, dignified, immaculately dressed man who was still driving his car at the age of eighty-nine. Over a cup of tea with me, he described his war experiences so vividly that the war came alive for me. Before our conversation, the war in which my father had fought had been just an abstraction that had death, killing and pain associated with it.

Joining the army was a political commitment for Fred: he knew that the Nazis had to be defeated. He was barely seventeen, which was underage, and he bluffed his way into the army because they needed signallers: he had worked at the post office so he had the requisite experience.

Fred became a radio officer in the Duke's 10th Brigade Signal Company. He was sent to East Africa and Abyssinia for a year and a half. The desert consisted of nothing but miles and miles of hot sand, scrubby grey bushes and sand dunes. The soldiers were badly sunburnt and it was hard to breathe in the swirling, stinging grains of the frequent sandstorms. Fighting was vicious. When Major Holloway, Fred and his signal company of fifteen men drove into the desert, the road was strewn with burnt-out vehicles and aeroplanes, corpses dotted across the landscape like ants. The stench of rotting bodies was as overpowering as the sound of bombs being dropped by aircraft and the staccato of machine guns. Fred and his fellow soldiers had to dig trenches to bury the cables and hide them so that they could receive radio signals. He knew that the lines of these trenches could be seen by enemy aircraft and that it was easy for the enemy to trace them to the signal office where he, Fred, was sitting, to drop their bombs. When he was not in the signal office, Fred took dispatches on Major Holloway's Harley-Davidson. In spite of the thrill of riding a huge motorbike as fast as it could go, he knew that he was an easy target and could be shot down at any moment.

Even in the stress of war, Fred was mindful of the underdog. Major Holloway had six Zulu batmen working for him. They were taught how to dig themselves a shell-slit below ground level to avoid being shot and were told how they should queue for food. Fred tried to persuade them to eat with the white soldiers: 'We are all doing the same job, so you must join the food line like the rest of us!' They always refused, and at every meal time the other soldiers would tease Fred, saying, 'Go on, invite the Zulus to join us.' But they never did.

When it looked as if the Germans were going to win, the major asked for twelve soldiers to volunteer to join a composite battalion going to the coastal port of Tobruk to fight it out. Fred volunteered. The Allied line had been stormed by the Germans under Erwin Rommel. The English kept changing their minds about what to do, and their troops retreated just as Major Holloway and his platoon came through Tobruk. Two days later, the major and his men were completely cut off from the rest. On 21 June 1942, Tobruk fell and General Klopper surrendered.

Fred's 10th Brigade Signal Company refused to surrender. Instead, they decided to escape. The major suggested they make a dash for it through the German lines in the two radio vans they had left, and the men agreed to take the chance. The lines were full of Germans singing triumphant songs of winning the battle, playing German music and waving flags with swastikas from the tops of their tanks. Major Holloway and the men decided to join, quietly, the German transport moving towards the desert – the Germans had captured so many enemy vehicles that other non-German vans joining the convoy could easily be overlooked. It worked: neither of the vans was noticed. The major had taken five men with him in his van, including Fred. Because Fred was a good artist, he sat beside the major sketching the insignia on the German vehicles around them as intelligence to identify the German troops in the event that they reached their own lines safely.

When the convoy halted, the major signalled to the second van, which was travelling behind them, that they were going off the road and through the desert bushes. It was then that they were spotted. A German armoured car fired at them and the second van was captured. They never saw their fellow soldiers again.

The Germans chased the remaining van, firing at it continuously, but Fred, Major Holloway and the three other men in the vehicle managed to escape. Four hours later, driving south with the aid only of the major's sun compass (they had been instructed to destroy their radios days before), they caught sight of four soldiers walking on their own. They were relieved to recognise them as other South Africans, who joined them. Continuing into the desert, they came across more German convoys going to El Alamein, but the Germans took no notice of the small van. They went on alone and during the afternoon caught up with two other trucks. Fred looked through some German binoculars, which he had taken off a dead body. 'There are black men in those trucks,' he said excitedly. 'Definitely not Germans. Yes, there are black chaps.' He dug out a white vest and waved it to attract attention. The trucks stopped: they were Allies. Major Holloway asked them how they could get back into their own lines. 'Wait until dusk and use your car lights to signal the letter D: dash, dot, dot,' was the reply.

It took the whole of the next day in the burning desert heat with limited water supplies to travel 120 miles to friendly lines. When Fred and his fellow soldiers reached safety, they realised that out of an original sixteen men, there were just five survivors.

The situation did not get any better. The next battle, the Battle of El Alamein, was one of the worst in the war. In a BBC project titled *World War 2: People's War*, a South African soldier named Douglas Baker narrates how he was driving shot-up trucks back from the Front for repair. The ground in front of him was boiling with mortars and shells and the noise was terrible. Baker saw an unending infantry row of South Africans starting to move forward. Fred, said Baker, was among them, and positioned to Baker's left. They were all looking for mines and there were tripwires everywhere. Baker flung himself into a shell hole, switching the Bren from single shots to automatic and engaging the machine-gun nests. The next moment, he said that 'Shorty' Carneson rushed up. 'A piece of shrapnel had hit him in the jaw. He was wide-eyed and scared stiff.' Baker used a handkerchief to staunch the blood flow and told Fred to take a pull at his side bottle. He then grabbed some Bren magazines from Fred's wobbling pouch and sent him on his way.

When my father had some time to himself during the war, he read, learnt languages and read or wrote poetry:

> Keep hushed the voice and
> softly tread
> on this unknown field where
> lie the dead
> in stiff unseemly attitudes
> of frozen fear
> No muffled beat of drums
> No bugles sounding clear
> No patriotic rhetoric to
> claim their cause was just!
> Only the moan of the
> unfelt wind and a pall
> of desert dust attends the shallow burial
> of erstwhile friends and foe
> Who dreamed of homes in
> distant lands a few
> short days ago

What kept Fred going was his vision that the communists would change the world for the better and his belief that the Internationalist Movement was an important part of this. He met other soldiers who shared his convictions and they became comrades. Taking part in life-threatening exercises deepened their friendship and trust in each other. When the Allies were preparing for the invasion of Italy, Fred and his friend Ivan Schermbrucker were among those who took a convoy from Egypt to Algeria and then to Sicily, landing at Salerno. From there they moved across the Italian Peninsula to Bari on the Adriatic coast and then worked their way to Alcona, where their company established its headquarters.

The Germans were still offering stiff resistance and Fred's unit moved up the coast at a fairly slow pace. 'On one occasion,' remembered my father, 'we were called upon to repair telegraph lines along the destroyed railway track running north. I worked with Ivan digging holes on the side of the track. To get to the track we had to cross a heavily mined area with safe paths marked out by strips of white cloth. A small team not far from us dug out a rock and it rolled down the embankment, triggering an antipersonnel mine that sprang into the air before exploding. One of the team was killed. We had been joking with him an hour before, and now he was just blood and bone spattered over the land.'

The men had to camouflage their tents to prevent being discovered. It had been raining steadily for days on end and there was a lot of mud with which to do the job. Fred and Ivan decided to mix military duty with propaganda. They smeared the canvas with hammer-and-sickle symbols, big and small: 'We got away with it – there was no adverse reaction from the higher-ups!' Fred chuckled. 'We were jubilant.'

While resting in their tents, there was enough time for passionate political debates that often continued right through the night. Fred and his army comrades held informal discussions on current international issues and discussed likely developments in South Africa after the war. They believed that the defeat of the Nazi army would signal the beginning of a different kind of struggle for freedom and democracy.

The strong group of communists in Fred's unit were all active in the Springbok Legion, which was formed to ensure that soldiers received better treatment during and after the Second World War than they had after the previous war. My father was furious about the way his father had returned from the First World War wounded, penniless and without support. Fred and his comrades tried to explain to troops the real objective of the war, which was to defeat fascism and the Nazis. They found that many people did not really know why they were fighting. They also believed that a version of fascism was emerging in South Africa because of the way in which people of colour were separated from whites and were allowed only menial jobs.

Towards the end of the war, Fred's unit was billeted at a small Italian village called Rosetta di Abruzzo, where the local socialists and communists were organising May Day celebrations. To show their solidarity, the South African communists hung a red banner from a window of Fred's billet and greeted the villagers gathered in the street below with shouts of 'Viva socialism!' and 'Viva communismo!', as well as their own ragged version of 'Bandiera Rossa'. The villagers were delighted and invited them to join their procession. 'This we did with gusto,' declared Fred, 'and a good time was had by all, in spite of the fact that at that stage none of us knew much Italian. Generous glasses of local red vino flowed all night long.'

It was during the war that my father first met Brian Bunting, a man who would become his best friend, comrade and work colleague for over sixty years. Brian and Fred met on a boat called the *Sibyak* going to Suez from Durban, where Fred had been on leave and had led a deputation to protest against the treatment and condition of soldiers. He was outraged that they had to sleep in hammocks and eat stale porridge crawling with maggots. On the boat they had endless discussions about politics and the work of the Party. When they reached Suez, they transferred to a troop train made up entirely of cattle trucks. They had to sleep on the floor and could perform natural functions only when the train stopped.

Brian and Fred were then parted, but joined up again at Alcona in northern Italy, where the fighting had ceased. Because Brian was in Intelligence, he had a truck at his disposal, which he enjoyed using when he and Fred were off duty. At Alcona they joined in local Communist Party celebrations – with factory girls, liquor, dancing and lots of fun. Fred was good at languages and soon picked up Italian, so he was popular with the women. He and Brian often used to sneak out of their billets on clandestine outings. On one of these excursions they were asked by the local Communist Party to wait in the dark by the truck at Jesse. They were not sure what the Italian Communist Party wanted them to do, but expected it would have to do with organising meetings. As it turned out, the Italian communists simply wanted Fred and Brian to transport a barrel of wine in Brian's truck from one area to another. Had they been caught, their punishment would have been harsh: they would not have been allowed out of their camp for weeks.

Fred's first commitment was to win the war. His second was to support the Soviet Union. He sincerely believed at that time that the Soviet Union was going to be a model of a better society for the rest of the world. He was extremely concerned that there would be a war between Britain, the United States and the Soviet Union – and not without reason. When ceasefire ended the Second World War, he and other South Africans were dispatched to the main communication centre in Cyprus. They were sent secret manuals and protocol to follow in case the Western Allies went to war with the Soviet Union. If the order was given, they were instructed to remove these from the safe and to pass on the directives to the appropriate military units. It was clear that the British army was expecting to go back to war. Fred instructed his co-signalmen not to transmit any such messages, as that would mean a continuation of a war that was now over. He could not allow war with the Soviet Union, despite being informed that his refusal would be unlawful and punishable by death. His response was to tell his colleagues that, if they were on duty when the order came, they should pretend to be ill and say that they had asked him to take over, so that he could bear full responsibility.

Fred loved politics. He also always loved women. He believed that the presence of a woman comforted him and provided him with relief from stress:

> There is lust in the eyes of men at midnight
> as they walk the neon streets of the city
> alone and lonely at midnight
> seeking Madonnas in doorways
> seeking the stolen heritage
> of woman warmth
> and all mankind.
>
> Between the working and the waking
> the desert of tonight and tomorrow
> and the working again
> the women stand in the doorways
> alone and lonely at midnight
> awaiting the desert travellers
> the men adrift in the night.

As a young man Fred was adventurous and he was fearless. He felt lucky to have survived the war, during which he developed his political beliefs and established long-lasting friendships with people like Wolfie Kodesh, Brian Bunting, Ivan Shermbrucker and Rusty Bernstein, which stood him in good stead until the day he died. Fun-loving, charming and witty, his great passions in life were learning, literature and communism. It was communism and a mutual love of poetry that drew Fred and Sarah together.

11

Courtship and Marriage

F RED AND SARAH met for the first time in 1936 in Pietermaritzburg, where Fred was living with his family. Sarah was working for the People's Book Shop in Johannesburg at the time and had come to Pietermaritzburg to buy copies of the *Moscow News*. A comrade called Mike Diamond used to buy copies of the newspaper from Moscow and pile them high in his barber's shop in Pietermaritzburg. Mike asked Sarah to help a young man who wanted to set up a Left Book Club. 'How can I get hold of him?' she asked. Mike said, 'He is around the corner, playing hockey. I told him to expect you.'

Sarah and her friend Dr Goonam Naidoo went to the hockey field to meet up with this young man. To her surprise, he was only in his teens! She was not impressed: 'He was a little scruffy chap with red hair, long skinny legs and red socks, one down, and one up.' He came bounding up to them and said, 'Hello, my name's Freddie.'

After talking to him about his ideas, Sarah's first impressions shifted: realising that he was 'enthusiastic and totally committed', she was suitably convinced of his ability to set up a book club and she offered to assist him. Fred, at that time, was interested in communism and had a number of friends who were communists, but he was not yet a member of the Communist Party.

Freddie asked Sarah if she had anywhere to stay. 'You can stay at my home,' he offered. 'My mum loves visitors.' It was a tiny railway house packed with children. Sarah slept on the couch, people coming in and out of the small living room throughout the evening. Aside from crucifixes and pictures of Mary, the walls were bare and the interior of the cottage sparse, but Sarah found the family to be warm and welcoming.

Sarah and Fred enjoyed talking about books, and particularly about Marxist theory. After she helped Freddie set up the book club, she returned to Johannesburg and soon forgot about the scruffy teenager. Little did she know that they were to have a lifelong future together.

In 1938 she saw Fred briefly again. They continued their conversations about communism and, although Fred had already decided that he wanted to become a member of the Communist Party, Sarah, independently, decided to recruit him. She helped him to establish the first Communist Party group in Pietermaritzburg. Freddie was eighteen and Sarah was twenty-one.

Soon after this, Fred joined the army and went to fight in the Second World War. Sarah continued working at the People's Book Shop in Johannesburg, a non-profit independent organisation that supplied people with political literature. One of Sarah's jobs was to send books to the troops in North Africa. She often received letters from soldiers asking for a book list so that they could order books. She recognised Fred's name on one of these letters and remembered that they had talked about poetry when they last met. Sarah knew that he loved poetry, so she sent him a book by Walt Whitman as a gift, together with the list of books.

Her act was the beginning of a three-year-long regular correspondence between them, Sarah in Johannesburg and Fred fighting in different places with the army. In their letters they shared their political views and their visions for a better world. They shared details about their lives, their hopes and their fears. Sarah was aware of how dangerous it was for Fred and his fellow soldiers. 'At that time, death was ever-present,' she remarked afterwards. They shared their favourite books and their favourite poetry, and over the years they grew fond of each other. Fred treasured her letters and Sarah was relieved to receive his, as it meant that, 'at least at the time he wrote, he was still alive'.

A much-loved poem of theirs was Walt Whitman's 'Among the Multitude':

Among the men and women the multitude,
I perceive one picking me out by secret and divine signs,
Acknowledging none else, not parent, wife, husband, brother, child, any
    nearer than I am,
Some are baffled, but that one is not – that one knows me.

Ah, lover and perfect equal,
I meant that you should discover me so, by my faint indirections,
And I when I meet you mean to discover you by the like in you.

In the late summer of 1943, Sarah was taking stock in the back of the shop and thinking about what to wear to a party she was going to that evening with her friend Pauline Naidoo. Suddenly Eddie, the shop assistant, rushed up to her, very excited: 'There's a man at the front of the shop. He says he wants to see you!'

Fred was on leave from Egypt and had travelled to Johannesburg to see Sarah. He was carrying a huge bunch of sweet-scented red carnations.

Sarah was amazed by how much he had changed: he had become a self-assured young man. 'He was very handsome in uniform and when I saw him I really fancied him,' she laughed. The feeling was mutual. They fell deeply in love and started an intense and urgent relationship – what Fred called an 'extremely physical whirlwind romance'. As soon as Sarah had time off work, they would go to a hotel to be by themselves. One day they came down for breakfast, and sitting at the next table was the book shop's most valued customer. They had to pretend that they were having a breakfast business meeting.

Two weeks later, they decided to get married and have a baby. Fred and Sarah were secretly married on 31 March 1943. Fred was twenty-three and Sarah was nearly twenty-six. Fred explained that, because of the circumstances, 'there was no fuss, no bother. Just a special-licence civil ceremony, with Jack Barnett and Sarah's sister Ida as witnesses.'

That day Sarah overstayed her lunch hour: 'When I got back to work they said, "You're late." I said, "Yes, I just got married", and they replied, "Look, it's not April Fool's Day yet!" There was no time for big splashes.' Fred would joke with his friends, saying, 'I went into the book shop to get a book and came out with a wife!'

After they were married, Fred stayed for a few months with Sarah in her parents' house before going back to the Front. After a few weeks, Sarah's mother asked her, 'When is he leaving?' Sarah replied, 'He's not leaving. He's my husband.'

I was conceived soon after the wedding. The doctor had warned Sarah against having a baby because of her heart condition, telling her that she might not survive a pregnancy. Sarah did not care: 'I wanted a baby so much that I decided it was worth taking a chance.' As soon as she knew she was pregnant, she sent a telegram to Fred. When he received the news he went to his commanding officer to ask for compassionate leave. 'My wife is going to have a baby,' he said, not mentioning that the baby was due in seven months' time. He returned to Johannesburg and he and Sarah continued their honeymoon in the Kruger National Park. Then he rejoined his unit and went up north, back to war.

Neither Sarah's nor Fred's parents approved of the marriage. Sarah's father said very little and wished them well. Her mother, Anna, was furious: 'What did you do, marrying a Catholic? You will have nothing but trouble. All they do is fight, smoke and drink, and breed like rabbits.' Sarah attempted to reassure her mother that Fred was an atheist and had progressive views, but Anna was not impressed.

Fred's parents were not happy about Sarah's Jewish-communist background. Anthony, Fred's father, hated Stalin, believing that he was as bad as the Nazis. In addition, Fred's and Sarah's grandfathers had fought on opposing sides during the Anglo-Boer War, which increased the tension. Fred and Sarah were too much in love to care. Later on, Sarah acknowledged, 'Had we taken their concerns seriously, we might have learnt that a lot of later clashes would arise because we came from different cultures and had different expectations. Perhaps we could have managed them better.'

Being pregnant did not prevent Sarah from continuing her political work, but she stayed out of the thick of things by helping to organise meetings rather than demonstrating in the street. Around that time there were constant, violent clashes between anti-fascist trade unionists and soldiers and the pro-fascist Greyshirts, the South African Nazi movement of the 1930s and 1940s. Every time there was a Communist Party meeting, the fascists, with the support of the police, would try to break it up. Often people would get badly beaten up and dragged away; their comrades would never see them again. If the Greyshirts knew that a particular person was active in the political movement, they would follow them, find out where they lived and do their best to intimidate them.

The anti-fascists were hostile towards all Germans. At that time there were a number of people who had come to South Africa to escape Hitler, either because they were Jewish or because they were German anti-Hitler protesters. Although Sarah felt helpless at the time, she later expressed guilt about them, saying, 'Perhaps we weren't sufficiently understanding of their personal problems when they arrived. When the government decided to support the Allies in the war, they interned people who were not South African nationals. They were put together with the fascists and beaten up terribly. They had a tough time of it.'

In the middle of all this turmoil I was born, on 24 January 1944.

To the doctor's great relief, Sarah's heart was not affected by the pregnancy, and she recovered from the birth quickly. Like all parents, she thought I was beautiful. Fred was very excited about having a child, but understood nothing about babies. On the day I was born, he sent Sarah a beautiful red cape with a hood as a present for me. The only problem was that he'd chosen a cape that would fit a three-year-old.

Having a baby of her own was a new experience for Sarah. 'It was at a time when people weren't casual about babies. You didn't simply look after them; you smothered them.' She took her new role as mother very seriously and followed the writings of Dr Tracy King, who believed that it was good for babies to cry. Sarah would let me cry for hours while she sat in the next room feeling terrible and having a good cry herself. Luckily her friend Dr Goonam Naidoo, who had graduated as the first Indian woman doctor in South Africa, came to visit and, on seeing my mother's state, threw Dr King's book away – to Sarah's great relief.

I did not see my father until I was eighteen months old. He was fascinated by his baby daughter and could not stop picking me up and walking around with me. 'I'll tell you what, Sarah,' he'd say, keen to feed me. 'Let me feed Lynnie. You go and have a rest.' For some reason he believed that eighteen-month-old babies ate only bananas. He continually fed me bananas until I spat them out all over him and threw tantrums. Sarah didn't have the courage to tell him that babies ate more than just bananas.

As soon as my father returned from the war, he and Sarah realised that they wanted a home of their own. It was almost impossible to find accommodation at that time: with so many people returning from the war and needing homes, there was a severe housing shortage. One day, Sarah's mother came back, excited: 'I have just heard that an alcoholic woman died in a drunk-driving accident. Her house in Observatory has become vacant. If you get there early, you might stand a chance.' Sarah braved the bitter cold and was first in the queue at five in the morning. By the time the seller of the house arrived at nine, the queue was winding around three blocks. The man asked Sarah why she wanted the house. She replied that her husband had just come back from the war and that they had a baby. 'The house is yours,' he said.

The house was filthy and took weeks to clean. A very thin wall divided it from the neighbours and, when I was teething, I kept not only my parents but all our neighbours up every night. One day, the neighbours came over with half a bottle of brandy. Delighted, Fred said, 'Thanks for the brandy; that is very kind of you.'

'No,' they responded, 'it's not for you. It's for the baby. Give her some at night and she will sleep soundly.' My mother gave me a small glass of brandy that night and she and my father fell asleep. I must have woken up soon after, because the neighbours complained that I sang all night.

My mother and father were generally happy together, but it was not easy. Sarah believed that soldiers who came home never recovered from the terrible effects of the war. 'When men came back from the war they were different,' she told me much later. 'They had to be different. A lot of them became indifferent to pain because they couldn't cope with their pain and the pain of others. Many of them, including Fred, took to drinking heavily and chain-smoking. His language was worse: he swore like a trooper. For the blokes that came back, life and death didn't mean the same thing. When Fred couldn't cope, he lost his temper and shouted. It was very easy to trigger him off.

'I was used to being independent, being responsible and earning my own wages. Then this man came into my life and tried to boss me around and take charge. So I told him if he wanted to use me as a dishrag like he did his mother, he could leave right now. Fred would tell me not to insult his mother.'

My parents used to argue but couldn't stay apart for very long. After a day or two, they would both apologise and make up. Then they would begin to quarrel again. One of their arguments centred on a newspaper article about a man who took his pregnant wife to court. The legal dispute arose because either the woman or the baby was going to have to die, and while the woman chose to sacrifice the child rather than her own life, her husband chose to sacrifice his wife. Fred agreed with the man. Sarah, who believed that a woman had the right to choose whether to keep a baby or not, was shocked: 'I told him that I disagreed, and he shouted, "You don't know what you're talking about."'

In spite of this, they were still very much in love, adored their baby and were both deeply committed to their ideals. Sarah was still organising campaigns, fighting for workers' rights and continuing her social work in the townships.

Fred and Brian Bunting decided to work together full-time to bring about political change, selecting the Springbok Legion as their focus because they believed it could make an impact in South Africa. The Springbok Legion helped soldiers readjust to civilian life by assisting them with finding work and claiming their rights. In addition, it worked to mobilise soldiers and former servicemen, as well as wider sections of the population, black and white, against the racist National Party, and it campaigned for equal rights for black soldiers – equal pay, equal living and working conditions, and the right to carry arms. Brian and Fred's paper, *Fighting Talk*, was very influential. Unfortunately they overlooked the fact that Afrikaners who were left-wing during the war reunited with their families after the war, returning to the right-wing National Party and the Dutch Reformed Church.

Brian and Fred also worked for the Communist Party. At the time, they felt that it was very important to defend the Soviet Union. Fred explained, 'If the Soviet Union had been defeated and Hitler had been victorious, our life in South Africa – and generally in the world – would have been very much harder. We really believed that the Soviet Union and communism would make the world a better place, especially for the oppressed and the very poor. We also genuinely felt that stories about atrocities under Stalin in the Soviet Union were anti-Soviet propaganda.'

While Fred was working at the Communist Party office he was offered a job as General Secretary for the Party in the Western Cape, which he accepted. This meant moving to Cape Town, which was slightly familiar to him because of his early childhood. For my mother, however, it meant relocating to a strange place with a toddler and no supportive family to help her.

12

Relatively Free

FRED AND SARAH arrived in Cape Town at the end of 1945 and rented a flat in Ludlow Road, Vredehoek. The ground-floor flat was painted dark cream, and was nestled right up against the mountain. It was tiny, with just two bedrooms, a living room and a kitchenette. 'Vredehoek' means 'corner of peace', but the southeaster wind blew with such force that, on one occasion, a window in the living room that had been left open slammed shut, smashing glass all over the floor.

I was a highly active two-year-old. On calm days I would play with other children from our block of flats. We used to collect *dennepitte* – pine nuts – smash their hard shells with rocks and then fight over how many each of us should have. My mother preferred us to be outside rather than bouncing on the settee inside. We would hear the fishmonger blowing his seaweed fish-horn as he came up the road, and on hot days we listened for the bell of Jimmy's ice-cream van.

Just after we moved into the flat and before my parents started painting it bright white, they decided to throw a party. The theme was 'Tramps', and their guests all arrived in their best tramp outfits. Because my parents were new to Cape Town, they didn't recognise some real bergies who had joined them until they sat down next to them and were overpowered by the smell. My parents would roar with laughter every time they remembered that night.

Fred was in his element. He claimed that he was a true Capetonian because he had been born in the Mother City. He threw himself into his work as General Secretary of the Western Cape Communist Party, which was based in Burg Street. Moses Kotane, the eminent black communist and ANC member, occupied an office below Fred's. Kotane used to get cross with the young communists who, he complained, were a great nuisance because they left the place in such a mess.

Fred and Sarah spoke at meetings, informing their audiences that the country's whole economy rested on the exploitation of black people. To counter this, my parents argued, they should join the Communist Party and the ANC to do something about their living and working conditions. They always made sure that there was a racial mix of speakers to promote the idea of multiracialism. By organising mass rallies in Athlone and in Langa and Nyanga, they helped to campaign for the rights of the poor. It was hard work as many black people believed that the South African government, then under the leadership of Jan Smuts, would physically smash them down if they protested. Fred and Sarah's first objective was to get people to understand that they deserved basic human rights and that their destiny lay in their own hands.

At twenty-six, Fred was passionate, enthusiastic, energetic and dedicated to helping the oppressed and creating a better world. He sparkled; he was a rough working-class diamond. He chain-smoked and swore, and poor people felt they could relate to him.

Fred worked hard. He stayed up late at night to keep up his languages and international contacts. He read widely. He also used to take days off to climb, with me on his shoulders, up Table Mountain or go fishing in the Indian Ocean. He was ecstatic about the beauty of the mountain and the sea, and particularly the taste of Cape brandy, which he kept in the drawer of his desk.

Because he was paid so little, as well as working for the Party he worked as a bookkeeper until the end of 1945, when he joined Brian Bunting at the pro-ANC, left-wing *Guardian* newspaper as manager, fund-raiser and occasional editor. The *Guardian*, a weekly paper with a small staff, was doing well and had a circulation of over 50 000. Fred also served on the Western Cape Council, after being elected by overwhelming majority as Native Representative in 1949. In this role, which he performed until 1952, he led delegations and petitioned on behalf of black people, working long hours. He was seldom home.

For Sarah, it was different. When she first arrived in Cape Town with me, aged two and a half, she was nervous, and she missed her family and friends. She felt as if the mountains were on top of her all the time and she longed for the wide-open spaces of the Transvaal. In Johannesburg her parents had helped to look after me and she had had domestic help to do the housework. In Cape Town she had to give up her full-time career to care for me and to make sure that Fred was properly fed and his clothes ironed. Although my mother believed that she should be there to look after me, she resented the fact that Fred could rush around when she had to stay at home. She deeply missed her job and was relieved when she was offered part-time work as General Secretary of the South African Railway and Harbour Workers' Union.

Once she settled in in Cape Town, she met people through Party meetings. Because she was genuinely interested in people, they found it easy to talk to her about themselves and their problems. She started a deep and lasting friendship with a Xhosa woman comrade called Dora Tamana, who lived on a bleak, windswept sand dune in a squatter camp called Vrygrond. Dora was worried about the number of orphans roaming the streets. She told Sarah: 'I feed the children for one penny a day but I can't continue doing this any longer. There are too many children. We need a crèche.' Sarah would take me with her when she visited Vrygrond in the evenings to help Dora and her community build the school. She often remarked on the sense of fellowship among the people, saying that 'there was a wonderful community spirit' in the township.

Dora and her comrades in Vrygrond noticed that Sarah was struggling to make ends meet. One day, when both Fred and Sarah were home, Dora arrived at the flat. 'We have a present for you,' she said. The Vrygrond community had saved the little money they had to give us a live scrawny chicken. My parents took it gratefully and put it in the backyard to fatten up.

It was the middle of winter. I was upset because the chicken was getting cold and wet. I cried my heart out, telling my parents that it was cruel to leave a chicken outside in that weather. To make me happy, they chased it all over the yard in the rain and wind, caught it and put it in the bath. When visitors came over, they would always emerge from the bathroom bewildered and surprised: 'Why is there a squawking chicken in the bath?' What with chicken droppings littering the flat, the smell, the noise and hunger, my parents decided one day to have chicken for dinner. They told me that the chicken had been lonely and that they had given it back to the farmer so that it could be with other chickens. I was happy and dinner was delicious.

I loved going to visit warm and welcoming Granny Dora in Vrygrond. She lived in a corrugated iron shack that was extraordinarily clean and tidy inside, mainly to prevent the onset of diseases like TB. There were two beds in the shack, one for her and one for her children; a table with four chairs; and a big round tin, which I would sit on. She would give me a huge hug, say 'Welcome!' and, when she saw me getting bored, would ask me to go to the tap to fetch water for tea. There was only one tap in that area and I queued up with a clean, empty cocoa tin. The other people in the queue were amazed to see a white child queuing for water. I had to pay a tickey (a silver coin worth about three pence) for it and would then run back to her shack very proud that I had not spilt a drop. We used to take Dora and the children fruit because she could not afford to buy any. On receiving the fruit, the children would hold out their cupped hands as if they were begging, do a little curtsy and say thank you, but my father told them that we were all equal and to enjoy the fruit; it belonged to them.

Once a week Fred and Sarah stood on different street corners to sell the *Guardian* and discuss people's rent, health and legal problems. Many working-class people would buy the paper. Sarah also used to go to District Six, the predominantly Cape Malay area, on Friday evenings, where she would knock on doors and the person answering the door would shout, 'The *Guardian* is here.'

At that time, as before, the policy of the Communist Party was to not encourage many people to join. Anyone who was invited to do so was carefully screened: quality and commitment were more important than quantity. Members were expected to be highly organised and available twenty-four hours a day. They needed to be well read, understand the theory and know what was happening in the rest of the world. They had to think strategically about how to mobilise the masses and understand when a country was ripe for revolution. In 1945, the Party knew that South African workers were not organised enough for widespread change and believed that education and mobilisation were necessary.

Fred went from door to door collecting money. There were also fund-raising parties and bazaars, to which my parents usually took me along. The best were the New Year's Eve parties, often at the Buntings' house on the mountain in Clifton, overlooking the white beaches and crashing waves. It was one of the few opportunities where people from different races could mix socially. Africans came in busloads from the townships; coloured people, both Christian and Muslim, came from District Six and the Malay quarters; and left-wing white friends of my parents came from the white parts of Cape Town. There was lots of food, wine, conversation and 'well, everything', as my mother described it. What I really enjoyed was the loud, live, rhythmic South African music. Sometimes people would sing freedom songs with deep joyful voices. I sang with them even though I did not understand the words. It was impossible not to dance, so I joined everyone else and danced until I got tired. My mother loved to gossip with friends in between dancing, while my father, who was quite wild, was the life and soul of the party and would dance erotically with the most beautiful women he could find. After the New Year was heralded by a seaweed horn that sounded like the loud moo of a cow and joyfully greeted by singing and cheering, I would happily go to sleep in a corner until someone picked me up and took me to a bedroom. Early the next morning, my parents would carry me down the long flight of stairs to the road to drive home.

By 1946 my father was a member of the Central Committee of the Communist Party. The international political climate was becoming increasingly hostile towards communists; capitalists feared that the Soviet Union wanted to take over the world. Churchill was anti-communist and the United Party under Smuts was too, while the Nationalist opposition party had already shown its support for the Nazis and its hatred of communists.

Anti-communist indoctrination was prevalent, and the *Guardian*'s circulation numbers went down. Advertisers withdrew, and sellers and workers were harassed by the police and landed up in jail. Cigarette in mouth, Fred was always swearing and shouting, his explosive temper coming to the fore. A sympathiser called Mr Kessling, who owned a hotel at the top of Hope Street, told Fred, 'I am worried because I think I have a Nationalist staying in my hotel.' Fred went red in the face and shouted, 'I joined the army during the war. You are a disgusting yellow rat. How can you house a Nazi like that?'

He never gave up. Even on the train to Cape Town Central Station he would chat about the *Guardian*, the Party and communism to anyone who seemed interested. He and Jean Bernadt would try to collect money every day, but as anti-communist pressure mounted, donations started drying up.

Early in 1946, the Communist Party supported the ANC and the trade unions in holding a miners' strike against poor wages and terrible working conditions. Fred was one of the leaders. He addressed the crowd: 'The working conditions are so bad you wouldn't take an animal down there. They get paid starvation wages, but when our comrades, the miners, asked Prime Minister Smuts for a wage rise, that bastard refused. What do you expect from colonialists?' It was a terrible strike with savage consequences: hundreds were injured and many were killed.

The United Party, under Smuts, argued that communists were using the strike as a front to mobilise the miners to overthrow the government. Members of the Central Committee of the Communist Party, including Fred, were arrested on a charge of sedition on 15 August. They were accused of creating revolutionary upheavals for the seizure of political power by the workers. Fred was dismissive, declaring later, 'That was bloody rubbish. We knew that the country wasn't ready for revolution. We also believed that it was right to work lawfully and non-violently within the system. We were deeply influenced by Gandhi's practice of passive resistance. None of us who had been in the army wanted violence or, indeed, anyone to be killed.'

Fred's August 1946 arrest was his first one. It was also the family's first experience of what was to become an all-too-familiar event. At 5.00 a.m. that day, the wind was howling around the flat. The windows were rattling so much that we did not hear the banging on the front door until it was so loud that it woke up the neighbours. My father went to the door and two enormous security policemen came in wearing belted beige raincoats and felt hats. They grabbed my father and marched him away. I was so shocked that my mother took me back to bed with her and cuddled me until I felt better. He was released later that day, pending trial.

During the next month the security police searched the offices of progressive organisations like the *Guardian* and the trade unions, including the one for which my mother worked. They returned to our flat four months later, on my third birthday, and searched it, taking away leaflets, books and letters. We had to step over the mess that they left, and my parents, unable to find the papers they were working on, were furious. I ran around the flat imitating them: 'They won't get away with it. They won't get away with it.' My father shouted, 'I didn't fight fascism in the war not to recognise it starting here.'

The second time, they came for my father in the evening. They allowed him to pack a case. Before they took him away I threw my arms around his legs and the police had to pull me off him; I was inconsolable. Even when he came back a few days later – there was not enough evidence for a case against him – I was anxious every time someone knocked at the door.

Things only got worse. In 1947, when I was three and a half, my parents had a terrible row and my mother left my father.

13

Lost and Found

Tension between my parents had been building up for some months. Fred would order Sarah to make him cups of tea or bring him his slippers. She refused, saying that she had not been born to serve him. When they discussed politics, he would get angry with her if she disagreed with him. She stood her ground and said that she had been brought up to be independent, to think and to argue. He would shout and tell her that she didn't know what she was talking about. She would then quote from Marx or Engels and Fred would find that she was often right. Because she was working part-time and also looking after me, she resented Fred for not helping with me, doing household chores or bringing in enough money to look after his family. She was constantly having to stop him from giving away what little they had. After they had an argument, he would say to her, 'You're not like my mother.' She would shout, 'Thank God I'm not a slave!'

Because Fred was a passionate, fiery young man with a wicked sense of humour, he was extremely attractive to the opposite sex. Women were always telling him that Sarah was 'too modern' for him and that she should treat him better. They constantly found excuses to spend time with him. Fred teased Sarah, saying, 'Why don't you line up with the other women to fight for my favours?' She did not speak to him for a week after that comment.

When my mother had bronchitis, the women in the office told her that she should move to Durban to recover. 'Not bloody likely,' she said. 'I knew they were trying to get rid of me.' Fred's aunts, Aunty Bella and Aunty Annie, who were very Catholic, came and cooked meals while my mother was sick and would take me out. One day they came back shocked: I had spent the afternoon swearing like my father. They told my mother to 'wash her mouth out with soap'.

While Sarah was recovering from bronchitis, the doorbell rang. On opening the door, the wife of a friend marched in. The woman folded her arms, stood with her legs apart and stared aggressively at Sarah. 'Fred and I are in love with each other,' she said. 'I want to move in with him, so you will have to find another place to live.' Sarah took her by the arm and threw her out.

That evening I was giving my teddy bear and my doll Pauline a tea party with my miniature tea set when I heard a terrible row going on in the lounge. 'It's not just work that's keeping you out late at night! You just see what it's like to be in day after day!' My mother stormed into their bedroom, came out with a suitcase and marched out the house, slamming the front door behind her. 'Where's Mom going?' I asked tearfully. 'She's just gone away for a few days,' my father replied. 'She'll be back soon.' But she was away for six long months.

Sarah found out that the affair had been going on for years. The woman and Fred were having passionate sex in Fred's office, and everyone knew about it except for Sarah and the woman's husband. Sarah was furious, confused, distressed and disturbed and did not know what to do. She realised that she did not really know or like my father. She just wanted to leave. A friend, Ruth Lazarus, offered her a job in Paris, working for the United Nations. She decided to go to Paris, start the job, establish herself and then come back to fetch me.

My father and I were left behind. He took me on a long two-day train ride to Johannesburg, where I first stayed with my Grandma Anna and Grandpa Zelic, who made a great fuss over me. I played with their dog, a huge, tawny Great Dane called Jock. He allowed me to ride on his back, but I wanted my parents. My grandparents decided that I would be less lonely if I went to my Aunt Ida, my mother's youngest sister who had two young boys, Jasper and Roland, who were a few years older than me. To them I was just a nuisance. My aunt was preoccupied with her husband, Manny, who was dying of cancer. I spent most of the time on my own, sucking my thumb and sitting outside on the polished red kitchen steps, watching processions of ants and avoiding the maids, who would step over me to hang out the washing.

I was there for over five months – an eternity for a three-and-a-half-year-old. Plenty of time to ask why, over and over again, I had been left all alone. Did Mommy and Daddy decide I was a mistake? Was that why I was at this house? Where were they, my mommy and daddy?

Meanwhile, Sarah had started work in Paris for the United Nations, to help the many starving and abandoned children who were roaming the streets. Paris was a bleak and unhappy place at the time, full of debris, rotten rubbish, rubble and bombed buildings. People were grey, gaunt and on strict food and clothing rationing. Sarah learnt to be very sparing when using water or electricity, and her friends were grateful for the chocolates, coffee and cigarettes that she brought from South Africa. She was distressed by the desperation of the children and sent letters to her sisters saying, 'These lost children are so full of anger and hatred. All they want to do is to fight and kill people.' She wrote that she missed me terribly and that as soon as she had sorted herself out she would come and fetch me.

While she was away, Brian Bunting took my father and the woman aside and told them that they were to stop their affair immediately. Fred should behave like a proper husband and father, he said. Fred, who was shocked that Sarah had left, found that he really missed her and his little daughter. He started sending her telegrams every day, asking her when she was coming home. Then every two days she received a contrite letter from him begging her to come back. He needed her support. There was no reference to the other woman in the letters. By then, my mother was also missing him and realised that she still had strong feelings for him. She also felt that it was wrong to take me away from him. She knew I adored my father and remembered how I used to throw my arms around him when he came home from work.

One very hot and humid day in Durban, in 1948, when I was four, I was sitting on the stairs listening to my aunts Kay and Ida talking about the terrible election results. 'We have a bunch of fascists ruling us. Things will get very bad from now on,' they were saying. The phone rang. My aunt Kay answered. It was a friend of my mother's phoning from Paris.

'It's Minnie Bodenstein,' Kay whispered. When she put the phone down, she told Ida: 'When Sarah heard about the Nationalists winning the election, she fainted. Fred and Sarah are getting back together again – apparently they are both determined to make the marriage work. Sarah's coming back to Cape Town in a week's time, and Fred will come and fetch Lynn to take her home in a few days.'

I was so excited that I drove everyone crazy by asking them every five minutes how much more time I would have to wait. But when my father came to fetch me, I ran away from him. He picked me up, saying, 'My, what a heavy girl you've become. Come on, give me a hug.'

During the train journey he told me that we were not going back to Vredehoek: 'Grandma Anna and Grandpa Zelic have helped us buy a large house that we can use as a guest house so we can have more money, because I'm not earning much with the paper. I am sure you will like it much better than the flat. It's called Mount Pleasant.'

Mount Pleasant was huge. To me, it was like a fairy-tale castle. It had a beautiful green gate made of iron with curling patterns on it. The gate was so tall that it towered above my head. A long path lined with cycads led to polished red steps, which ascended graciously to the large wooden front door, whose shining brass keyhole and handle offset the dark-red tiles of the roof.

We walked up the path and passed two lawns as big as fields. I was hopping and jumping beside my father, who held me by one hand and carried my case with the other. He was shouting very loudly: 'Sarah, Sarah, where are you?' He pushed on the shining brass bell at the side of the door, producing a lovely deep chime. The generous front hall had shiny black-and-white floor tiles and in the corner was a large brass pot filled with ferns. Above was a magical crystal chandelier, shimmering pink and blue and all the colours of the rainbow as it glinted in the sun.

My mother rushed up. She picked me up and held me tightly. When she put me down, I put her hand into my father's and they both held me. I never wanted to be separated from them again. I was so happy to be with both of them again that it never occurred to me to resent their absence.

14

The *Guardian*

THE YEAR 1948, when D.F. Malan and his new National Party came into power, was a time of unwelcome change. The comrades debated how quickly the Afrikaner Nationalists, with their belief in white supremacy, would fulfil their election promises. The Nationalists promised to 'maintain the rule, the purity and the civilisation of the European race'. They would 'save the whites from coloured blood, the black peril and the red menace of communism', which they would do by 'dissolving the Communist Party, deporting Indians, segregate the Coloureds with privileges over the Africans, do away with the Native Representative Council and provide separate education for Africans'. They would also evict Africans who were redundant from the towns (Malan's election platform, 26 April 1948).

The Nationalists were not the only whites who were anti-communist. The English-speaking United Party wanted a law passed according to which communism was punishable by death. They gave the Nationalists lists of communists and progressives, which they had compiled as material for the sedition trial in 1946. All the people listed were branded as dangerous, including Fred and Sarah.

The *Guardian* fought back, publishing an article in which the following appeared: 'What Germany experienced under the Hitler regime will be experienced by South Africa under Malan's regime. No good will come from a regime that is based on fear and hate.'

The comrades decided to work lawfully and non-violently within the system for as long as they could, and to focus on educating the people. They ran educational classes to help black people with literacy and political consciousness. They promoted democracy, workers' unity, racial equality and socialism wherever and whenever they could. They challenged the Nationalists' insistence on 'total apartheid' and separate development based on 'white supremacy' that stemmed from their belief that they were 'bastions of white civilization'. 'That is definitely not what I call these fascist bastards,' said Fred.

In 1949 the Unemployment Amendment Act excluded most Africans from unemployment benefits unless they owned their own homes or had a certain income. There was racial segregation on trains, buses, benches and even in post offices. The Prohibition of Mixed Marriages Act, which commenced in the same year, made mixed marriages unlawful. Our friends H.A. and Pauline Naidoo were in deep trouble: as an Indian, H.A. could no longer live with Pauline, who was white, and their children. He came to live secretly for a while in a hut in our garden. It was difficult for his wife and children to see him as they were constantly watched by the security police, so Pauline and the children, Sandra and Karen, used to sneak out to meet him.

In spite of forebodings, Fred was his usual optimistic, argumentative self. Sarah's cousin Alex and his wife invited them to a dinner party when they were visiting Johannesburg. There was a heated discussion about communism and the ANC. Fred was convinced that 'black people can rule the country. There are some very intelligent leaders among these people.' The white guests told him that he was 'stark, staring, raving mad'.

Fred was still Native Representative for the Western Cape Council. Long queues outside our house formed from early in the mornings of poorly dressed, undernourished, patient black people needing legal advice or social help.

The comrades were furious about the imposition of the colour bar. Fred and a fellow communist, Sam Kahn, a Member of Parliament, would sit over cups of coffee and discuss what to do. They were amused when they discovered a white Nationalist MP to have coloured ancestry. Sam mentioned this in Parliament. Fred chuckled, 'They were so angry that the speaker ordered it to be struck off Hansard – so there is no record of his [the MP's] past.'

After the elections Fred spoke at many large meetings in African townships and on the Parade in the centre of Cape Town. Even then, police informers were following him and writing reports about him. One police report stated:

> After the war he pops up out of the blue as a speaker at communist meetings and speaks to big groups of Africans in locations and on the Parade in Cape Town ... He is an especially good speaker and easily

sweeps his listeners to a high ... The character of his speeches was always without exception the typical communist kind that whips up the non-whites in a very subtle way against the whites. He always tries to encourage a feeling of dissatisfaction among the non-whites by telling them how weak they are economically, socially and politically, compared to the whites ... He usually emphasises the importance that non-whites should 'fight' for their rights; that they have the 'strongest power' in the country ... and that [they] should unite and join organisations such as the African National Congress and especially the Communist Party ... Whenever he incites the non-whites against the government it is clear that he also means [against] the whites, because he said the government consists only of whites.   – Translated from the Afrikaans police files

Fred was given an anonymous tip-off about the last point in the above report, which, he was told, had been given to the security police by an informer. Fred laughed. If logically considered, he said, they expected him to slaughter his own family and friends, which was ludicrous.

15

Named

The depth and importance of true comradeship can never be underestimated. Neither can the devastating effects of social isolation when that comradeship is forbidden.

— LYNN CARNESON

ONE EVENING IN June 1950, my father was reading the *Cape Times* with a cup of coffee in his hand. 'Suppression of Communism Act Is Out', 'Communist Party Unlawful', 'Communists Publicly Listed', read the headlines. Fred was furious: 'It's reds under the beds from now on, but we'll show them.'

I was puzzled. What did he mean, 'reds under the beds'? I went into the bedrooms and looked under my bed and my parents' bed and even under the settee, but there was nothing but dust and a ball I had lost the week before. I thought, being six years old, that I should know everything.

My parents were in such a bad mood that I decided to go back across the road to play with my two friends. We had been playing 'doctor, doctor' and I was the nurse. I went across the road and rang the bell. 'Can I play with Julian, please?' His mother looked at me as if I had done something very naughty. 'No. You can't play here any more. Filthy communists; I don't want anything to do with the lot of you.' She slammed the door in my face. I felt the door shaking, but soon realised that it was me who was trembling. I turned around and ran home, then walked slowly up the path to my house. I really could not understand what I had done wrong. Tears streamed down my face; I kept thinking, 'I don't understand; I don't understand at all.'

On hearing the story, my mother hugged me. 'There is nothing wrong with you,' she reassured me. 'The government is being silly and many white people don't like people like us helping the Africans.' My father lifted me onto his knee, saying, 'Things will be hard for a little while. You must be brave. Very brave. Don't give them the pleasure of seeing you upset.'

The next day when I went to school – Good Hope, in Gardens – my teacher, Miss Vaughan, called me up in front of the class. 'Put out your hands,' she barked. She picked up her ruler from the desk and hit me hard on my right hand. 'That is for having communist parents.' Then she hit me on the other hand. 'That's for having parents who are kaffir lovers. You will stay after school and write one hundred lines: "I must not love kaffirs." That will teach you.' Both hands had angry red stripes on them. They stung. 'I will never cry. I will never cry,' I repeated to myself. During break time I walked around on my own because suddenly no one would play with me any more.

When I arrived home that afternoon, I was still fighting hard not to cry, and found myself sniffing loudly instead. My mother gave me a handkerchief. 'Are you coming down with a cold?' she asked, looking at me with concern.

I sniffed again. 'No. I'm all right.'

'Then what's wrong?'

'They're saying at school that Dad is going to poison them.'

'Oh. That's rubbish,' she replied. 'Mr Swart, the Minister of Justice, said that communists have started a secret organisation to poison white people's water and stop electricity on a certain day. He also said that we are teaching Africans to kill as many whites as possible. Of course it's not true. Can you see Dad, or me, or any of our friends doing anything like that?'

I shook my head but couldn't stop sniffing: 'I don't want to go to school any more.' Because I knew I had to be brave, I didn't tell her that the teacher had hit me or that the other children wouldn't play with me, but my mother probably realised that I was having a tough time. She said that I had to go to school to learn things, but that I could stay at home the next day and perhaps my nanny Minna could do something with me.

I loved Minna. She was soft and comforting, with a big bottom and skin the colour of milk chocolate. She used to tell me stories of her ancestors, the Bushmen, who came from the Kalahari Desert. She said that because there was so little water and food available they had big bottoms to store fat for the lean times. She told me about how the Bushmen lived and how they sipped liquid from the stems of plants.

Minna asked my mother if she could take me to Rhodes Memorial to see the deer. My mother gave her some money for the bus ride. Minna looked unhappy. 'What is it, Minna?'

'How to go on the bus? I can't go in a *"blankes alleen* [whites only]" bus.'

'Then take her on the "non-white" bus; she is used to being with Africans.'

When we arrived at Rhodes Memorial, we climbed up the hill to where the pine forest began. 'First look around at the trees,' Minna said. 'What do you see?'

'Some of the bark has been rubbed off.'

'That's the deer, shedding their antlers or scratching when new ones begin. Look.' She pointed at something lying in the grass further up the mountain. I saw a pair of horns, the tip of one horn broken off. 'Now, you see, these tell a story. This buck has been in a fight with another buck during the mating season. They both want to mate the female deer, but only one can.'

'Why?'

'That's how they are. Now sit very, very quietly.' We squatted for a long time. Minna sat comfortably but I was getting cramps and started to move. Then Minna pointed. There, in the distance, were five deer. She beckoned to me. I moved very quietly and we started circling the deer on their left till we were behind them. Copying Minna, I crawled on my tummy so that we could get closer to the quietly grazing animals. I held my breath and tried to be so still that I would be invisible. After a very long time, a baby deer came close. I held my breath. It had large brown eyes and long, long eyelashes. Its brown hair met in a point at its chest. It had tiny shiny hooves, and it stood still, sniffed and then ran away, all the other deer running with it. Minna smiled. 'Now, I'll teach you how to do that again. First you have to ask the wind not to tell them you are there. The wind will help you trick them into not knowing you are there. Then, when you are close, you talk to the deer with your mind and tell them they are safe with you. If they believe you and feel like it, they might come up to you again. You have been very lucky today.'

I couldn't wait to get home to tell my parents all about it. My times with Minna were such a pleasant contrast to the hostility I was experiencing at school. Over and above that, however, Minna gave me a lifelong ability to calm myself by observing nature.

As an only child at that stage, I was lonely a lot of the time, so my father used to take me with him on his rounds to raise money for the paper and the Party. We would sometimes stop at the home of Alex and Blanche La

Guma, coloured comrades of my parents who lived in a small bungalow painted white with brightly coloured pot plants inside. Blanche was very beautiful; she looked like a princess and had straight black shining hair that she tied in a knot at the back. She was a nurse and always looked spic and span in her white uniform and white shoes, even when she rode her bicycle. Alex was very tall and thin. He worked on the paper with my father. When we visited, I would sit next to him on the couch and he would tell me stories about the tokoloshe, a naughty imp who played tricks on you at night if you weren't careful. When I got bored, he would tell me about Shaka, the great Zulu warrior. 'He was a truly great man,' Alex would say.

We often visited an Indian family called Chetty. They offered me bright green and pink sweets made of milk, sugar and coconut. My father, who loved chillies, always enjoyed their curry. Even so, he would drink lots of water with his curry. We also visited a Malay family, the Jaffers, who gave my father money for the paper. Like the Indian women, the Malay women wore bright clothes and scarves on their heads. During Eid, the religious festival marking the end of Ramadan, we were invited to celebrations where the whole community would prepare a banquet. I used to stuff myself with delicious biryani and samoosas. When we drove home, I would ask my father questions: Why do some Indians have gods that are elephants? Why do Muslims sometimes have more than one wife? Why are some coloured people Christian and not Muslim? Why do the Jewish people celebrate Passover? My father said that I asked so many questions that I would turn into a giant question mark if I didn't stop.

We often went into the townships to visit our African friends; not to raise money, but to organise meetings and demonstrations for the ANC. I could smell the township before we drew near. The place smelt so bitter and strong that I often felt I was going to be sick. My father said that it was a mixture of paraffin, the singeing of chicken feathers and poor sanitation: 'They don't have proper toilets so it doesn't smell very nice,' he told me. When the car bumped around on the sandy roads, I would cough because of the dust in my eyes, nose and throat. When I asked my father why they lived like that, he replied, 'Because this apartheid governance does not allow them to earn enough money to improve their lives. It's not fair – so that's why we work so hard to make their lives better.'

Every year I looked forward to the annual visit by my Grandma Anna and Grandpa Zelic. They used to take a long boat trip from Durban to

Mozambique and then down the east coast to Cape Town. In 1951, four days before they were due to arrive at the docks, I found my mother crying. Her nose was red and her eyes puffy. She told me that Grandma and Grandpa had gone on a long boat trip to Mozambique and that Grandpa had had a heart attack and died on the boat. She said that he would never be back to stay with us again. I ran into the garden and stood staring at the fountain.

Soon, Minna came rushing out. I burst out sobbing. 'Minna, my grandpa's dead.' She held me tight and crooned a little song. Then she took me by the hand. 'Come, I want to show you something.' We went through the back of the house to a small glade in the woods where the sun was shining on the pine needles between the trees. The trees were rustling. 'Listen! Can you hear the woods singing?' I shut my eyes and listened to the wind and the cooing doves. 'Those trees,' she said. 'What do you see?'

'Trees,' I replied.

'What do you hear?'

'I hear the wind.'

She smiled. 'Ah,' she said. 'Listen again. Trees sing and laugh and dance and cry.'

'How?' I asked.

'I'll tell you a story. Underneath the ground you walk on are very beautiful rivers of all colours. Rivers of song. They carry every song and story that was ever sung. Sometimes the songs are sad; sometimes they are happy. Each song has a line of its own, like a thread. When you or anyone dies, your song gets sung in the river. And your parents and their parents before them and those before them and those before them.' We sat down under a tall pine tree.

'Well,' she continued, 'one day there was a very wise old man called Xtumi. Xtumi put his ear to the ground and heard the river singing the songs. But he couldn't understand what they were saying. He lay with his ear to the earth to hear better, but he was very uncomfortable. He found that he was lying on the root of the tree. It felt as if the root was trying to tell him something. He looked at the tree and then he knew.'

'What did he know?'

'He saw ribbons like light coming from the river into the tree and the tree started moving, dancing and rustling and singing. And he just knew that one of his ancestors and the tree were singing his ancestor's song.'

'What did the song say?'

'It said that the ancestors were very wise and knew many answers to many, many problems. If he wanted to know anything, he should ask the tree to ask the ancestor and if the ancestor said "yes" and the tree said "yes", then the song would be sung through the tree.'

'But I can't hear any song.'

'That's because you need to ask the tree a question, or ask it to help you. Listen to it sing and you will know the answer. Watch it move, and it will show you the way to go. It will wake up the knowing that is in you and you will either know or the right thing will happen. First, you must always leave a gift for the tree and the ancestors to know you are grateful, or nothing will happen. Trees have feelings too, you know.'

'Minna, what is an ancestor?'

'People who have gone into another world and now live in another way.'

'Is my grandpa an ancestor? Is he a spirit?'

'Yes, that's right.'

'Can I talk to my grandpa?'

'Yes, of course.'

I ran inside to fetch the delicate little gold bracelet my grandfather had made for me. When he made it, he showed me how he plaited gold threads together to make beautiful patterns. Together Minna and I buried the bracelet under my favourite pine tree and sat and listened to the trees.

'Now you know what to do if you want to speak to your grandpa,' said Minna, and she began to sing a long song full of strange clicks and sounds. I tried without success to copy her. When the song finished, it was quiet. I felt my grandfather there with me, even though I couldn't see him. I knew that he would always be there for me, in the trees.

Minna collected some stones and put them around me in a circle. 'That is to ask the stones to protect you, so no harm will come to you in this place. If you sit still, you can hear the earth breathe. Lie on the ground and listen.' I put my ear to the ground and was amazed by the many sounds I could hear. 'Now lie on your tummy with your head still. Be very, very quiet. What can you hear?'

'I can hear myself breathing.'

'Ah,' she said. 'Listen again. If you really listen, you will hear the earth breathing through you and that is a truly wonderful thing.'

When I went back to the tree the next day, the bracelet was gone. Years later my mother told me that she had followed us and rescued the bracelet after Minna and I had gone inside.

Minna said that, often, if there is a death, there will also be a birth: 'That is how life works.' That was true for our family: on 9 August 1951, my baby brother John was born. My mother came home from the hospital three days later carrying a red-faced, fuzzy-haired bundle. He would cry lustily and then gurgle with delight after he was fed. After Johnny's arrival I received very little attention and, although I was not sure whether I liked him at first, soon I couldn't imagine how I could live without him.

My father was very busy during that time, working with the comrades and for the newspaper. The only days he would take off were Sundays, when he would take me up the mountain, either along the Pipe Track or around Lion's Head, from where we could see the dark-blue Atlantic Ocean. Then, on Mondays, very early, he was off to the *Guardian* again.

16

56 Barrack Street

Shortly before the commencement of the Suppression of Communism Act in June 1950, the Communist Party of South Africa, perceiving danger, disbanded. They were to emerge again as the renamed South African Communist Party, which was forced to work underground or face major penalties.

Both Fred and Sarah were prohibited from continuing with their 'communist' work, Fred for the Western Cape Provincial Council and Sarah for her trade union. It had become impossible for communists to find jobs. Not only did anti-communist propaganda build up anti-communist sentiment, but people became nervous of associating with known communists for fear of being treated in the same way. This meant that doors that were open before were now closed to anyone named as a communist.

Fred and Brian worked well together as a team. The comrades were amused by the differences in character between them. Brian was quiet, thoughtful, considered and slightly withdrawn. He was formally well educated and had come from a learned upper-middle-class English family that believed in the importance of thought and the values of dignity and equality of all people. Brian made a dramatic shift during the war from this world to complete involvement in the communist cause.

Although he had similar values, Fred, by contrast, was extroverted, buoyant, full of good humour and quick to offer his views and opinions. Highly emotional when it came to certain issues, he would refuse to let things pass, challenging anyone who, in his opinion, had not thought things through. Jovially highlighting the discrepancies between his and Brian's educational backgrounds, he would say when prompted, 'Of course I've been to university; I used to deliver telegrams there.'

Fred's office was on the second floor of 56 Barrack Street. It was a shabby room, furnished with second-hand furniture and piles of papers, journals, leaflets and documents. When Brian was ill or away, Fred would take over as editor. His desk was always strewn with papers – details of the new laws coming out, legal papers telling him what the newspaper could and could not do, political leaflets, books, articles and petitions. On the wall behind him loomed a large poster proclaiming, 'One man, one vote', and next to his desk were stacks of cards arranged in alphabetical order that listed subscribers to the paper. When Fred was not frantically typing on his typewriter, he was on the phone listening to news from the reporters or organising campaigns or fund-raising events. All the while he would be puffing on a cigarette and taking the occasional swig from his half-empty brandy bottle. Reporters and voluntary newspaper sellers were in and out of Fred's office and, with others, would turn up and sit around the table when there was a hot topic. There they'd debate the issues and Fred would join in, offering his opinions and provoking heated arguments among these fiery personalities, many of whom were young students that Fred had recruited into the Party.

There were numerous issues to discuss and fight against. More than ever, the *Guardian* was the vehicle both for reporting what was going on and for communicating forthcoming political events to members of the disbanded Communist Party and the ANC. The early fifties heralded many of the most vicious pro-apartheid racist laws. The Immorality Amendment Act outlawed any kind of sexual relationship between races, the classification of which was formalised in the Population Registration Act. The Group Areas Act forced people to live in designated areas according to race, which resulted in the forced removal of thousands of coloured and black people from their homes to barren areas that were often far from their places of work. The Suppression of Communism Act, which so affected Fred and Sarah, banned the Communist Party; named communists were forbidden to speak to other members of the Party, and involvement in associated political activities was prohibited, as was joining any organisation considered 'communist' by the government. In 1951 the Bantu Authorities Act provided for the establishment of separate black homelands and regional authorities, supplying the legal basis for the deportation of blacks to these rural 'Bantustans'. To promote self-government in the homelands, the Act abolished the Native Representative Council. The following year, the pass laws made it compulsory for black people to carry with them at *all* times a pass book that contained their identification and employment information. An invalid pass book, or failure to produce a pass when required to do so by officials, was a criminal offence and could lead to arrest, imprisonment and often hard labour.

In 1952, the nationwide Defiance Campaign started with a national day of pledge and prayer on 26 June. The campaign, which was advertised in the *Guardian* and drew support from thousands of ordinary people of many races, protested against all forms of discrimination, including the unjust laws enforcing the subjugation of vast portions of the population.

Fred and the comrades were concerned about what would happen if the *Guardian* was banned. Luckily there was no shortage of lawyers to find loopholes in the law. When the *Guardian* was indeed banned in 1952, it was renamed the *Clarion*, which, in turn, was banned and subsequently renamed *Advance*. The newspaper's next name, in 1953, was *New Age*, which then became *Spark*. Fred ran the paper for ten years.

Fred loved finding, screening and recruiting members to the Communist Party. Many of them became long-time family friends. Denis Goldberg was the son of comrade Annie Goldberg, and he was inducted into politics at a very young age. When he was a teenager, Fred asked him to design stalls for the Annual Bazaar, where he would be fund-raising for *New Age*. Denis idolised Fred: he made a sketch of what was needed, and Fred built the stalls accordingly. It was a great success. Fred wrote to Denis on an official letterhead to thank him for his efforts and to say how good the stalls had looked. Denis was so thrilled that he kept the letter for years behind the mirror in his wardrobe. The Special Branch never found it. 'If the wardrobe still exists,' Denis remarked, 'the letter is probably still there.'

Mary Butcher was a quiet, tall, attractive young student at the University of Cape Town. She came from a Christian Scientist background, but her belief that the system was unjust led to her involvement in the Party in 1952, which is when she met Fred. Because of the banning of the CPSA, members of the newly named SACP were forced to meet secretly in cells of four, as it was easier to avoid arrest in smaller numbers. Someone would provide them with a discussion paper and instructions for getting involved in campaigns, such as leafleteering or recruiting new members.

Fred offered Mary a job at *New Age* as a cub reporter. He was her mentor and she was very fond of him but, in spite of his past history with women, he never made a pass at her. Instead, he protected her, especially when one of the comrades reputed to be the 'great fast-and-loose lover' invited her out. Fred told her that she did not have to get mixed up with him and that he had a 'bad reputation'.

Mary met Ben Turok at a meeting when he was student chair of the Modern Youth Society (which was, in essence, the Socialist Party). They started going out when Mary was working on *New Age* with Fred. Ben, who came from an intellectual Jewish family, was fairly short, charismatic and outspoken. He was like a terrier when it came to arguments, and he loved coming into the newspaper's office to take part in the discussions. Before he joined the SACP, he finished his studies and completed postgraduate training in economics overseas. When he returned to South Africa he joined the Party and committed his life unequivocally to the struggle. He became a trade unionist and then worked as a full-time organiser for the Congress of the People. As soon as he returned, he and Mary decided to get married. Ben knew that his Jewish parents and Mary's Christian parents strongly disapproved of the marriage, so they eloped and got married very suddenly, grabbing Fred to be one of the witnesses at their wedding. Fred, remembering the speed and secrecy of his own wedding, and the reactions of his Catholic family and Sarah's Jewish family, wholeheartedly supported them.

Ben and Fred would often argue just for the fun of it; Albie Sachs would stop them after a while and tell them that they were wasting time – everyone knew that they actually agreed with each other. Albie was a tall, gangly young man who did his homework, read the literature and would always come out with a well-considered response. He respected Fred's grasp of Marx and Lenin, as well as his political guidance. Fred was about ten years older than Albie, who had been in school while the servicemen like Fred were fighting in the war. He was also impressed because Fred was streetwise. One day, while walking with Fred along Barrack Street, a man who looked a little drunk bumped into Fred. Fred's arm shot out and grabbed him, and he took back what the man had stolen from his pocket: Fred was not to be outsmarted by some crook in the street.

Among the many black and coloured people coming in and out of the office was Zolli Malindi, a reporter and fund-raiser. Always cheerful, he was down to earth and he understood his people, knowing what would work for them. Another comrade, Greenwood, was a member of the Central Committee. He would visit us at Mount Pleasant, a tall, elegant young black man who delivered our newspapers. My parents would rush to the door and take him into the kitchen, giving him something to eat and a cup of coffee. I was confused: 'newspaper boys' were not normally offered coffee. I liked Greenwood. He was always friendly to me and often asked me how I was doing at school. He was studying to be a lawyer through a correspondence course, and he would talk about his studies and his future with my parents, who helped him with his fees. Eventually Greenwood disappeared. We never found out what had happened to him.

Fred's passionate and outspoken nature, so appreciated at the *Guardian*, got him into trouble – and not just with the security police. On the night of 23 May 1951, when my mother was pregnant with John, she was waiting for Fred to come home for supper. By nine o'clock she was fed up. She decided to lock him out, saying, 'He can sleep outside.' Then the phone rang. It was the Woodstock hospital: 'Your husband said you were pregnant and we mustn't worry you, but he has had an accident. Someone cut his face. He is all right now but he will have to stay overnight. You don't have to come right now as he is sleeping.'

The next morning Sarah rushed to the hospital. Fred's face was all stitched up and disfigured. It was a terrible shock. She felt that he would be better cared for if she took him home, but when they got there, a reporter from the Nationalist paper, *Die Burger*, was waiting to take pictures. Sarah was so angry that she ordered him to leave at once. Her small stature belied the power of her voice, and the reporter left immediately.

My mother asked Fred what had happened, and he explained that he had been coming home from work on the bus when the man sitting next to him started insulting Jews. Fred became angry and said to the man, 'My wife's Jewish and I won't have you insulting the Jews.' According to Fred, 'The guy just took out a cut-throat razor blade and slit my face.'

My father looked extremely pale. A dark gash ran down his face, bristly stitches holding it all together. He smelled strongly of friar's balsam. I was seven at the time and my shock must have shown. He tried to smile, but it turned into a wince. Then he said out of the corner of his mouth, 'Don't worry, I've had far worse than this happen to me and I survived.' Fred wanted to bring a case against the man, wishing to expose the man's anti-Semitism, but he was persuaded not to take legal action.

Denis Goldberg wondered whether Fred had been drinking: 'Fred liked to tipple. He was quite well known for being outspoken and could be extremely argumentative. He was pugnacious and always ready to defend his beliefs. At the time there was a huge sympathy for him, but some thought he had probably provoked the man. In the end the case was withdrawn and settled because the man's defence was going to be that Fred had had too much to drink and had attacked him. This would have been damaging to Fred as a member of the Provincial Council.'

The irony of it was that my father swore to my mother that he had not had anything to drink that day. In spite of the fact that he was a heavy drinker, my mother believed him: he never lied about events relating to racism or his political activities.

17

Banned

THE BEGINNING OF 1952 was a happy time for me. I had won first prize as a *Guardian* angel at a fancy-dress fund-raising party, and had a certificate to prove it. My mother had made a long white dress out of an old sheet and enormous wings that said 'Guardian' on them. I had also won gold and silver medals in the Cape Town Eisteddfod for ballet. To make that time perfect, my sister Ruth was born on 18 January 1953, six days before my ninth birthday. I thought that she was beautiful and carried her around like a doll.

A few months later, Fred and Sarah were banned for the first time. Both were given banning orders that prohibited them from belonging to a long list of specified organisations for life. Sarah was forbidden to take part in any trade union work. She was furious. 'That means, at thirty-seven, that my career as a trade unionist is over,' she fumed. The Minister of Justice, Dr Colin Steyn, told her in a letter that she and her fellow conspirators 'wrongly championed the cause of racial equality and liberty for all South Africans. Separate development is the only sensible path to take.'

Fred was banned for a number of months and had to stop working for the paper until the end of 1953, when he was unbanned. The newspaper had been through a number of names before becoming *New Age* at the end of that year. Fred had been forbidden to work for the *Guardian*, but not *New Age*, which he then edited. While he was banned, Fred had to earn money by selling encyclopaedias. In spite of the enthusiasm he shared with me about the books' contents, it wore him out.

All left-wing literature was banned and there were frequent raids in offices and homes by the security police, who were searching for illegal literature. It became my job at home to hide any books, leaflets or papers when we received a tip-off that there was going to be a raid. My parents hid most of their books – some of them successfully, as I still have them on my shelves.

The Nationalist government was fulfilling its promises. Africans were no longer free to live in the towns, and had to obtain a permit from the local authorities if they wanted to leave a rural area for an urban one. They were made to carry pass books (called *dompasse*) which they had to produce at any time; they were segregated by law from the white population in every conceivable way, including living space, physical proximity, and friendly or sexual relations. In the streets, there were mile-long queues of black people waiting to show their pass books to the police. Many people were arrested and beaten up. Whenever there was an incident, I would keep my eyes shut as I could not bear to watch people being dragged away.

Fred and Sarah were busier than usual, helping the ANC to organise a general strike, distributing leaflets, raising money and talking to people in the streets. They were campaigning for the end of the labour colour bar and for social security for all. They also helped to introduce the idea of the Freedom Charter, where people of all races would be asked as equals to help formulate a charter for a free South Africa.

During this time I went to an anti-pass demonstration with my father in Langa, where I witnessed police send Alsatians to tear a man apart. I also saw a child shot dead with dumdum bullets; the bullets exploded inside him and burst out of his skin as he screamed, and then died. My father had not realised how vicious the government had become; had he known, he said, he would never have taken me into the township.

I was terribly sad when my friend Sandra and her parents H.A. and Pauline Naidoo decided to leave South Africa because they were prohibited from living together. They decided to go to Hungary, where they believed they would live in peace in a model socialist state. The next devastating loss for me was that my beloved nanny Minna and her husband, Amos, had to leave because Amos came from Rhodesia and had been ordered to leave Cape Town. It was a deeply upsetting and unsettling time. People were being wrenched from their homes and from their loved ones. They were anxious about where they would be forced to go next and uncertain about what awaited them far from familiar surroundings. A sense of loss pervaded and there was terrible confusion.

Fred was happy to be back at the paper. As a family, we enjoyed a brief period of relaxation and time with comrades when we went camping together by the golden-brown, velvety Breede River, with its shining sands flowing down to the sea.

For the short time that their banning orders were lifted, Fred and Sarah continued to campaign actively and publicly against the pass laws. To keep one step ahead of the police, they organised small group meetings for members of the SACP in different homes to discuss strategies for helping the ANC to hold mass demonstrations. They wrote and circulated leaflets, and went door to door persuading people to contribute to the Freedom Charter and to campaign against the pass laws. Fred and his comrades spoke at many meetings in Nyanga, Langa, Athlone and Cape Town to mobilise people to take part in campaigns against the many unjust laws that were being brutally enforced. Our house was raided at all times of the day and night and police confiscated leaflets and banned books to use as incriminating evidence. Lying in bed waiting for the knock on the door, my worst fears were often realised.

On the night of 24 June, I was fast asleep when I woke up with a jerk. It felt as though there was something or someone in the room staring at me. I half-opened my eyes. A large shape loomed on the armchair opposite me. 'I must be dreaming,' I thought. I knew that my clothes, draped over the chair, could look like monsters. I held my breath and wondered whether I should get out of bed to check that this dark presence was indeed merely my clothing metamorphosed. Suddenly, the enormous black shape stood up, shifted smoothly across the room and switched on the lights. A huge Special Branch man wearing a hat and a beige raincoat was frowning at me. I quickly shut my eyes. Silence. 'Oh, God, please let me be dreaming.'

His voice was very loud. 'Lynn, where are your parents? When are they coming back?' I kept my eyes tightly closed. 'Listen here, I want your parents. Where are they?'

'I don't know.' I held tightly onto my sheets. He walked up to my bed, took hold of the sheets and pulled them off. I lay frozen in my nightdress and folded my arms across my chest to keep warm. 'Get out,' the man said. I stood on the cold polished-teak floorboards holding my doll and shivering. The Special Branch man took out a penknife and slowly unfolded the blade. 'Listen when I talk to you. If you don't tell me where they are, you know what I'll do? First, I'll slash your bed into little tiny shreds. Then I'll do the same to you.' I couldn't breathe. The intruder looked around my room. Then he went up to my bookshelf and started looking at my books. 'Ah,' he said, as if he had found treasure. 'You have two banned books: *Black Beauty* and *African Queen*. I'll take them. You can go to jail for this.' *Black Beauty* was the name of a horse. *African Queen* was the name of a boat. He took them simply because they had the words 'black' and 'African' on the cover.

The Special Branch man tipped all my books out of the bookshelf so that they clattered loudly onto the floor. I listened to see if he had woken the younger children or the maid. But there was silence. 'Watch out. Like father, like daughter. We will get you.'

I heard the door slamming as he left. I ran to the window to check that he was really going, and listened for the car to drive off. I shakily tried to remake the bed, but when I climbed in, it felt dirty and uncomfortable. I decided to get into my parents' bed, where I waited, trembling, for them to come home. I had no idea where they were. By that time I had been trained never to ask where my parents were going; it was too dangerous.

When they got back, my parents were shocked and angry. They put all my books back in the shelf. My father, furiously, said, 'Why are books about horses and boats banned?' My mother explained to me, 'Lynn, the government is doing terrible things to many people, which is why we have to go out to fight them, so that the world is a better place for you and everyone else. You need to be brave.' It was only when we talked about the danger many years later that my mother said to me, 'If we had really thought about the danger to you and John and Ruth, we would never have been able to do the work we did.'

That night, my parents let me sleep with them, and their presence during the night comforted me. The next week I was beside myself with joy when they presented me with a pitch-black puppy called Inky, who was a cross between a hunting poodle and a Dalmatian. My father said, 'Here is a friend for you. Look at how he wags his tail and jumps up at you; he likes you. From now on you won't feel so lonely.' The dog was to be my constant protector and companion for many years, but not even Inky could protect us from the security police.

18

Defiance

In 1954, Fred and Sarah were banned again. This time it was to last for fourteen years, and their banning orders were far worse. In addition to the list of organisations in which they could not be involved, they were not permitted to be part of a 'gathering', which constituted two or more people in the same place. (They were granted special permission to live together and with us.) They were also confined within a small part of Cape Town, to shop, and had to get permission to move outside that area. They were prohibited from printing or publishing anything, and had to report once a week at a specified time to the police station. Their banning affected family life immensely, particularly as they were not allowed to come to our schools. Forbidden from talking to anyone else who was named or banned, they were completely isolated from their comrades and close friends. A consequence of this for me was that I lost those friends who were the children of other banned people.

The hardest part of the banning orders was remembering to report to the police station. It was always inconvenient and because my parents resented going they often forgot, and then had to rush out at the last moment or be arrested.

I refused to tell anyone where they were or what they were doing. The first time my parents were banned, they had gone for a walk to discuss what to do. Himie Bernadt, their friend and lawyer, pitched up to see them while they were out. 'Sorry,' I told Himie, 'I don't know where they are, who they are with or when they are coming back.'

'You are well trained,' he said.

Being banned did not stop Sarah from running a secret communist cell at the house. Blanche La Guma and Ruth Gosschalk came every week, rain or shine, and Sarah would secretly get hold of Marxist literature for them to discuss. They would plan how to distribute leaflets or put up posters to advertise mass meetings. They were so underground that, although they knew Fred and their husbands to be involved in communist activity, they had no idea what the men were up to. The degree of the secrecy of their operations was highlighted when, one day, Sarah was instructed to meet a comrade at a certain street corner for the handover of some political papers. She arrived at the appointed place only to find that the comrade was Fred!

Running a guest house was extremely hard work, and meant getting up at six o'clock in the morning to organise breakfast. Fred and Sarah also provided evening meals for the guests – there were very few restaurants in Oranjezicht at the time. They constantly worried that the security police would upset and deter guests with their continual raids of the house. In addition to their frequent searches, the Special Branch approached guests to get them to spy on us. Not all of the guests were spies, though. One Afrikaans woman was invited to have tea with a member of the Special Branch at Stuttafords department store to discuss a matter of national importance. Being curious, she decided to go. While she was sipping her tea, the man told her that she should keep an eye on Fred and Sarah and report all their comings and goings to the security police. The woman, loyal to her hosts and outraged by the security policeman's request, got up, asked the waitress how much the tea came to, slammed the money down on the table and walked out.

Sarah's mother, Anna, had given Fred a radio that could transmit as well as receive. My parents had no idea how to use it for transmission, so they ignored that feature and didn't think of the radio as a possible security threat. One afternoon, the security police arrived, saw the radio and declared that they would be confiscating it. Fred hung on to it, shouting, 'Don't you dare touch my radio.' The security men sent for some experts to see what Fred and Sarah were using the radio for. The argument continued throughout the afternoon and more and more people arrived; a large number of police vans and cars drew up outside the house. The neighbours couldn't understand what was happening. In the end, the security police realised that the radio was not a threat to national security and they did not confiscate it – although, as it was a hideous metal-grey colour, Sarah would have been quite happy to see it go.

When my Grandma Anna came to stay with us to help run Mount Pleasant, there was always tension. She disliked Fred – unless he was in jail, when he transformed into a hero. He smoked and drank and did not support the family. She was also possessive, wanting her daughter for herself. She would say to Sarah, 'Let's go for a walk, but not with Fred.' Sarah, loyal to Fred, would insist, 'I'm sorry, it's me *and* Fred. There's no choice.' Fred got his own back. His mother-in-law used to cook very rich Eastern European meals, after which he would burp and take out a whole packet of Rennies. He'd take pleasure in munching them as loudly as he could.

The combination of tension between Anna and Fred, the extremely hard work of running Mount Pleasant and the constant harassment of the security police became hard to bear. On top of this, Fred and Sarah were aware of the fact that they were not spending enough time with the children. They started to explore the possibility of moving out of Mount Pleasant. Things came to a head when Sarah was so busy one day that she couldn't watch Johnny, so she sent the maid out with him. The maid was drunk and left Johnny, who was just learning to walk, on his own on the veranda. Johnny fell down the steep stairs and hurt himself. Sarah felt, 'No matter what happened, nothing was worth risking the lives of our children.' So they rented out Mount Pleasant – it temporarily became the Czech embassy – and moved to a small house in Rondebosch East.

I hated living in a tiny rectangular house with a small lawn. The only compensation was that I moved to a wonderful primary school called Golden Grove, where Mr Holmes, the head teacher, taught me division by getting me to divide a big block of cheese into the same number of squares for each child in the class. I would then take the cheese to the rest of the children before break time. Like my father, I started to get into scraps when children called me a kaffir lover. When they described black people as 'dirty, filthy kaffirs', I would shout, 'They're Africans, not kaffirs, and they are *not* dirty.' In particular, I fought with a girl called Lucille. When Mr Holmes saw us literally tearing each other's hair out, he gave us boxing gloves and told us to fight it out in front of the whole school at the assembly the next morning. We stood sheepishly in front of over a hundred expectant faces and had to shake hands. Lucille and I did in fact eventually become friends.

My parents refused to stop going to meetings, even though they were banned. On one occasion, I remember going with them to a field outside Langa, where there were huge bonfires and thousands of people singing and throwing their passes into the fire. It was one of the most inspiring events I had ever been to. The spirit of joyful defiance ended abruptly as the sound of police whistles pierced the voices raised in song. Everyone scattered and started running away, and my father scooped me up and raced to where our car was parked, a block away. He drove off triumphant, singing, 'We got away with it, we got away with it'. I joined in. For me, it was like a game, but I had seen what the police could do to people, so I realised the seriousness of the situation.

The burning of passes was one of many protests leading up to one of the greatest events of the time – the adoption of the Freedom Charter at the Congress of the People in Kliptown on 26 June 1955.

19

The Freedom Charter

We, the People of South Africa, declare for all our country and the world to know, that South Africa belongs to all who live in it, black and white, and that no government can justly claim authority unless it is based on the will of all the people ... And we pledge ourselves to strive together.
— THE FREEDOM CHARTER, ADOPTED ON 26 JUNE 1955

IN 1955, AGED ELEVEN, I helped my mother to prepare for the Congress of the People, a momentous gathering at which the Congress Alliance – made up of representatives from a diverse selection of racial groups, all in opposition to apartheid – presented their demands for the kind of South Africa they wanted. We had been folding leaflets and putting them in envelopes, and my tongue hurt from licking the envelopes. I soon discovered that I could use a sponge to do the job, after which my fingers became sticky. As a reward for the hard work, my mother said that if I promised to stay away from trouble I could go with them to one of the meetings running up to the Congress of the People. It was going to be very important, she explained. All over the country, Africans, Indians, coloureds and whites had been electing delegates to come together to decide on what they believed to be fundamental to South Africa and its people. There was going to be a special meeting the next day and we would have to get up early to join people from across the Western Province. The wishes they put forward would be taken to Kliptown in the Transvaal in June, when a single document – the Freedom Charter – would be produced that would express what most people wanted.

I woke up at four-thirty the next morning to the feel of my father gently pulling my ears. 'Wake up; time to go. Dress warmly. It's still very early.' We drove across Cape Town to Athlone. Most of the city was still asleep so there were no cars on the road, but when we arrived in Athlone, a meeting point, there were lots of trucks and vans, the majority of them very old. My father went up to a green van where people were beginning to get in. 'Hello, Comrade Malindi, do you think you could take care of my daughter?' my father asked Zolli Malindi, our family friend who worked for the paper. Zolli replied, 'Comrade Fred, we will take good care of her. Here, sit here.'

I was lifted into the crowded van and given a coat to sit on. The floor was made of steel with ridges; it was very hard and uncomfortable. I leant against the wall of the vehicle as we all squashed together. Then the doors closed and it was suddenly dark, but I could see the white of people's teeth as they smiled. The van started up and we bounced and jolted and swayed over every bump. Soon the men started to sing freedom songs. Then one woman led the singing and lifted her voice above the men's. I sang as loudly as I could, and at the end of each song we all raised our fists and shouted: '*Amandla ngawethu! Matla ke a rona!*' – Power to the people! Victory is certain! Although the van ride was so bumpy, we were having such a good time that I hoped the final meeting place was a long way away.

Most of the day was an anticlimax for me. It was cold and drizzling, and I was too small to see the speakers, who went on and on. I was extremely bored. As soon as I could, I ran off and found some other children. We played tag with each other but were told to be quiet at the end of the day, when we were all asked to stand and sing the ANC anthem, 'Nkosi Sikelel' iAfrika'. It was beautiful, thousands of men and women singing their hearts out in different harmonies. I fell asleep that night happy and exhausted, even before I had had supper, the dullness of the speeches long forgotten.

On 26 June 1955 we waited for news of what had happened in Kliptown. Fred chain-smoked at least three packets of cigarettes. Then the phone rang and Fred cheered loudly: 'It has been a tremendous success! There were 3 000 delegates and 3 000 other people.' Sarah was overjoyed. 'Do you realise,' she announced, 'that we have just been part of one of the most democratic and historic events in the history of this country?'

Shortly afterwards, Fred and Sarah worked behind the scenes in organising the famous Women's March to protest against the pass laws. Sarah would visit Vrygrond and together with Dora Tamana would go from shack to shack telling people of the significance of this event and the importance of rallying support for it. On 9 August 1956, my brother Johnny's fifth birthday, 20 000 women marched to the Union Buildings in Pretoria singing, 'Strijdom [prime minister at the time], you have struck a rock'. The 7 000 individually signed anti–pass law petitions were ignored by the prime minister, who refused even to greet the women. But because of the sheer number of people that took part in the demonstration, Fred was convinced of ultimate triumph. 'They will never defeat us,' he declared. 'The people will never take oppression lying down.'

During that period, when my father was not busy with his political activities, he discovered that he could smoke delicious fish. He converted two large fridges for this purpose. The aroma of freshly smoked fish was so tantalising that neighbours would turn up when it was dinner time. One day he told us that an eminent guest was coming for lunch, Chief Albert Luthuli, then president of the ANC. Chief Luthuli was looking forward to spending the day with our family, and my father wanted to treat him to his special smoked fish, which he started smoking early in the morning. True to form, an Afrikaans neighbour showed up for a visit just before lunch time. My father invited her to stay for lunch and introduced her to the chief. She had never met a black man socially, and certainly not at the table. Hunger got the better of her. She sat down opposite the chief. The next minute, she got up, rushed to the toilet and was sick. I went to see whether she was all right and she said, 'I don't feel too well', and left immediately. Racism was so deeply embedded in her that sharing a meal with a black man made her violently ill. I was deeply upset by this incident and found it difficult to greet the woman after that. Fortunately we moved from the house a short while later.

20

Treason

My family returned to Mount Pleasant at the end of 1956 for a short time: the tenants had left and Sarah had to get the house ready for the next tenants. We were in a constant state of anxiety, as my father had had tip-offs that something big was going to happen. At seven o'clock in the morning on 5 December 1956, when I was twelve, I took my dog Inky for a walk down the hill towards the reservoir. The wind was blowing so strongly that on the way down it lifted him right off his feet. To struggle up the steep hill against the wind on the return trip was a real battle. I reached the corner of the road, and then I saw them: six Special Branch men were walking through our front gate. I let myself in through the back gate as silently as possible, but Inky started barking. I quickly locked him inside, telling him to be quiet. There was a loud knock on the front door and my father went to answer it. Six men filed in and surrounded my father as Van Wyk, the senior security man, handcuffed him. 'We are arresting you,' he said in a loud voice.

'What for?' asked my father.

'You will find out at the station. Come,' Van Wyk said, pulling my father towards the door. 'Say goodbye to your family. You won't see them for some time.'

Little Ruthie, aged three, hung on to Fred and howled. My mother had to pull her off. Johnny, then five, just stood and stared. I was worried that the security police had also come for my mother but, much to my relief, they left her alone. She looked furious, saying under her breath, 'I knew something like this would happen.' I just felt helpless; there was nothing I could do to stop them. As they escorted my father out of the house, two men walked in front of him, two behind him and one on each side. There were three Volkswagens parked outside the front gate, and they forced him into the middle car, a light-grey one. I waved at my father but he didn't see me; he was looking straight ahead. The cars pulled off and there was nothing outside to show that anything had happened. Except that, as usual, neighbours were watching from behind their curtains.

Blanche La Guma phoned to say that her husband, Alex, who worked with my father, had also been arrested. At eight o'clock that morning, only an hour after Fred had been arrested, Dora Tamana arrived at the house to find out if both my mother and my father had been arrested and, if so, how the children were coping; she had been worried that we might be on our own. A neighbour was looking after Dora's own children. She had left Vrygrond at six to get to us, as soon as she had heard the news of the arrests on the radio. All day long the phone rang. My mother gave the same answer: 'They have rounded up a lot of people all over the country, but I don't know what's happening.'

Later that morning, when the papers were delivered, the headlines were full of the story: 'Carneson Arrested for Treason'; 'People All Over Country Arrested for Plotting to Overthrow Government'. Over the next few months, security forces arrested 156 political leaders of all races from across the country and transported them to Johannesburg's Old Fort prison, where they were detained on charges of treason. Trialists included journalists, trade union leaders, lawyers – including Nelson Mandela – academics, members of the clergy and officials of banned organisations such as the SACP and the ANC.

The preparatory examination for the Treason Trial started at the Drill Hall, Johannesburg, in 1957. *New Age* complained about the violence of the police against the demonstrators who stood outside the Drill Hall singing loudly and holding placards that proclaimed, 'We stand by our leaders'. Most of our family friends were accused: Brian and Sonia Bunting, Alex La Guma, Jackie Arenstein, Hymie Barsel, Rusty Bernstein, Paul Joseph, Moses Kotane, Chief Albert Luthuli, Ruth First and Joe Slovo, and too many others for me to remember.

I read in the papers that if you were guilty of treason, you could be handed the death sentence. My mother told me not to worry. 'There is a very good chance that they will be found not guilty,' she said, 'especially if the judges are fair.'

'When will we know?'

'I don't know. It will take time for the trial to start and then time to hear the evidence. It could be months.' In fact, it took four long years.

I missed my father. To make matters worse, my friend and companion Inky had attacked a Special Branch man and had to be put down. I suffered an inconsolable sense of loss but refused to get another dog because, I said, 'he would just be taken away'.

Before he was tried in the Drill Hall, my father was taken to Roeland Street Prison in Cape Town. Because I had turned twelve, the minimum visiting age, I was allowed to visit him in prison. My Grandma Anna took me; my mother could not come with us because the prison was outside the area to which her banning order confined her. When we arrived, there was a long line of people outside the jail, singing freedom songs as they waited their turn to enter. We joined the queue and Grandma Anna took out her knitting and clicked away, reminding me of Madame Defarge in Dickens's *A Tale of Two Cities*, waiting for the storming of the Bastille. To ward off boredom, I took out some paper and a pencil and wrote a poem:

> Like Madame Defarge
> My Granny stands outside
> the doors
> of Roeland Street Jail.
> We wait
> a bedraggled line
> of thirty people
> and one child, me,
> waiting to be let in.
> I hear the clanking of
> keys.
> The turning of
> One
> Two
> Three
> Four
> Five keys.
> And the warder,
> grim-faced,
> clanks open
> the heavy studded wooden doors.
> My Granny
> is knitting a grey-green jersey
> for my Dad
> in case he is away a long time
> and winter is cold.

A petition was written by the children of political prisoners for the release of their parents – arrested for ninety-day periods without trial during the state of emergency – to try to draw the public's attention to what was happening, 1960. From left: Ruth Fischer, Hilly Goldberg, Lisa Thorne and Lynn

An excerpt from Sarah's description of the disgusting conditions at Roeland Street Prison for women detained without trial, 1960

A year of 1960 will never be forgotten in the History, when thousands of people of the whole South Africa were arrested. Men, women, children, infants and pregnant women, as I was arrested by two European men and one African man wearing private clothes, from my home to the Police Station.

I was searched by the European woman with private clothes. After a certain time Police van took us to Roeland Street Jail. I was searched again by European woman with uniform. She told me to take of all my clothes until I was naked, takes the clothes from me, every one which has been searched thrown on the floor; after all told me to lie down on the floor; and this is called 'Tauza'. From there to the cell I was given two old blankets and one mat like grassy mat and cold porridge for my supper. It was about 4 p.m. as I came in the cell. The women were crowded and singing. I stood and look, did not know where to get space for myself. The women talked to others to move and I can get space. So crowded an open bucket was here as 'Toilet Room'. An open dish of water to drink was also here.

Photos of Lynn, John and Ruth by Eli Weinberg, a prominent photographer who worked for the newspaper and who took pictures of the children to send to Sarah in jail and Fred in hiding, 1960

Lynn Carneson,
"Rogues' Den",
Travers Road,
NEWLANDS. C.P.

23rd May, 1960.

The Secretary for Justice,
PRETORIA.

Dear Sir,

My mother, Mrs. Sarah Carneson, was arrested on the 8th April, 1960, and was first detained in Roeland Street prison and now in Bien Donne prison at Simondium under the Emergency Regulations.

I do not know where my father is.

I am sixteen years old and have a little brother Johnny aged 8 and sister Ruth aged 7.

We have had no means of support and the two younger children are staying with one family and I am staying with another family who have been good enough to keep us for the time being.

Our home has been broken up and we are very unhappy and uncertain about what is going to happen to us.

I have been able to visit my mother but the younger children have not yet been able to get permission.

I am sure that my mother has not done anything wrong. I know that she is a good person, we love her dearly and miss her very much. The younger children are pining for her and we can't understand why she has been taken away from us.

When I visit her, we are very upset as she can't tell me why she is there or when she will be able to come back. She and others have told me that she is waiting to know whether she will be charged or not. It is taking such a long time and I thought that I would write to you to ask you please to deal with the case urgently so that she may be released and start a home again for us.

I have seen in the press that other detainees have been released who have been detained at the same time or after her.

I hope that you will be able to let me have a reply as quickly as possible.

Yours faithfully,

Lynn's letter to the Department of Justice, asking why her mother was in prison. She did not receive a reply

UNION OF SOUTH AFRICA.

TO: ...... *Sarah Carneson* ....

CERTIFICATE OF RELEASE.

(Regulation 4(2)/19(2) of the Emergency Regulations)

You are hereby notified that the Honourable the Minister of Justice of the Union of South Africa has authorised your release from detention in terms of the Emergency Regulations promulgated by Proclamation No. 91 of 1960 / Proclamation No. 93 of 1960 / Proclamation No. 91 of 1960 read with Proclamation No. 124 of 1960, subject to the undermentioned conditions:-

1. That you do not participate in, or associate yourself in any way with the activities of any organisation or attend any meeting or gathering without the prior approval of the Magistrate, *Cape Town*.

2. That you do not visit or in any way communicate with any person who is being or was detained in terms of the Emergency Regulations or who was a member of any organisation declared unlawful by or in terms of any law.

3. That you do not publish or cause to be published or supply to any person any information relating to your detention or the detention of any other person in terms of the Emergency Regulations.

4. That you do not leave the Magisterial district of *The Cape, Wynberg, Simonstown and Bellville* or change your place of employment or residence without the prior approval of the Magistrate, *Cape Town*.

5. That you do not absent yourself from your place of residence between the hours of 8 p.m. and 6 a.m. daily, without the prior approval of the Magistrate.

6. That you report in person to the Police Station every Monday between the hours of 9 a.m. and 10 a.m., or at such other places and at times approved by the Magistrate,

Your attention is invited to regulation 4(4)/19(2) read with regulation 25(1) in terms whereof a contravention of any of these conditions or any failure to comply therewith is an offence and punishable with a fine not exceeding £500 or imprisonment for a period not exceeding 5 years or with such imprisonment without the option of a fine or with both such fine and such imprisonment.

— 1 JUL 1960

SECRETARY FOR JUSTICE.

ACKNOWLEDGMENT.

I, *Sarah Carneson* hereby certify that I have received a copy of the above certificate and that the contents thereof have been explained to me.

Date: ....

Place: ...... *8.-7-.1960* ......

Sarah Carneson

BIEN DONNE GEVANGENIS
P.O. SIMONDIUM
BIEN DONNE PRISON

1 Sarah's certificate of release from prison

United again: Fred and Sarah in Kirstenbosch botanical gardens after Sarah's release from prison and Fred's return from hiding, 1961

© UWC–Robben Island Museum Mayibuye Archives

When it was banned, the *Guardian* changed its name a number of times and eventually became *New Age*, and then *Spark*, which was banned in 1963. Fred was editor of the newspaper from 1953 to 1962

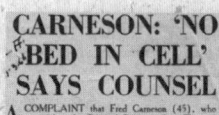

When Fred was arrested in 1965 on charges of sabotage and belonging to the Communist Party, he lived in solitary confinement for over five months in a tiny, brightly lit cell with no bed and round-the-clock surveillance by guards. St Mungo Court at Clifton, which he used as a hideout and office before his arrest, was finally discovered in 1966 and labelled 'Red H.Q.'

Letter to Fred from Thabo Mbeki, 1966, who wrote that he hoped to 'be writing to you under normal conditions' soon

After receiving this telegram with Fred's verdict, the family was so delighted that Fred had not been given a life sentence that it took a while to realise that even five years and nine months was a long time

Not entirely happy: Ruth, Sarah and John at home after the trial, showing signs of strain, 1966

Lynn, twenty-one, in London, 1966. For her, the end of Fred's trial was a relief, but she knew that the waiting was not yet over

John, aged fifteen, goes to England as political refugee and follows in his father's footsteps by taking part in interviews about South Africa, 1967

JOHN (15) ON 'POLICE STATE'

Jan 9 Southampton

"Echo" Staff Reporter

A 15-YEAR-OLD political refugee, John Carneson, from Cape Town, was met by his sister, Lyn, this morning when he arrived in Southampton in the liner Edinburgh Castle. He tried to describe what it was like to be the of politically-suspect parents in "a police state".

John's father, Mr. Fred Carneson, was the former editor of the now banned South African newspaper "New Age," also called "Spark." John said his father was imprisoned under the 180-Day Act, and he was interrogated to such an extent that he had to be put in an oxygen tent in order to ensure that he would live through further torture. He was now serving a five-year sentence under the Suppression of Communism Act.

John's mother was under house arrest; she must not leave a two-mile area around their home, and had to report to the police at least once a week.

She was not allowed to be with more than two people under the same roof at any one time or she might be arrested for holding an illegal gathering.

"So if I bring friends home," John said. "I have to hurry them from room to room, so that when my mother comes in there are not more than two of us in the same place."

House "bugged"

He continued: "Wherever I go I am followed by plain clothes policemen. Our house has shot into without any reason except to frighten us.

"It is bugged,' and I cannot deny that the recordings will be used as evidence against parents, talk either about chemical experiments at school, even discuss the French relation regardless of the content.

The threat of having the house raided is always present and every time I hear a footstep outside the door I say to myself. 'This is it.' They have come for my mother."

John commented: "This is the first time in months that I have felt free to speak like this to anyone.

A few weeks ago his sister, came to this country four years ago, sent a telegram telling John she had found him a place at a Quaker boarding school at Leighton Park, Reading – where his fees would be paid by the school itself.

Within days of receiving the news that he had somewhere to go to in England John packed and was, as he put it, "on a boat to freedom."

John on his arrival today. —"Echo" photo.

Ruth and Sarah emerge from court laughing about how, when Sarah was accused of breaking her banning order, a Special Branch agent described how he had sat in a dripping fig tree to observe her taking Ruth to a party, 1967

Sad and brave, Sarah and Ruth are pictured here for the final time before Ruth leaves for London, 1967. Sarah was devastated by the loss of her children; Ruth put on a brave face

Mrs. Carneson leaves S.A.

-7 SEP 1967 1st ED

Mrs. Sarah Carneson, wife of the former Cape M.P.C., left South Africa in the S.A. Vaal yesterday on an exit permit.

Her husband, Mr. Fred Carneson, former editor of the banned Left-wing newspaper 'New Age,' is serving a prison sentence of five years and nine months for contraventions of the Suppression of Communism Act. His sentence has about five years to run.

Mrs. Carneson, who will not be able to return to South Africa, has gone to join her three children in Britain.

Forced to leave, Sarah knew she might never return and did not know when she would see Fred again, 1967

Fred was forbidden from seeing a letter and the above photo sent by John in 1967, because the prison authorities objected to John's long hair

The continued cruelty of censorship went on year after year and meant that what could be said was always strictly limited

Wedding greetings from Lynn's extended family – Fred and his fellow political prisoners – at Pretoria Central Prison, 1968

During the four years of the trial, Fred was able to come home to Cape Town only infrequently, when the proceedings were adjourned for more than a week. It was during one of these times that we moved to a single-storey Victorian house in Protea Road, Claremont. My parents explained that they wanted me to go to a brand-new senior school nearby called Westerford: 'We think that it is the best school in Cape Town at the moment because the headmaster, Mr Taylor, is progressive.' We all loved the house in Protea Road. It had character. There were sweet-smelling lemon and naartjie trees outside my bedroom window. When the naartjies were ripe and juicy, I would lean out of my window and pick them.

Fred loved the house but was not there very often. It was too expensive to come down from Pretoria for weekends and short breaks. Instead, between sessions at the Drill Hall he travelled to areas around Johannesburg with his old wartime friend and comrade Ivan Schermbrucker to raise money for the Party and the paper. Because the SACP was banned, all of their activity was highly secretive so that they – and the people they approached – would not be recognised by security police.

When Fred came home it was always a joyful occasion and we would go for picnics on the beach or in the woods in Tokai. When he had to leave us, he wrote as often as possible. His first letter was written two days after he was arrested and transported to Johannesburg to await trial.

From the Remand Cells
The Fort
Johannesburg
7 December 1956

Sarah darling
We only managed to organise some notepaper today, hence the delay in writing.

First of all to soothe any fears you may have as to our health: we are all very fit and in excellent spirits. There are long periods when there is just nothing else to do. We have no complaints to make in regard to treatment. The food, though monotonous, is both well prepared and more than adequate. Food parcels from outside are freely allowed and we therefore get plenty of variety. Please don't send me anything. Our people are well organised up here and we can get anything we want.

We are not permitted to discuss life in prison in our letters, so the details will have to wait until I get back.

One other thing: we are separated from prisoners charged with criminal offences and are on our own, two to a cell. I'm sharing one with Benny Turok who, thank heavens, doesn't snore.

The Cape Town, Durban and Port Elizabeth crowd all appeared in court this morning, where we were remanded to the 19th, when the preparatory examination is due to begin. Bail has been refused, but our attorneys are reasonably certain that we shall be granted bail by the 21st, or perhaps even on the 19th. Until then we shall just have to sit.

In so far as the kids are concerned, try to keep the news from the little ones if possible. Lynn, no doubt, is devouring every item of news she can lay eyes on. To her I say: Don't worry about Daddy. I've got a lot more space and freedom than your poor budgie Gordy has in his little apology for a cage! Another thing, Lynn: your mummy has to handle a lot just now, so please be as helpful as you can, especially with Johnny and Ruth.

To get back to other things. Tell Brian I did not have time to call on any of the town regulars. They must be seen soon otherwise we'll lose money. Let him rope in a few helpers for the office while I'm away. Tell the staff not to take advantage of my absence. Don't forget the rent for the office on the 17th. We won't have enough money in the bank for it. Maybe Himie Bernadt will make a short-term loan, but in any case borrow as little as possible.

In regard to the Xmas Eve party, everything should go as arranged. We shall, as I have indicated, probably be out by then and I would like to have a good time there. Try to get the Xmas tree for the kids and go ahead with all arrangements just as if I were home. Please don't forget to run the car a little each day, in order to keep the battery charged.

As for the arrests themselves, I think the government has blundered badly. From what we hear, there is widespread sympathy and support. Thousands have already been collected for bail and a strong Defence Committee has been set up. I am confident that, whatever minor victory the government may score, we shall be the winners.

For one thing is certain: nothing on earth will ever prevent the people from winning their just rights; neither prison, nor even death itself can change either history or the simple facts of life. As long as things are what they are there will always be South Africans, of all races and creeds, willing to oppose tyranny and injustice.

It was a thrill to hear in court today almost every language in our country: Zulu, Sesotho, Xhosa, Bavenda, English and, last but not least,

Afrikaans. Each of those languages was heard in turn as we answered to our names. To those with any sense to see, we are the true South Africans, fighting for that unity which alone can make our country a strong and happy land for all its peoples.

But that's enough now. I understand that, although our letters are censored, we may send and receive as many as we please.

Write soon. Kiss all the kids for me. Chin and thumbs up.

All my love, darling,

Fred

My father did not come home that Christmas, or the following one. We missed him terribly. And all the time the possibility of a death sentence was not far from my mind.

When Fred was at the Old Fort in Johannesburg, he had the chance to meet up with many comrades from other parts of South Africa whom he had been forbidden to communicate with while he was named and banned. Afterwards he would exclaim, 'I don't know what the Nats were doing, putting us together, on State expenses. An excellent opportunity to plan our next steps.'

In the June holidays of 1957, I went up to Johannesburg to stay with my aunt so that I could see my father. I used to go to the Drill Hall with him to observe the trial in progress. All the accused were seated on hard, uncomfortable benches and the court proceedings went on and on. It was difficult for me to sit still for hours at a time. One day I sat between my father and Nelson Mandela, who shook hands with me and gave me a toffee. 'You should bring a cushion next time you come,' he told me.

My father was in good fighting spirit. Ben Turok, my father's cellmate and fellow accused, said afterwards that 'Fred was the life and soul of the party in a big way. He used to joke and play the fool. Very few outside the Cape, where he had status, realised that he had a good brain. He was the sort of man who would slap you on the back and say, "Hello, mate". He didn't demand respect, admiration or adulation.'

There were times, however, when Fred did take the lead. Early on in the trial, the officials put the accused in an enormous wire cage. Fred lost his temper, shouting, 'You can't do this. We are being treated worse than animals.' He ranted and raved and everyone applauded. The officials threatened him with contempt of court. My mother, equally angry on hearing about the prisoners' treatment, joined others in Cape Town to protest against the cage. Eventually it was removed. Reporting the incident in a letter home on 8 September 1957, he wrote, 'Last week I was so cross I landed myself in a spot of bother. They put people in cages depending on their colour and I really lost my temper ... It all turned out well in the end, so don't worry.'

Fred never stopped protesting. Three judges were appointed to the Treason Trial: Judge Frans Rumpff, Judge Alexander Kennedy and Judge Joe Ludorf. On the opening day of the trial, the defence team applied for the recusal of Judge Ludorf, as he had represented the government as lawyer for the police in a previous case, as well as Judge Rumpff, who had been the judge in the 1952 Defiance Trial. While Judge Ludorf recused himself, Judge Rumpff did not. When Rumpff walked into the court, the accused decided to protest by not standing up for him. Fred led the protest. Walter Sisulu, former Secretary-General of the ANC, who witnessed the event, was impressed. 'The judge threatened to arrest all those defying him,' he said. 'It was a dramatic affair and made all the Treason Trialists associate themselves closely with Carneson.'

The fact that white people were accused in the Treason Trial made a huge impression on the black population. Because they fought side by side with the Africans, the Africans realised that not all whites were oppressors. It made a difference to people like Mazolo Mafu, a black freedom fighter who reflected, 'Being a black South African, I deeply mistrusted whites, including those that said they were non-racist. But through the readings and proceedings of the Treason Trial, we saw that there were some whites that practically embodied non-racism and were also part of the struggle. Fred belonged to that group.'

The trial dragged on. On 28 February 1958, eight months after I visited him, Fred wrote, 'The case still goes on. We thought that it would become more interesting when evidence of meetings began, but it is not really much different. Our bottoms still get tired of the benches. And at the slow rate the witnesses are coming and going, they will get a lot more tired before all the proceedings are over.'

The prolonged four-year trial made it impossible for the accused, including Fred, to earn a proper living. Luckily for us as a family, professional people like doctors, dentists and lawyers gave their services free. Sarah found a job organising the Cape Town Eisteddfod every year, which brought in a little money, and her family also helped. She was aware that the black families of trialists were far worse off and helped to raise funds for them.

She was also on the Committee for the Banished, which assisted black political people who were exiled to rural areas and who were starving.

Sarah kept her secret Party cell going with Ruth Gosschalk and Blanche La Guma. The three women became very close friends and comrades. Both Blanche and Ruth had to check whether they were being followed whenever they met with Sarah because they would have been arrested had they been caught. They were highly disciplined: 'You made sure that when an arrangement was made, you would be there,' they explained much later. 'It was commitment, duty bound. You did it even if it was raining or bitterly cold. We were never caught. The Special Branch at that time was not so vigilant.'

Blanche had to work many hours a day as a nurse and midwife to support her children. She didn't have a car, so had to take a bus and a train to Oranjezicht. One freezing winter she was cold and wet for much of the time and contracted severe bronchitis. Fred had come back during a short break from the Treason Trial. Even though he was banned and not supposed to be in the same room as them, he entered the room when he heard Blanche cough. 'You are dying on your feet,' he said to her. 'We must organise for you to get a car. Can you drive?'

'No, I can't,' she replied.

'You can learn to drive.' My parents and some other comrades got together enough money to buy Blanche a car. Despite his banning order, Fred drove her around looking for a second-hand car until one eventually turned up. Another comrade gave Blanche driving lessons. It changed her life.

When my father was home between sessions and fund-raising, we had some wonderful times – picnicking, walking, fishing and picking mushrooms. By then we had learnt the names of most of the mushrooms: we picked pine rings, cep or shaggy ink-cap mushrooms. My father would cook them for breakfast with scrambled eggs when they were fresh and tasty. When we didn't recognise a mushroom we took it to an expert called Miss Stephens, who used to say, 'Well, I'll taste it and if you find me dead tomorrow, don't eat it.' I used to worry that she might poison herself. We also went often to a beautiful beach at Fish Hoek. When the men brought the nets in they would give us a free fish for helping them haul in their catch. My father would braai the fish on the beach, and it always tasted delicious.

One of our favourite places was a flat rock called Rooikrantz overlooking the sea at Cape Point. My mother had a terrible fear of heights but was game to go anywhere. One day we wanted to go fishing at Rooikrantz. The path down to the rock was quite steep and my mother slid down on her bottom, refusing to accept help. We were amused because a troop of baboons was fascinated by this and watched her slide down with us. She finally made it and we all cheered and clapped.

My Grandma Anna frequently visited us in Cape Town. When she and my father were in the house at the same time, we still expected fireworks – and often got them. On one occasion, just before my father was going back to Pretoria for the trial, he said that he was going via Pietermaritzburg to visit his family. My grandmother left the room and came back with two brown-paper packets. 'These are for your family,' she said, presenting the packets to my father. He looked inside: they were full of condoms. My father nearly hit her, but managed to control himself and went red instead, looking as though he were about to explode.

On another occasion, just before Inky was put down, we all went on an outing, leaving the dog to run after the car, as my grandmother believed that dogs should not be allowed inside the house or car with people. When Inky started to lag behind, we pleaded with my father to let him in. 'If you let that dog in the car,' my grandmother threatened, 'it's either him or me.' My father stopped the car. 'Then it's the dog,' he said. 'Would you like to step out of the car?' As children, we found the clash of these two strong characters extremely amusing and we used to shriek with laughter. This only made both of them angrier, but at least it stopped them fighting with each other. My mother put the heated arguments down to the stress under which we were all living.

As the trial progressed, Fred was able to come home for longer periods of time. When home, he went back to work on *New Age*, also continuing to raise money and recruit more members into the Party. During this time he recruited a nineteen-year-old coloured man called Dougie Brown. Dougie used to sell *New Age* on the docks, where he worked, and met Fred frequently in the *New Age* office on Saturday mornings, when he came to collect papers to sell. Fred would sit him down and explain things like the Freedom Charter. Dougie was hungry to learn: 'Whenever I left the office, I felt I knew more than when I went there,' he said. Dougie read *New Age* avidly. What impressed him was that reading *New Age* gave him his first real insight into the ANC. He was excited by the fact that black people could play a political role, and would go to demonstrations on the Parade where black people would ask about Fred: 'What's that white chap doing here?'

Dougie decided that he wanted to join the Party, and told Fred of his decision. A few months later Dougie was approached by a comrade called Alf Wannenberg, who said to him that he wanted to introduce him secretly to someone at a certain street corner at eight o'clock that night. When Dougie got there, a car arrived. Dougie got in the back. Fred was sitting in the car and said, 'Repeat after me: "I will abide by the rules of the Communist Party." Then give me a rand.' Dougie repeated the words and paid him, and joined the Communist Party. He felt very proud; it was not easy to become a Party member.

In 1959, my father was investigating a serious matter with Ruth First, a journalist and political activist, but would not discuss it in front of me because, he said, I was too young. He got up at five in the morning and read newspapers. Then he would go and make himself a cup of coffee. Being curious, I used to sneak into the room to see what he was up to. I once found a terrible photograph of a dead man hunched up in the boot of a car, full of injuries and bruises. Shortly afterwards, the front page of *New Age* was full of the story of Bethel farmers who had beaten, starved and massacred over thirty farm labourers. Because of this exposure in *New Age*, there was a mass boycott of potatoes. The price of potatoes fell and the farmers were investigated. At least sometimes, I thought, there is some justice in the world.

Around that time I had an intense personal experience of the terrible human suffering that apartheid and racism caused. Blacks were treated with utter contempt and paid minimum wages. The majority of black farm workers, including coloured workers in the Cape, were illiterate. On the wine farms many were alcoholics because of the 'dop' system, where workers were paid with wine. When I was fifteen, I went on holiday to visit friends of my parents, Tebby and Joan, who were farmers in Klapmuts near Paarl in the Western Cape. Although they paid reasonable wages, most of the farm workers drank heavily. Joan offered literacy classes but these were seldom attended. One evening, a farm labourer's wife knocked on the back door. The woman said that her baby was sick. Joan examined the baby and told her that the baby had dysentery and was dehydrated, and that she should feed the baby a solution of sugar and water every two hours. The women went off with a pot for boiling the water and a bag of sugar. The next day she returned and said that the baby was dead. She had had no understanding of the importance of what Joan had told her. Joan said that she had tried to help mothers like this one, but it often made no difference. Later, when I was about to go fishing at the lake, I saw the mother holding the baby in her arms, just rocking backwards and forwards. I helped her to bury her baby in my towel, just a tiny baby that was so thin you could see her bones, but with a large distended stomach. I did not feel like fishing after that. I collected stones and carefully positioned them right around the lake to show that children who died were not forgotten. That day I sat and stared at the water and wondered whether, as a white person, I should feel guilt for the death of that baby.

When I asked my mother about it, she said, 'Of course not. You have done nothing wrong.'

'But, Mom,' I said, 'I don't understand. I don't understand. I really don't.'

'It's very difficult to understand why people do the things that they do,' she responded.

'But I really want to understand,' I said to her.

She left the room and came back with five books. 'I have been waiting to give you these,' she said. 'You have to work things out for yourself. You have to think for yourself; no one can do it for you. In these books you will find four different kinds of belief. Read them and think about them. It takes many years to make your own sense of it, but this is a beginning.'

The books she gave me were the Old Testament, the book of the Jewish faith; the New Testament, believed in by the Christians; the Koran, the Muslims' holy book; and *The Communist Manifesto*, which, she said, was banned, so I had to hide it away.

'What do you believe?' I asked.

'Well,' she said, 'there are many good things that all of them have in common, but you have to find those yourself.'

She then gave me the fifth book. I was growing up, she said to me, and it would answer any other questions that I wanted to ask: it was a book for teenagers about love and sex. The one about love and sex seemed to be the most interesting, so I started that one first.

The books my mother gave me that night started years of searching for a spiritual belief. At the time I thought I would try praying in case it helped. I prayed that the Treason Trial would not end with a death sentence for the accused, especially my father. I was obsessed with what would happen if he was sentenced to death. Would he hang? Then what would happen to us? However much I tried not to think about it, my fantasies were full of how I could help him escape, knowing full well that whatever I tried would be hopeless. The signs were promising, however. As the Treason

Trial progressed, more and more people were being acquitted. By the end of the trial on 29 March 1961, there were only thirty-one accused left, including Fred. Oliver Tambo and Chief Luthuli had been released for lack of evidence, but Ahmed Kathrada, Helen Joseph, Walter Sisulu, Nelson Mandela and others formed part of the final group of accused. They were all acquitted. We were relieved and felt that a victory had been won. But the four years had taken a toll on the families, especially as many of the men had been breadwinners before the trial.

The naming, the banning, the witnessing of atrocities on the street and the Treason Trial had made the fifties a difficult decade. Little did we know that those years were only a forerunner of worse things.

21

State of Emergency

On 21 March 1960 the phone rang. My mother picked up: 'Zolli, is that you? Zolli, what's the matter?' It was Zolli Malindi, friend and reporter of my father's who was covering a mass demonstration at Sharpeville. 'What did you say? Oh my God, they're beating up demonstrators? They're shooting at them?' She heard guns being fired, and what could have been a machine gun. People were screaming. Then the phone went dead. That day, sixty-nine demonstrators, who were protesting in a planned anti-pass campaign, were killed in Sharpeville, two were killed in Langa, and many more were injured. Reporters were phoning in almost every minute. My father was hysterical: 'They are going into people's houses, beating them up and shooting them down.'

During dinner four days later, on 25 March, the phone rang. 'Trouble,' said my father. When he came back from answering the phone he was furious. 'Jesus, mother of mercy, these bastards will never stop their nonsense. I've just been tipped off that I'm likely to be arrested.' He took a deep breath. 'Not this time. They won't get me. I must go away for a short while until this blows over. I'll keep in touch, don't worry,' he added, seeing our alarmed expressions. My father asked me to climb over the wall in the garden to ask our neighbours, the Wieners, to help him escape without being observed. They smuggled him out in the boot of their car, but they were extremely nervous.

From that day my mother and I were followed all the time. I was tailed by two Special Branch men in a white Volkswagen, wearing their felt hats, fawn raincoats, moustaches and brown shoes. They were the same two who had raided our house looking for illegal literature. They followed me to school, to piano and judo lessons and back from school every day. One day I had had enough and went to an ordinary policeman on the beat. I complained, 'There are two men following me. Could you please help me?' I watched him stride up to the two Special Branch men and say something to them. I quickly hid behind a large tree, watching as the two security policemen walked past me and down the road. I had shaken them off – for one day, at least.

On 8 April my mother was arrested at six o'clock in the morning. The government had declared a state of emergency; they could now arrest anyone without trial for up to ninety days at a time. She was forty-three then. John was nine and Ruth was seven. I was sixteen. We saw the police van outside but did not know that Jean Bernadt was already in the vehicle. The Special Branch men said that my mother could pack a case and say goodbye to us. She must have known that her arrest was a possibility because the evening before she had gone into John and Ruth's bedroom and held them for a long time. When she left with the police, she hugged us, saying, 'You must be brave and good. It will be all right. You must go to school as normal and someone will be here after school to take care of you.' She picked up a small brown suitcase. Ruth rushed out and cried, 'Mommy, please come back. Where are you going?'

When I came home from school, Johnny and Ruthie were sitting forlornly on the front steps of the house with the maid, Iris. No one knew where the keys to the house were, so we could not get in. I had just enough money on me to take us by train to friends of my parents called Maurice and Rita Tabakin. They had room for only one of us, so Natie and Crystal Horovitz took John and Ruth. They clung to me and let go only when I said that I would be over as soon as I found out where Mom was. I was not going to leave them. I desperately wanted to find the keys so that I could go back to the house with them and we could be together, but I could not find the house keys anywhere. With no change of clothes and no money, we all had to wear borrowed clothes – mine were much too large. We didn't know how long this was going to last and were desperate to get in touch with my father, but no one knew where he was.

John was completely confused and kept saying, 'Something is wrong. What is going on? What has happened to Mom and Dad? When are they coming home?' Ruth, too, was bewildered. She couldn't understand the situation. 'Now Mom has been taken away. Both Mom and Dad are gone. I want them back. I don't want to be brave,' she sobbed. She and John stuck closely together even though everyone was kind to them and gave them lots of sweets and toys. While separated from our parents, Ruth wrote poems that I found very sad. She was especially proud of a poem she had picked up at school and revised:

No one loves me
Everybody hates me
Going down to the garden to eat some worms
Big fat hairy ones, long thin slimy ones
Long thin slimy ones slip down easily
But big fat hairy ones stick in your throat
And the juice runs down.

I tried to visit Johnny and Ruthie every day after school, which was difficult without enough money for transport. If I couldn't see them I phoned them in the evening. Although John was trying hard to be brave, I knew he was distressed: he was absent-minded and kept stubbing his toes or burning himself with hot water from the tap. Ruth would rush around noisily showing me toys she had been given. She would then suddenly go to sit on her bed and suck her thumb. She clung to me when I visited and I could see that John wanted to do likewise, but thought he was too grown up. I gave them lots of hugs and then cried myself to sleep every night.

One day Basil Jaffe, our family doctor and friend, came to visit. He had a message from my father concealed in his medical bag. Dad was still in hiding, he was well and he was missing us. Could we please write as often as possible and send him some photos? After that more messages arrived with instructions on how to get our letters to him.

By then we had been told that my mother and other comrades were being held in Roeland Street Prison in Cape Town and that they could receive letters. From then on my time with John and Ruth was spent making cards, presents or writing letters to either my mother or my father. It was not easy; sometimes the children were reluctant and sometimes I felt I had nothing interesting to say. John's first letter to my father contained the words, 'It's sad but true. Mom's in jail.'

At the Tabakins', where I was staying, I was treated like one of the family. They had two sons, Roger and Dennis, and I enjoyed having two older boys around the house. But I found it difficult to sleep at night and would often get up to make myself a cup of tea. Dennis was also often up late at night. He had a collection of jazz records including Charlie Parker and Dizzy Gillespie, and we would sit in his room and listen to music until one or other of us got sleepy and went to bed. He probably had no idea how those sessions helped me to cope with what was going on. What also helped me was that, because I loved drama, my mother had arranged for me to have private sessions with Joyce Crawford, a brilliant speech and drama teacher. She and I went through all the major poets and playwrights. I learnt some of them off by heart and then read them aloud until the meaning came across perfectly. I discovered that the intensity of my pain was shared by famous writers, and drew comfort from the fact that I was not totally alone. One of my favourites was Gerard Manley Hopkins, whose poetry reflected many of my own feelings. He so vividly described that emotional pain from which it is impossible to escape:

> My own heart let me more have pity on; let
> Me live to my sad self hereafter kind,
> Charitable; not live this tormented mind
> With this tormented mind tormenting yet.
> I cast for comfort I can no more get
> By groping round my comfortless, then blind
> Eyes in their dark can day or thirst can find
> Thirst's all-in-all in all a world of wet.

My mother and her fellow prisoners – Annie Goldberg, Jean Bernadt, Nancy Dick, Celia Rosenberg, Joan Shchedrin and Dora Alexander – had been detained without trial. No one had any idea of when they might eventually be released.

At the end of May, I was granted permission to visit my mother, first in Roeland Street Prison and then later in Bien Donné, another prison in the countryside near Paarl. I was allowed to go twice a week, sometimes only once. The visits meant getting permission to be off school at Westerford. At first, the headmaster, Mr Taylor, was sympathetic and supportive, but this changed as the security police put pressure on him. He threatened to expel anyone who was 'found fraternising with a native'. He also told me that he didn't want 'progressive' children in his school any more – they were too much trouble. For me, school was not the safe place it used to be.

My grandmother came back to Cape Town from Johannesburg to stay in Mount Pleasant between tenants and keep an eye on us. We could not stay with her because Mount Pleasant was too far from our schools. She used to go with me to Roeland Street Prison to visit my mother. When we were let in to the prison, the stink of dank walls, stale sweat and strong, bitter floor cleaner overwhelmed us. I had to sit opposite my mother at one end of a large table with a member of the security police sitting between us. My mother repeatedly asked me to bring her her clothes and never seemed to understand that I couldn't get into the house to get them; she was quite irritated that I brought her borrowed clothing. She didn't seem to realise that the house keys were missing, even though I told her every time I saw her.

On the way back from school every day, the security police used to ask me where my father was. Once I was taken into Caledon Square Police Station and questioned for six hours by four security policemen. 'Where is your father?' they asked, over and over again. I told them that I knew absolutely nothing. They threatened to hurt Johnny and Ruthie if I did not give them information. They shone hot bright lights into my eyes, saying, 'You know, we can keep you locked up for as long as we want if we find that you are telling lies.' Fifty years later, I still have trauma spots in my eyes from that time. I was quite proud that I said nothing. I just pretended that I was looking at a film in which the security men were tiny figures.

Bien Donné was close to the farm of our family friends Joan and Tebby Sachs, with whom I'd stayed when I'd witnessed the death of the ill, malnourished baby. During holidays I would stay with them and they would drive me the short distance to the prison. Otherwise, family friends would drive me from Cape Town – a three-hour round trip. We were always followed by the same two security men allocated to our family. On one occasion I was travelling with Sadie Foreman, a comrade and old friend of the family, and we stopped to have lunch in a café halfway to the prison. The fat security man was sitting across the room. At one point I looked in his direction and he winked at me lewdly. I felt extremely uncomfortable. I made sure that I was never on my own when he was around, even when I went to the toilet.

My parents kept asking for photographs of John, Ruth and me. Eli Weinberg, a friend who worked as a photographer for the paper, came and took photos of us. By then we had been separated from our parents for over six weeks. We put on brave faces for the photographer in an effort to look happy, so that they would not be worried about us.

John and Ruth were allowed to visit my mother only twice during her detention. They were too young to understand why she was there. 'I had a sense that the country was in turmoil and that her arrest was connected with this,' John later said, but he failed to grasp why exactly she had been arrested. When he saw my mother, he broke down and sobbed. A friend who had taken him to the prison tried to comfort him, but he was still crying when he got back to Natie and Crystal's house. All I could do was hug him. It was during this time that John started suffering severe recurrent nightmares that went on for years: 'A giant dark and dangerous rhino smashes into my room through the door no matter what I do,' he told me. 'I wake up covered in sweat.' I felt terrible because there was nothing I could do to comfort him.

One of the visits to my mother was on her birthday, 17 June. We made presents for her, and my father sent a message asking me to buy a dozen roses to take to her from him. I babysat and earned enough money to buy her the roses and a colourful jersey. We had all had permission to visit her on her birthday, so I dressed John and Ruth in their best borrowed clothes. We took her cards, pictures and presents as well as a birthday cake. When she saw the roses and was told she could keep them, she knew who they were from and burst into tears.

Before the visit, I had said to Johnny and Ruthie, 'You must be brave and good.' Ruth told herself to smile, 'to let Mommy know that I am happy'. Like John, she was extremely disturbed and unhappy after the visit. It was difficult for me to know whether they should visit her or not: I knew that my mother needed to see them and to know that they were all right. But I knew, too, that prisons were not good places for children.

My mother was overcome by the visit. In her thank-you letter, she must have said something that the authorities did not like because one-third of the letter was cut out. Some of it was blotched with tears.

21 June 1960

My darlings

I had meant to write sooner, but it has been so cold and miserable that it has been difficult to sit down and write.

First I must thank you for your wonderful gifts. Ruthie, your box is beautiful and I shall keep all my letters in it, and your flowers were lovely – won't you send me more on Friday, and put plenty of wet paper around the flowers to keep them alive. John dear, I shall wear your earrings on my first day at home. They are very sweet. Lynn dear, thank you for your lovely gift, and please thank all the friends who sent me gifts and birthday greetings. I hope that it will not be long now when I shall be able to thank them myself.

I have been told that there is no news yet about my release, and that I must make arrangements for you all to be taken care of by people other than myself. I would suggest you phone the farm and ask if it would be convenient for you and the children to spend the first part of your holiday there as I am not keen on your spending much time at Granny. I think the little ones will be a bit too much for her.

[Text censored]

I don't play chess any more and I am not too keen on jigsaws, so I have spent all day reading and making little squares.

Lynn darling, how about sitting down and writing me a long letter with lots of news? We feel dreadfully cut off and are hungry for news.

I feel as though I am in for flu, so please forgive this rather short, scrappy letter. I'm afraid some of the letter had to come out after the warden read it and did not like it.

All my love my dear ones, and my love to our very dear friends.

Sarah was not allowed to talk about the prison conditions or the treatment of prisoners in her letters. It was only much later that she described to us what had happened.

After her arrest she was taken to Caledon Square Police Station in Cape Town with other detainees. They were fingerprinted but not charged. Then they were all taken to Roeland Street and searched by a white woman in a uniform. She screamed at Sarah, 'Take off all your clothes – underwear as well.' Then she searched every piece, threw it all down and told her to lie naked on the filthy floor. At about 4.00 p.m. she was taken to a tiny cell crowded with other political detainees. There was an open bucket called the 'Toilet Room' next to an open dish of drinking water. The women started singing freedom songs in defiance.

They slept on the floor. Everyone had two smelly, dirty blankets and one grass mat that was placed on the cold cement. No pillow. No window except for the ventilator high up on the wall. They had to breathe in the smell of the stinking bucket. The food was, to my mother's mind, 'not fit for humans': breakfast consisted of porridge with salt, no sugar, no milk and no spoons – they were forced to use their fingers. Lunch and supper were similarly unappetising. The detainees were locked up for seventeen hours at a time and allowed to read only the Bible. Sarah later said that she 'learnt more about the Bible during that period than at any other time of my life'.

After just over a month at Roeland Street Prison the women were moved to Bien Donné, which was very different. There was a proper toilet and a water tap, glass doors and windows with iron bars – they had a view – and a bathroom with hot and cold water. Breakfast was coffee, dry bread and porridge, while lunch consisted of samp, meat and carrots, and was eaten with plastic spoons. For supper they were fed dry bread, soup, coffee and some grit. The food was better than at Roeland Street, but the menu did not change; it was the same every day, day after day. Although the women had new blankets and thin mats, they had to sleep on an icy-cold cement floor with no sheets or pillows. They were locked in there for fifteen hours each day, from 4.00 p.m. to 7.00 a.m. They were, at least, allowed to read books from the prison library.

Later, the security police isolated them and instructed them not to talk to each other. They questioned each person about their organisations, their leaders, the constitutions of their organisations and their involvement in fighting the pass laws. Questioning went slowly – sometimes only two or three people were questioned in one week. They were told that if they did not answer questions they would stay in prison for the rest of their lives, or at least for fifteen to twenty years. They were watched all the time and told not even to look at each other. It was terrible, not to be able to look at the other detainees.

My mother and her fellow inmates had no idea how long they would remain locked up. Someone from the Party smuggled in a message to say that all detainees should go on a hunger strike to protest against the injustice of detaining people without charge. After a week of this, Sarah became ill and suffered badly from bronchitis. She was determined not to give in until there were instructions from the Central Committee to stop the strike. When I visited her and saw her in this state, I was shocked and said to her, 'Mom, you look terrible; please take care of your health.' But she responded defiantly: 'They'll have to take me out in a box first.'

A week later, my grandmother visited her. She yelled, 'It's no more Yom Kippur, no more Yom Kippur any more.' Grandma Anna's reference to Yom Kippur – the Jewish Day of Atonement, when Jews traditionally fast – was a message to them to end the hunger strike. The strike had served its purpose in successfully publicising the conditions under which prisoners were kept. Because it was so dangerous, messages were secretly conveyed in all sorts of ways. Much later, my grandmother told me that someone had slipped the message into her shopping bag while she was out buying groceries. She did not see who it was.

When the women ended the hunger strike, it was so cold that they had to sleep with their stockings on. My aunt Ida was given permission to send my mother a brightly coloured blanket that she had crocheted for her. It was greatly appreciated, not only for the much-needed warmth it provided, but also for its colour. Colour of any kind was missed so much that the prisoners would order coloured toilet paper so that they could decorate the cells.

Sarah tried as hard as she could to stay cheerful. She would tell the other inmates not to worry because it would all be all right in the end. One of her fellow prisoners, Amy Reitstein, found that she had to revise her opinions about Sarah as a friendly little domestic housewife. She discovered that Sarah was a very involved activist who was good at keeping her activities strictly underground. Because Fred had the reputation of being quite a 'ladies' man', the other women were surprised at the wonderful love letters he sent her. Posted from different parts of the country to confuse the police about his whereabouts, the letters gave Sarah an enormous amount of pleasure and self-confidence. The other women found Fred's letters deeply moving and romantic.

12 April 1960

Sarah darling
Please forgive me if I do not write much of my personal feelings. They are all locked up inside me, hammering away to break out and giving me little peace, day or night. In fact, I'm sure I feel very much as you do. Courage, my love, my dear one. The world has not come to an end. We shall build anew on better foundations. Our future will be richer for the experience of today.

Try not to worry about the children. They will be well looked after and surrounded with love and care. However hard the present may be for them, they will be able to hold their heads high and proud, knowing that their parents did not fail their country in the dark days. The clouds, black as they are now, will clear, the sun will shine again and the sound of singing drowns the thunder. Remember the words of Walt Whitman, that glorious singer of democracy:

> What we believe in waits latent forever through all the continents
> Invites no one, promises nothing, sits in calmness and light, is
>   positive and composed, knows no discouragement,
> Waiting patiently, waiting its time.

My heart is too full to write more. Wherever you may be, my love reaches out to you. I have never loved you more than I do now. Loved ones may be locked up but never love itself.

* * *

20 April 1960

I seem to have lived most of my life writing letters which I know will be subjected to scrutiny and censorship by some third party. It certainly cramps one's style, so please forgive me if my letters are dull. We shall have to leave the real tit-bits for better times.

As for me, you needn't worry. It's almost like being back in the army again, only the food is better and my shirts and socks are in a small suitcase and not a haversack. And I'm ready to move at a moment's notice: a real 'here-today-and-gone-tomorrow' existence. The worst part about this sort of life is not being able to do anything to help you directly. I can only hope that you have enough warm clothes, enough good things to eat, all the toilet necessities and so on. The only consolation is that I'm confident others will do their best to cater for that aspect …

My impatience to be home grows by the hour, the closer we come to the end of the month. Why these sons of bitches have to wait until then to lift the emergency I just don't know. They are quite incapable of any kind of graciousness. In the meantime, the people in prison can rot as far as they are concerned. It's simply unnecessary, malicious punishment – an absolute scandal.

I dream of all the things we'll do together. If we get round to doing even half of them life would be one long pleasure. The spring sparkle will soon be dancing on the sea, luring the summer fish out of the depths, to where Johnny and I can get at them. It's good to think we'll be home in time for all the good things that spring and summer bring.

As time dragged on, it was obvious that my mother was trying hard to keep her morale up. While the love letters from Fred gave her a tremendous boost, she was missing John, Ruth and me, and was terribly worried about how her children were coping without her. She had had to get special permission to see John and Ruth because they were so young. Sometimes she would allocate one of her visits to them, hoping that the officials would allow them to see her. No permission would be forthcoming, however, and she had to miss her precious visit completely. Visits were the best part of her life in prison, and she referred to them often in her letters:

9 May 1960

I am writing to tell you that visits have changed once more and are now on Wednesdays and Fridays. In the meantime, parcels and particularly letters are the highlight of our lives. Letters are common property and are read by all with much love and warmth, and we never, never get enough news from home.

A little Cape canary comes to say hello to us. He is a cheeky little fellow. He sticks his chest out and struts around with an air of great conceit. There is a piet-my-vrou, a red-chested cuckoo, that passes us on his way home every evening. It is raining and cold, but in spite of the wet weather we can still hear the birds. I would love to be able to sit outside and watch them. There seems to be quite a variety of them from the different notes we hear. You must write and tell me of the walks you go for in the woods and what you see there.

I am writing for permission for John and Ruth to see me but in addition to my asking, the authorities say I must now get a letter from the other parent or from an appointed guardian for permission, so please discuss this with our lawyer and let me know if he can do so.

* * *

19 May 1960

My darlings

The day has been cold and crisp, but the sky is clear so we have been able to spend most of the day in the courtyard walking or sitting in the sun and knitting. The day always passes much quicker when we are able to do this. Today has also had its excitement because the other women had visitors and you know how wonderfully this cheers everyone up. The day visitors come is always a big day and preparations for this day must not be taken lightly. We wake up in time to have a wash before breakfast. We wash ourselves with the soap that has the strongest stink and then cover ourselves with powder and perfume. Also the clothes we wear for visitors are kept for this special occasion, and we usually complete our dressing up when we have finished the chores for the day.

Lynn darling, your letters and your visits are wonderful, your bits and pieces of news make me remember that there is a world outside and that I still belong to it. It helps me dream of the wonderful times we will have together – all of us. Perhaps it will be in time to gather mushrooms…

The months passed slowly and I walked around with my stomach tied in painful knots. I had no idea where my father was but fervently hoped he would not get caught. Because letters arrived from Swaziland, we thought that that was where he must be hiding. However, as we were soon to find out, he had been much closer to us than we believed.

Basil Jaffe continued to carry messages from my father to us in his little black medical bag. One day he arrived at the house where I was staying and said that my father wanted to meet me. Fred had been in Cape Town the whole time, hidden by Harold and Lisa Ruben. Lisa was an artist: she taught my father how to disguise himself so well that he was never caught.

The meeting between my father and me took an enormous amount of complicated planning so that I could avoid being followed by the police. I was extremely excited to be seeing him but terrified that he would be caught. A small part of me also enjoyed the adventure. On the day, I paired up with another girl who was the same size as me and had similar colouring. We both wore black slacks, a T-shirt and sunglasses. Two identical white Triumph Herald cars pulled up. I got into one of them and the driver managed to slip away from the police car long enough for me to get out of the car and climb into the other Triumph Herald. We waited around a corner until the police car caught up and started following the other car, which was carrying my lookalike. The security police followed her almost right around the Cape Peninsula for two and a half hours before realising that it was not me in the car. I went to Kirstenbosch to meet my father. We had arranged to meet at a favourite place by a small waterfall on the mountain. Ten minutes after I was due to meet him, a tramp approached me. I felt alone and vulnerable and unsure of what to do. It was only after the tramp started whistling that I recognised him as my father.

He later arranged for John and Ruth to meet him there in secret. His hair was longer, but they recognised him, and he gave them a present that they treasured – a tea towel with a picture of a bright rooster on it. Fred was amused and saddened by Ruth's reaction to the visit: 'I asked them to be silent about the visit because if they talked about it, I would be caught and arrested. Ruth's response was, "Oh goody, goody, then you can be with Mom and she won't feel so lonely."' After John and Ruth's visit with Fred,

I asked them how it had gone. Johnny told me that it had been a 'great adventure' but that he wished 'we were all back home again'. Ruthie sucked her thumb more than usual. I hugged them, saying, 'We will all be home together, soon.'

When Fred was in hiding, he worked closely with Albie Sachs, who visited him at the Rubens'. Albie, working underground as well as on political legal cases, would meet my father at their cottage but park his car a block or two away. They discussed what their strategy would be when the emergency was lifted. Harold Ruben was a concert pianist; the beautiful music he played while they talked left a sense of profound peace in a time of intense turmoil.

22

No Going Back

ON 31 AUGUST 1960 the state of emergency was lifted and my mother was released from prison. The Protea Road house was about to be sold so we returned to Mount Pleasant. A month later my father came out of hiding. Fred and Sarah were temporarily free from banning orders, but the security police continued to observe their daily activities. Sarah was extremely frustrated, but the fear of rearrest or persecution for her political activity was eclipsed by deep anger. She later said, 'It was no fun looking over one's shoulder all the time and living in a country where there was so much tension, cruelty and unhappiness. We were so angry about what was happening that fear was the lesser emotion.'

Fred was back working at *New Age*, and Sarah and her comrades were busy again – mainly with leafleteering and fund-raising. They sent illegal literature by post and wore gloves when handling all material, but later found out that their fingerprints went through the gloves, so the precautionary measure was of little use. They stood on street corners talking to people about the importance of the struggle and why the paper needed support. They had to scatter when the police arrived. Living was a cat-and-mouse game: at the *New Age* offices illegal literature that had been left around by staff had to be hidden constantly; talking on the phone was risky because all our phones, at home and at the office, were tapped.

The townships were under siege. They were surrounded by barbed-wire fences, and helicopters circled in the sky above. People were starting to starve – getting food into the townships was a major problem. One day my mother received a message from an acquaintance who asked how he could help. Thinking of the food crisis in the townships, Sarah suggested that he provide some food for people there. When a van arrived stuffed with boxes of food, Sarah was immensely taken aback. The boxes filled the kitchen and had to be cleared quickly, before the guests became suspicious and alerted the security police. John Morley-Turner, an old army comrade of Fred's, owned a van and had privileged access to the townships. He was able to pick up the food within an hour and deliver it straight to its intended destination. Sarah pretended, when speaking on the phone to Morley-Turner, that the initial delivery had been made by mistake.

It was not easy as a family to get back to normal after having been separated for so many months. John was nervous, clingy and accident-prone. Ruth was unhappy. 'I felt very lonely,' she later told me. 'Mom was like a stranger and I didn't want to talk to her. I stopped eating; food was tasteless. I was also very upset when I heard that the Wieners, our neighbours in Protea Road who had helped Dad escape, had packed up with their children and moved to Australia because they felt they would be safer there.' We were like lepers, isolated from the ordinary white community in which we lived, aware that certain neighbours were only too happy to keep watch and phone the police if they saw unusual activity. Not all our neighbours were hostile, however; sometimes we did receive unexpected support. One day, a white neighbour came to the front door and introduced herself. 'How can I help? What can I do?' she asked, before offering to take John and Ruth out for the afternoon. My mother was intrigued by this offer from someone she had never met before – the woman could have been an informer. She wanted to know: 'Why do you feel you have to help me?' The woman replied, 'I'm a Hollander and I remember the Nazis marching into the town I lived in and how I felt about it. When I came to this country, I didn't feel any different about persecution and the injustice of it.' She hated the persecution of Jews and those who opposed the Nazis, she said, and was just as strongly against the persecutions of both blacks and those who opposed it.

In spite of the danger, in 1961 a few comrades, including Greenwood and Looksmart – before they disappeared or were arrested – did come to visit. They always had time to talk to us, and Ruthie and Johnny adored them. They loved to sit on Looksmart's lap and play with his beard. They climbed all over both Greenwood and Looksmart demanding attention. The comrades were very patient, good-natured and fond of the children. Walter Sisulu also came to see us during that time. On one occasion Johnny and Ruthie were playing football with some of the neighbours' children. A big argument arose about who should have the ball. 'I had it first,' said one of them. 'No, I had it!' shouted another. 'But it belongs to me,' argued a third. Walter stepped in, took them seriously and listened to each child before saying, 'Why don't you play together and share the ball.'

Because he treated the children with so much respect, they thought he was brilliant.

Sarah and Fred started arguing about money again. Sarah thought that Fred should help to support the family, while he wanted to be totally committed to the struggle. They didn't argue at home; instead they tried to discuss things in a pub or somewhere with lots of people. This was difficult because Fred would start yelling, and everyone in earshot would hear their problems. Sarah soon realised that his way of dealing with the stress was to shout. At a secret meeting in the house one day, the comrades in attendance were discussing Soviet dominance over Eastern European countries. Fred started shouting so loudly that Sarah walked out. She knew that he was extremely disturbed by what was going on, but felt that he had to toe the Party line, which was to support the Soviet Union. One of the reasons he was so tense was that he was terrified that she would get picked up again.

One day, the atmosphere between my parents was unusually strained. Unbeknown to me, they had had a terrible argument about my future. My time at high school was coming to an end and I was worried about my exams. Their argument began the previous evening while on their way back from a party at the Buntings', where there had been a discussion about how everyone would have to make more sacrifices. Afterwards, my mother brought up the subject of saving for my further education, and my father snapped back, 'How can you talk about that? We all have to make sacrifices now.' My mother was furious and shouted, 'Who are Brian and Sonia to talk about sacrifices? They have their own income. I will not sacrifice my daughter's future because you obey everything they say.' It was the closest that my father ever came to hitting my mother. He raised his hand and she said, 'Don't you dare! Stop the car right now.' Even though they were miles away from home, she got out of the car and started walking. She refused to get back in and eventually my father drove off. When she arrived home, still fuming, in the early hours of the morning, my father was beside himself with anxiety about her safety. They went to bed without talking to each other.

My mother spent the next day phoning her family, who said they would help. My uncle Eli offered to pay for my first year of studies. My aunt Kate said that she and her husband would take care of me if I came to England. I was keen to study drama at the Central School of Speech and Drama in London, but to qualify I would have to pass two British A-Level examinations. My mother had no idea how they could find the money for tutors in Cape Town, as A-Levels were very different and more difficult than the South African matric exams. To her surprise, once my father had calmed down and seen that she was determined, his attitude changed completely. Within two weeks he had found lecturers at the University of Cape Town who agreed to tutor me, free of charge, for as long as it took.

It was one of the best learning experiences of my life. One of the subjects was Chaucer's *Canterbury Tales*, about pilgrims who journeyed together, telling stories along the way. Some of the tales were a little naughty and my father would tease me that I was too young to read them. He would snatch the book and run off giggling and I would chase him round the house until he returned it. He told me that he was actually pleased that I might have a chance of a good tertiary education. My mother changed her mind about him, saying, 'What a wonderful father Fred can be.'

This short interlude of near-normality did not last. The nature of the struggle was about to change: it was going to move into its next – even more dangerous – phase.

23

Umkhonto we Sizwe

South Africa was not the only country in the throes of a liberation struggle. Many countries in Africa and elsewhere were fighting for liberation and, after long and bloody battles, some had gained independence. Fred was extremely upset when Patrice Lumumba, the first black president of the Congo, was assassinated that year, on 17 January 1961. When he heard the news he shouted, 'The bastards. The fucking bastards. They murdered him!' At about this time, people involved in the struggle in South Africa started to consider armed combat.

The people were getting restless and angry. There were growing demands for violence against the whites, and the SACP and the ANC were repeatedly told, 'Don't give us leaflets. Give us guns.' The two organisations were criticised for not responding adequately to the increase of oppression and, as a result, were losing their standing as leaders in the struggle to other parties, including the Pan Africanist Congress, which was seriously talking violence. A palpable fear of a bloody civil war circulated. Fred was against any killing, particularly indiscriminate killing. He and his comrades had urgent secret meetings which were sometimes held at our house. I was told that it was dangerous for me to invite friends home, as it might compromise the secrecy of their activity.

At a meeting of the SACP Central Committee, attended by Fred, it was decided to back the ANC's setting up of an armed force rather than lose mass support. Backed by the SACP, the ANC decided that, if violence was going to be inevitable, *controlled* violence would be best so that loss of life could be prevented. They were still very much influenced by the heritage of non-violence and the belief in racial harmony.

Umkhonto we Sizwe – Spear of the Nation – was launched in December 1961. In his statement from the dock at the opening of the defence case in the Rivonia Trial on 20 April 1964, Nelson Mandela explained the thinking behind MK. He stated that sabotage targeting industrial and state installations was preferable to more violent forms of warfare such as terrorism, which he condemned. 'Sabotage did not involve loss of life,' he explained, 'and it offered the best hope for the future and race relations ... Umkhonto was to perform sabotage, and strict instructions were given to its members right from the start, that on no account were they to injure or kill people in planning or carrying out their operations.' Only in the case of a real threat of civil war would guerrilla warfare be adopted. The strategy was to build up small regional leadership groups of highly trained people to ensure that the campaign was disciplined and in line with MK policy. Mandela distinguished clearly between the ANC and MK, describing the ANC as a peaceful mass political organisation and MK as 'a small organisation recruiting its members from different races and organisations and trying to achieve its own particular object'. One of the organisations from which it recruited was the SACP.

Because everything was so clandestine and urgent, I knew that something important was in the making. Being extremely curious, I started searching in the places where my parents hid papers. On 19 December 1961, I got up at three o'clock one morning, emptied a jar of coffee beans and found a lengthy document. It was the MK Manifesto, dated 16 December 1961. I started to read, glancing up furtively to check that my father was not around:

> The time comes in the life of any nation when there remain only two choices: submit or fight. That time has now come to South Africa. We shall not submit and we have no choice but to hit back by all means within our power in defence of our people, our future and our freedom.
>
> We of Umkhonto we Sizwe have always sought ... to achieve liberation without bloodshed and civil clash. We do so still. We hope – even at this late hour – that our first actions will awaken everyone to a realisation of the disastrous situation to which the Nationalist policy is leading. We hope that we will bring the government and its supporters to their senses before it is too late, so that both the government and its policies can be changed before matters reach the desperate stage of civil war.

The next morning I told my father I wanted to be involved. He told me to pass my exams first, that I was too young and that he would see.

Fred was asked to join MK as a 'political commissar' for the Western

Cape. It was a tremendous honour to be chosen. For safety purposes, not even Sarah was told. Fred and Looksmart Ngudle were the senior people for the regional command of the Western Cape. The political commissar was deputy commander for Political Affairs. The rationale for the role was based on a similar structure used in the Military Revolutionary Committee of the Bolshevik Revolution. The job of the South African commissar was to infuse everybody with the political consciousness of the ANC.

Fred and Looksmart had to screen and recruit MK members and turn them into fully fledged political and then military cadres. The political commissar had to have advanced, unparalleled political consciousness, impeccable credentials and the ability to convey the heart and soul of MK. Fred's job was to work on the well-being – the spirit and soul – of the cadres, teaching them how they should live their lives and relate to others as MK soldiers and representatives. In his role as political commissar, he therefore had to be exemplary and beyond dispute. He had to have the capacity to motivate the worst coward to go forward into war.

Armed action would proceed in phases – the first phase was a carefully planned campaign against selected government installations. Comrades were instructed to avoid actions that would lead to injury or loss of life.

One of the ways in which Fred recruited MK soldiers was to approach comrades he already knew well. He also recruited certain university students when he was invited, as a former soldier of the Second World War and member of the Springbok Legion, to give talks at the University of Cape Town about the effects of the war. Using the platform to his advantage, he had to speak in such a way to keep on the right side of the law. Black students at the time, including Pallo Jordan, were impressed by Fred's down-to-earth, non-reactionary nature. Fred had a good reputation among left-wing students. He was still editing *New Age*, which was considered to have extremely high standards of coverage and debate and was eagerly read by young politically aware students wanting news of the ANC. A comprehensive paper, *New Age* contained stories unavailable elsewhere and good editorial opinion.

When the students received pamphlets calling for action or describing different forms of armed struggle, they were unable to trace the source of these pamphlets, although they had a good idea where they came from. They knew that the pamphlets were illegal and that those distributing them were working underground. Neither could they trace the secret circulation of a banned book by Crane Brinton, *Anatomy of a Revolution*. The students, who were involved in various political youth groups, discovered the source of the pamphlets and other material only when people were arrested and accused.

Left-wing students held private political meetings on campus. The students invited Fred to talk about his war experiences and about methods of struggle. In 1962 everyone sat up sharply as Fred, who had been talking about the history of the struggle and the policy of non-violence, towards the end added, 'You should also be thinking about armed struggle.' He had started by discussing a particular African woman who had been assaulted by the police, and had moved on to talk about the routine violence of the apartheid government. 'The system depends on violence,' he said. 'Let me ask you: in a situation in which violence is used in a routine fashion to keep people repressed, what can be expected of them in response?'

Denis Goldberg was one of the people recruited into MK by Fred. Denis had already joined the SACP. He was told to wait on a bench at the South African National Art Gallery in Cape Town. Fred approached him and said, 'We would like you to be technical officer for MK in Cape Town. We want you to think about it.' Responding immediately, Denis said, 'Yes.'

'Yes what?' asked Fred, confused.

'Yes, I will be technical officer!' replied Denis with enthusiasm.

'But you have to think about it,' said Fred.

'I have been arguing for armed struggle for a year. I have already thought about it,' said Denis conclusively.

Fred and Denis would meet in the woods above Mount Pleasant in Oranjezicht. On one occasion Denis had been told that at the next gathering he would be meeting someone from Johannesburg. Denis got onto a trolley bus in St James Street and saw a well-turned-out black man with an expensive-looking raincoat and umbrella looking at him. He resembled a Special Branch agent, so Denis got off the bus and walked all the way up the long, steep hill to the woods behind Mount Pleasant. When he arrived, there was Fred with the same man that he had seen on the bus – Elias Motsoaledi. Elias was in Cape Town to teach the MK group that Fred had recruited to make explosives. Fred facilitated this meeting dressed like a tweedy country squire with a walking stick. They talked hidden in the shadows of the trees. When the lights of police vans flashed over them, Fred said, 'Stand still. They have less chance if they don't see movement.' The small group stood stock-still and the police vans eventually went away.

Albie Sachs was another MK recruit who worked closely with my father.

It was extremely difficult and dangerous to meet because most of them were under banning orders. In addition to congregating in the Oranjezicht woods, they used to meet at Newlands Forest. It was an advantageous meeting place because it could be approached from several different routes. Often it would be raining or drizzling and they'd convene under a big oak tree. Fred would be jovial and would exclaim, 'Welcome to our boardroom!' Meetings were very quick: Fred, Brian, Albie, Chris Hani, Archie Sibeko, Alex La Guma, Reggie September and Achmat Osman would appear and almost as quickly disappear, with instructions.

Fred, Brian, Bernie Gosschalk and one or two other comrades would also meet above Kirstenbosch Gardens on Sunday mornings. Fred and Brian would read aloud Party documents from Johannesburg to keep some degree of unity among the different Party groups. Sometimes, Bernie, Archie Sibeko and Ray Alexander would meet at night on the slopes of Devil's Peak, on a hidden forest track. On one particular occasion, one of them must have been followed by the Special Branch. After the meeting, as they walked down the mountain track through the pines, they saw two men coming up the moonlit path. Bernie whispered to Fred, 'Now we are all for the high jump.' The men approached Fred and the rest of the group and flashed torches into their faces. They didn't say a word and carried on walking up the track. Fred and the others scattered as fast as they could. The Special Branch had allowed them to carry on, having discovered who to keep tabs on in the future.

It was not just left-wing comrades that Fred tried to recruit. Ralph Rubin, the son of my mother's brother, was a young Zionist. He had a friend called David Ben-Uziel, a twenty-three-year-old officer in the Israeli parachute regiment. David stayed at Mount Pleasant when my Grandma Anna was helping my parents run the guest house. He was continually arguing with the pro-white guests and was obviously against apartheid. One day Fred asked to speak to David privately, upstairs in his room. He closed the door and said to the young Israeli, 'We know that you are an officer from the Israeli commando unit. We need someone like you to train our units and to teach us how to produce Molotov cocktails. Would you consider doing this?' David replied immediately: 'The South African government will kill you all.'

'We will be killed in any case,' said Fred.

David was uncertain, and Fred did not put pressure on him. Several months later, David was invited to dinner with one of the Zionist leaders of Cape Town. During supper the host of the house asked him, 'Where do you live?' He answered, 'I'm living in Mount Pleasant with Grandma Anna Rubin.'

'Oh yes, we know her well,' his host exclaimed. 'Her son-in-law, Fred Carneson, helped support us in 1948 for our war of independence.' In spite of this knowledge, David was persuaded by the Zionists in Cape Town not to get involved with MK.

During these highly dangerous times, it was all too easy to take life too seriously. The cadres were very solemn. They were immersed in their studies, learning about the international revolutionary movement and being inspired by resistance fighters from all over the world. They felt very responsible and had to be extremely careful to avoid arrest. Fred was quite the opposite. He sparkled. He was passionate and emotional. He didn't rationalise everything down to theoretical terms. He was bright, energetic, active and fun. 'Fun isn't a word one would associate with having to meet on the mountain in the rain waiting for the police to turn up,' says Albie Sachs. 'Fred would joke. He was amused by the circumstances and it lifted all of us.'

Government pressure was mounting. More people were being arrested, tortured and killed. As life became unbearable, many left the country and continued the struggle from abroad. Ray Alexander and her husband, Jack Simons, went to Lusaka, Zambia. Brian Bunting left for England, having been asked to edit the *African Communist* in London. Chris Hani and Archie Sibeko were arrested in 1962 and sentenced to imprisonment. They escaped while on bail and disappeared. Reggie September left too, and Alex La Guma was placed under strict house arrest. One by one they fled, leaving a severely diminished group behind. The only remaining full-time operator was Fred. Albie, who was one of the last to leave, said, 'I knew Fred was carrying on and would be caught. The security police were waiting to pounce on him.'

24

Split in Half

AT SIXTEEN AND A HALF, I believed that I was old enough to get more involved in MK. Because Fred would not allow me to join MK at the time, I bought a pistol from a friend and took shooting lessons at a gun club. I hated it because I could not bear to think of actually shooting anyone. I was also worried that I had not studied hard enough to pass my matric and A-Level exams. Peter, the first love of my life, had been screened by the comrades and was allowed to visit again after having been told to stay away in case he discovered something and informed the police. We were passionately involved with each other to the exclusion of everyone else. Johnny and Ruthie drove us crazy. They would hide behind the settee where we were sitting and jump out to surprise us just as we started kissing. Shrieking and giggling, they would run away and we'd chase them. One day I heard Johnny squealing loudly. He had provoked Peter so much that Peter's temper got the better of him and he held John by the feet over the toilet, threatening to flush the chain. After a short while, Peter put Johnny down and Johnny drew himself up. With dignity he said, 'Well, that's enough of that. I'm going to my room to play with my chemistry set.'

John had been given a large chemistry set for his birthday. He loved to make explosives and bombs, purely for fun. Fred caught him one day. 'What the hell are you doing?' he exclaimed. 'You don't make things like that; they are dangerous. And you mustn't leave this set in full view.' He marched over to the carpet next to John's bed, lifted it and pointed underneath. He instructed John, 'Hide it under the floorboards over here when you finish playing.' One evening just before Johnny fell asleep, he heard a noise. It was Denis Goldberg tiptoeing into his bedroom. He saw Denis move straight to the loose floorboards under the carpet, lift them and take out the chemistry set. He then removed a couple of test tubes and put the set back. Johnny knew that Denis was named and should not be there. He'd also learnt enough to know not to mention it to anyone. He was cross, however, because the chemicals he needed to make his explosives were gone.

At school Johnny was treated as an outsider. Whenever he said he supported black people, most of his schoolfriends would walk away, leaving just two loyal friends by his side. He was becoming aware of the poor treatment of black people: he had watched a coloured family being thrown out of a drive-in; he had seen a convict being brutally beaten on the lawn of the prime minister's residence; he had witnessed small children move up and down the train tracks begging for food. Because everything my parents did was secret, they did not explain the political situation to him. As a result, he didn't connect these incidents with the way the police harassed his own family.

Johnny's school and peers were a source of strong pressure to conform to apartheid thinking. This reached its highest point on 31 May 1961, the day South Africa became a republic. All schools had a special event where the children were handed a gold chocolate medallion and a flag. The day before, Fred had told John, 'Don't accept anything from those bastards. The government is changing for the worse and there is nothing to celebrate.' John didn't understand what Fred was talking about so he accepted the tokens, but felt bad when he did so. One day he needed a lift home from Kloof Nek, so he phoned Fred to ask if he'd fetch him. Fred arrived hysterical with anger: 'People are being hanged, and you have to bother me for a lift!' John was too young to know that that was the day Vuyisile Mini and others were hanged for political offences. Fred, who had been trying his best to help save them, was so devastated that he did not realise the effect that his anger had on John.

After I'd passed my school exams and my English A-Level exams, I was restless. I handed out anti-government leaflets, put up posters and sprayed slogans on walls. I also passed secret messages to some of the comrades. I was very frightened when a security policeman approached me one afternoon. 'We know all about your activities,' he said to me. 'If you carry on like this, you will get arrested. Either stop your activities or leave the country.'

'Why are you so bothered about what happens to me?' I asked him.

'I would hate to see you hurt,' he replied, surprising me. 'This job isn't for me any more and I am thinking about leaving the country myself.' I wondered whether he was setting me a trap, but after that I was more careful.

When I was in Cape Town I would wistfully watch the passenger liners departing from the harbour and wish that I was on one of them. My aunt wrote to reissue her invitation for me stay with them in London. I was still undecided, so went down to Clifton Third Beach and tossed a coin. 'Heads I stay here and do what I can. Tails I leave.' It was tails.

I left on the passenger ship MS *Jaegersfontein* on 22 July 1962 for London, to study drama teaching at the Central School of Speech and Drama. My father, mother, John, Ruth and Peter stood on the quay waving goodbye as I waved from the ship's deck. We were all crying. As the ship moved away they got smaller and smaller and eventually disappeared completely. I was split in half, my conflicting emotions tearing through me: I felt that I was abandoning my family and my country, yet I wanted to study and to see the world. I knew that one day I would return.

The boat journey from Cape Town to Southampton, England, took two weeks. I loved watching the white wash of the water at the back of the boat and, when we reached the equator, huge albatrosses circled around the ship. We had dinner dances every night and I made long-lasting friends. On the day I arrived in England, it was grey and rainy. It was a very different place from what I had expected. I took a train to Victoria Station in London, and a porter took my case. He said something to me, and it was completely unintelligible. Total panic; I thought they spoke English in this country! My uncle Sol, who met me at the station, was amused. 'He comes from Glasgow in Scotland. Not even I can understand him,' he reassured me.

I stayed with Aunt Kate and Uncle Sol in Cornwood House, in Cornwood Close, Hampstead Garden Suburb. They spoilt me. Drama school provided a holistic education with three hours of physical and voice exercises every day, including fencing, which I loved. There was history of the theatre, psychology, educational theory and the study of plays and poetry. It was the time of hippies, flower power, liberation and loud music, and there was lots of dancing, reading of authors that were banned in South Africa and going to films that had also been banned at home. Over the months I had the opportunity to travel to countries such as France, Italy, Greece and Israel. It was paradise – once I had adjusted to a different culture and way of life. During the first few months of my new life in London I kept a diary about my experiences.

9 September 1962
Yesterday when I was at Trafalgar Square, I panicked. I saw a black man holding hands with a white girl in public! Then I realised that they wouldn't get arrested in this country. In the last few days I have

developed a bad habit. I love the policemen. Solid and good-natured in their blue uniforms, helmets, shiny shoes and buttons. No guns. I just can't help going up to every policemen I see to ask him either the time or the way! Kate stands in the distance and pretends she doesn't know me.

A few weeks ago I committed my first faux pas. When I arrived, Kate prepared a delicious meal. Chicken soup followed by succulent lamb chops, potatoes and peas plus gooseberry fool. Then she offered me a bowl of fruit with a large bunch of grapes, some peaches, apples and bananas. In Cape Town fruit is cheap and abundant so I finished all the grapes, the peaches and the bananas. At breakfast she poured the tea and then told me how much fruit costs in England. I was terribly embarrassed.

14 September
My first week at drama school! The Central School of Speech and Drama is in a side road in Swiss Cottage in the north of London. There is a coffee bar run by a friendly man called Gerry. He serves frothy coffee which leaves a moustache of foam on your lips. I can't bear the way everyone calls each other 'darling' all the time, hugging, kissing and slobbering all over each other.

Our first improvisation was about a gas stove which is leaking in a locked room. I didn't know that you can use gas for cooking or that it can be dangerous. Then I was asked to mime walking through snow to an iced pool and to skate across it. As I have never seen snow or ice, I just stood there. Cicely Berry, our teacher, asked, 'What's the matter? Lost your nerve? Come on, duckie, you have to do better than that.' I felt very foolish when I explained that I don't know what snow or ice is like. 'Don't worry, duckie, we'll soon change all that as well as that dreadful accent you have.' It is true. My South African accent stands out like a carbuncle on someone's nose.

16 October
There are lots of parties and I am allowed to go to them as long as I get home by midnight. Last week I met a friendly man called Christopher Logue who writes poetry. He has offered to show me 'that part of London that really counts'. He took me to a poetry reading at an enormous round concert hall called the Royal Albert Hall, which is like a tiered wedding cake, only decorated with deep-red velvet. Very British Empire! Dad would never approve. We stood, hemmed in by the smelly

crowd in the middle of the hall. A strange young woman dressed in white floated around as if she were in another world! There were two very dirty long-haired Americans called Allen Ginsberg and Jack Kerouac performing. Their poetry is raw and exciting, about journeys you take through life. Allen Ginsberg is shocking because every word is a swear-word. The person I wanted to hear was Robert Graves, who was the star. He wore a bright maroon-spotted cravat. His voice and poetry were electric, but I was disappointed because he was fat and flabby and very old.

Before we went to the Albert Hall, we went to a dingy, dark flat to pick up some friends of Christopher's. They were all wearing army uniforms, imitating Fidel Castro and Che Guevara, whom we had studied secretly in the political cell I went to just before I came here. One of them is a tall horsey woman called Vanessa Redgrave. She calls herself a true revolutionary! She struts about and tells everybody loudly what is right and wrong. Treats me as if I have just climbed down from the trees, only slightly advanced from a chimpanzee. She doesn't know what she is talking about. But as I am a guest, I politely keep quiet.

I found London liberating. Everything was new and exciting. The only problem was that I missed my family and Peter terribly and was worried about John and Ruth, with me so far away. I was sure that at some point one or both of my parents would be arrested again.

25

Banned Again

It was spring in Cape Town in 1963. Fred had a date to meet secretly with Looksmart Ngudle. Looksmart, who was always punctual, did not turn up: he had been arrested. Fred was extremely worried: he knew that Looksmart's life was in danger. He did what he could, but it was of no use. Looksmart, who was gentle, caring and full of fun, and who loved our family, was killed in detention in September 1963, aged forty-one. He died a terrible death. The security police tortured him severely. They pulled his beard off his face, skinning him alive. According to the accounts of other prisoners, they beat him, electrocuted him and inflicted many other horrific forms of torture. Looksmart's best friend and fellow activist, Bernard Huna, had also been arrested. My mother was told by a trusted comrade that he was forced to stand outside Looksmart's cell and made to listen to his screams outside the cell door. I was in London when I heard the news and felt sick. My father was beside himself with grief and rage. I wished that I was with my family, and worried about Johnny's and Ruthie's reactions to the news of Looksmart's death, as they had been so fond of him.

Most of the MK leadership had been arrested on 11 July 1963, when a squad of armed detectives raided Liliesleaf farm in the northern Johannesburg suburb of Rivonia. Liliesleaf was used by the ANC as a secret meeting place. At the time of the raid, almost all of the MK leadership was present, including Walter Sisulu, Govan Mbeki, Raymond Mhlaba, Ahmed Kathrada, Rusty Bernstein and Bob Hepple. After the raid a number of other activists were taken into custody; Nelson Mandela was already serving a five-year prison sentence for incitement and having illegally left the country. Detained under the ninety-day law, the suspects were placed in solitary confinement, interrogated and tortured. Ten accused charged on four counts of guerrilla warfare appeared in the Pretoria Supreme Court from October 1963 in what became known as the Rivonia Trial. Mandela, Denis Goldberg and Elias Motsoaledi were among those who joined the accused.

On 12 June 1964, after seven long months, the trial ended. All apart from Bernstein were found guilty and sentenced to life imprisonment at the maximum security prison on Robben Island. Denis Goldberg, the only white person, was taken to Pretoria Central Prison. Over 2000 demonstrators saw the convicted prisoners off from the court, singing 'Nkosi Sikelel' iAfrica' and shouting '*Amandla!*' as their leaders made the fist-and-thumb gesture of the ANC through the bars of the police-van windows.

When I saw the news in the papers, I phoned my mother. She could not say much because of the tapped phone but I could hear the strain and anger in her voice. It was a desperately sad day. To my relief my father had not been among the trialists, but I knew his freedom would not last long.

While attention had been focused on Pretoria, in Cape Town *New Age* had been banned and had reappeared as *Spark*. Fred was still editor. Then the Minister of Justice served banning notices on my father and everyone who worked for the newspaper. The staff all lost their jobs. When Fred suggested keeping the paper going by employing staff who were not named or banned, the printer, Len Lee-Warden, refused to print under people he did not know. *Spark* and that long line of newspapers came to an end, the last edition going out on 28 March 1963. It was inevitable but it left a great void; when I heard the news, I cried all night. It was a great loss for the struggle, as people could no longer be informed of what was really happening other than by word of mouth. The end of *Spark* contributed to the total media ban on what was going on. It was also an enormous personal loss for Fred. In the last issue of *Spark* there was a promise: 'We shall be back.' Years later, in 2007, Pallo Jordan, then Minister of Culture, said, 'We are still waiting.'

Sarah was also banned. Both of my parents were virtually under house arrest and the Special Branch tried to make life as difficult as possible for them. Sarah was outraged and wrote to me in a letter:

> Now we are our own prisoners. We can't go to meetings or have visitors or talk to any of our comrades. We have to get permission to discuss John or Ruth's education or fetch them from school if anything happens. Unless we have permission, we can't go outside of our small restricted area. Fred is out almost all the time. I have to rely on others to do shopping for me. There are very few people around. They are either arrested or too scared to go out. Fred and I had to get permission again to talk to each other and to be with John and Ruth because Fred and I

and the two of them are an illegal 'gathering of more than two people'. In fact, Fred and I were briefly arrested yesterday for being in the presence of a listed communist. It was me talking to Fred! Some idiot did not check that we were married and had permission to be with each other!

Almost all the guests at Mount Pleasant at that time were asked by the security police to spy on Fred and Sarah – some were even paid to do so. The police and the Special Branch continually raided the house and terrorised the children, threatening to do terrible things to them. My parents were frequently arrested for breaking banning orders; the house was under twenty-four-hour surveillance; every room was bugged; and servants were forced to plant illegal literature in the house. Fred went out to carry on underground activities even though it was extremely dangerous. On top of this unbearably tense living situation, it was difficult for Fred and Sarah to earn a living. After the demise of *Spark*, Fred endlessly wrote letters, without success, to the authorities, asking for restrictions on his movements to be lifted so that he could find suitable work to support the family. These were ignored.

Johnny, aged thirteen and a half, and Ruthie aged eleven, were even more socially isolated. Their closest friends' parents were scared: the security police had warned them that their children 'must stay away from the Carnesons'. They were also singled out and ostracised at school because their parents were communists. Ruth was punished for sucking her thumb in class at Good Hope School. 'That was horrible,' she remembered. 'I couldn't go to school. I used to bunk off school all the time and run home crying every day. I would come home, get into bed and go to sleep.' She was getting into constant trouble and started to do badly at her lessons. From being bright and doing well, her marks plummeted. She just stopped coping: 'I became this naughty child – not doing my schoolwork and playing the fool to get attention. I couldn't concentrate and just gave up. I was expelled for being cheeky to the headmistress. She told me to pack my bags and go. So I left.'

Although he still lived officially at Mount Pleasant, Fred was spending less and less time at home. He was leading a double life, operating under the name Dick Turnbull, who supposedly lived in St Mungo Court, a run-down flat in Clifton. Fred used the flat as a secret office from which to carry out illegal political activities and as a place that he could escape to if he had to go into hiding. In order to create the impression that he was still living at Mount Pleasant, he came home infrequently. He was so busy that he had almost no time to spend with the children. John missed him terribly and grieved over the good times had by the family when we were all together, especially the long drives to the beach when Fred would tell drawn-out stories. 'The Man with the Silver Belly Button' was a favourite, and Fred used to embellish it and spin it out for as long as possible.

The Man with the Silver Belly Button
There once was a man with a silver belly button. When he went to the beach people used to stare and point and he was very embarrassed. So the man went to a car mechanic and asked him to take the belly button off. But the mechanic couldn't. So he asked the doctor if he could get rid of the silver belly button, but he couldn't. Then he asked the dentist and the electrician. All of them tried and tried, but couldn't.

Just as the man was giving up in despair, this very old witch with a thin face and a beard hobbled up to him, croaking, 'You want to get rid of your belly button?'

'Yes, please. I will do anything you want.'

'Then you must go up to the top of Devil's Peak when the moon is full and pray to the Moon Fairy to come and take your belly button.'

So the man climbed up the steep slopes of Devil's Peak and lay on his back and prayed to the Moon Fairy. After a long time, just before the first birds sang at dawn, he heard a tinkling noise. There above him was a silver thread drawing his belly button up into the sky.

'What happened then?' we'd ask, knowing the answer.

'His bottom fell off!'

We would all shriek with laughter and say it was a terrible story. Then: Can we have it again?

All this was a thing of the past. The happy family outings had been replaced by a terrible sense of isolation in an unfriendly environment. There was absolutely no psychological support, only a growing sense of dread and fear. Johnny and Ruthie used to tremble in their beds at night when the police searched the house, which was surrounded at all times by openly hostile armed men.

26

Snipers

THE YEAR 1964 was nail-biting. After the harrowing experience of the Rivonia Trial, which dominated the first half of the year, we had been mildly relieved when the accused were found guilty and sentenced to life imprisonment – although life really did mean life as far as the government was concerned. We suspected that the convicted Rivonia trialists were being kept alive so that they could be persuaded to act as future state witnesses against other people who had not yet been arrested or tried, including my father. The very next day, 13 June, the death penalty was extended to anyone who had had sabotage training. Then, in September that year, Bram Fischer and other Party members were indicted under the Suppression of Communism Act. Fischer skipped bail and went underground for several months before being captured again. He was also sentenced to life imprisonment.

One Saturday evening in October 1964, when John, Ruth and a friend were quietly playing in the living room, snipers fired into our house. They missed Johnny's head by about an inch. Their violent action was part of a campaign to intimidate activists. That evening, on one of the rare occasions Fred had come back to Mount Pleasant from his office-hideout at St Mungo Court, he and my mother arrived home after going for a short walk to find three traumatised children. My father was furious about the danger in which the snipers had placed my family, as well as our friend and guests. Not to be deterred by the attack, he wrote a strong letter of complaint to the Attorney-General:

20 October 1964

Dear Sir

At about 9.15 p.m. on Saturday 17 October 1964, an unknown gunman fired a shot into our living room, apparently from the direction of the corner of Belmont Avenue and Forest Road. The bullet penetrated the wooden shutter, holed the window and lodged in the picture rail on the opposite wall.

My two children were alone in our living quarters together with a young friend when the incident occurred, we being out at the time, returning immediately on receiving a report from one of our lodgers.

The living room was well lighted at the time the shot was fired, though the shutters were closed. My son was sitting reading on a couch; some of the glass splinters from the shattered windowpane fell on his head and on the couch. Though it is unlikely that the gunman fired at any living target, the fact remains that my son was in danger of serious injury. The bullet, incidentally, entered the window at breast height and lodged in the living room wall one inch above my son's head. From the size of the slug it appears that the shot was fired from a high-velocity .22 revolver or a .22 rifle.

We reported the incident to the police almost immediately on our return home, and we must record that they acted with promptitude, sending first a squad car then, later, several members of the CID to investigate. The police also posted a man on guard for the rest of the night.

As is now known, at least three similar incidents occurred on the same night in different parts of Cape Town, indicating that the attacks were carefully planned, possibly by more than one group of assailants.

Numerous other incidents in Cape Town – and elsewhere in the country – over the last few months all point to the existence of a well-organised and well-informed group working on the principle of 'taking the law into their own hands' when it comes to terrorising (or rather, attempting to terrorise) political opponents of the government.

Because of the nature of the information upon which this group has often acted (knowledge of not generally known residential addresses, unlisted telephone numbers, exact location of particular rooms, etc.), it is my strong suspicion that some members of the security police, here and elsewhere, are working in close collusion with the culprits, feeding them with information gathered by the security police during the course of their official investigations. (I have already voiced these suspicions to Captain Rousseau of the security police, who gave me the categorical assurance that his department would not countenance any such behaviour, and would severely punish any one of their men found doing so.)

It seems to me that the lawless acts complained of fall within the scope of the Sabotage Act, and should therefore be viewed in a serious light. Unless the culprits are soon apprehended and brought before the courts, the situation may well get out of hand and inevitably result in loss of life, senseless retaliation and the rest of it.

I therefore respectfully urge you, Sir, to use your powers as Attorney-General to order a thorough inquiry by the competent and responsible authorities into all aspects of this disturbing development.

Yours sincerely
Fred Carneson

When I heard about the snipers incident, my concern for my family's safety intensified. Although I was separated from them by many miles and a huge ocean, not a minute passed that I was not with them in spirit, sharing their anxieties. In England I had realised that there was a whole other world where people lived different lives from us. There was relative peace, stability and the opportunity to flourish as a person, but because of the Cold War between the Soviet Union and powers of the Western world, including the United States, there was the constant underlying threat of nuclear war. If there was such a war, we were told, we would have a four-minute warning. We used to imagine what we would do in the four minutes before certain death.

In August 1964, I was elected United Nations student representative to accompany five Buddhist monks on a three-month peace march across Europe. The monks had come from Hiroshima and Nagasaki, where the Americans had dropped the atomic bombs during the Second World War and killed over 200 000 people. We started in England and travelled through France, Belgium, Holland, Germany, Italy and Switzerland, staying in school halls and hostels.

The monks wore saffron robes and walked barefoot, banging drums and tambourines. They marched without coats in rain and wind and slept on hard floors much of the time, yet I never saw them unhappy, tired or angry. In fact, they seemed to be in a continuous state of bliss. One day, while straining through driving rain, blisters chafing step after painful step, I thought, 'I'm not going to survive this. I'm going to ask if I can go back to London.' I looked at the leader, Reverend Sato. He was peacefully smiling a little private smile to himself. All of a sudden, I felt that everything was all right; the world was a wonderful place. I realised that if I could ever achieve even a small amount of that tranquillity I would be a lucky person. When I asked him how he reached and maintained that state, Reverend Sato said to me, 'It is not luck; it is hard work. Discipline.' When I then asked, 'How do I start?' he smiled and said, 'What do you think?' I felt stupid: it seemed that I should already know the answer.

Before I met the monks, I believed that the deep emotional pain and anxiety I was experiencing about the cruelty and human-rights violations occurring in South Africa was unavoidable. I realised that it would not be easy, but it would be worthwhile and necessary to attempt to achieve a similar inner peace to that of the monks. The three-month march across Europe was the beginning of a long spiritual and emotional journey to try to attain the compassionate detachment that I saw in Reverend Sato.

Compassionate detachment and a state of bliss were not, however, what I felt a few months later when I heard that my parents had been arrested – yet again – for breaking their banning orders.

27

Underground

On 8 February 1965, Fred and Sarah could not resist the temptation to visit friends. Caroline de Crespigny, who had met my parents at a fund-raising bazaar a few years earlier, had been recruited by Fred. When she joined the Party, she opened a bank account for Fred in the name of Dick Turnbull, and paid the rent for St Mungo Court, the flat in Clifton. Fred, Amy Reitstein and Caroline used the flat to run off Communist Party leaflets and put them into ready-typed envelopes for posting. Caroline remembers, 'I can still feel the nervousness that gripped me as we went down the narrow winding steps to that dingy one-roomed flat.' Although Caroline was known to the Special Branch, she had not been arrested or listed: she came from the prestigious Macmillan family in England – the police files indicated that 'she should be handled with utmost delicacy'.

Caroline had invited my parents to dinner. Because she was not listed, it was legal for one of them to visit her. On that night, however, they felt it would be safe for both of them to go because they thought they would be the only people visiting: they could therefore be in separate rooms. (By that time they also suspected that they would be arrested whether guilty or not.) They were indeed arrested, but the events had all the makings of a farce.

After my parents turned up, Amy Reitstein, also banned, dropped in without knowing Fred and Sarah were there. Fred decided to have a quick word with her and they both went into Caroline's bedroom. Then Gillian Jewell, also banned, turned up. When she saw who else was there, she said she had to leave at once. All the same, she lingered a little in the sitting room, talking to Sarah and Caroline.

Suddenly there was a loud knocking on the front door. Fred hurried back into the sitting room, Amy darted out onto the veranda and Gillian went into Caroline's bedroom.

Sarah went downstairs to the flat at the bottom of the house, as she knew the man living there was not in. She sat at his desk and started writing furiously, hoping the Special Branch would think that she wasn't part of the group.

The knocking was extraordinarily loud and aggressive. Caroline moved slowly downstairs. Opening the door, she was faced by a jostling crowd of men, all wearing suits and hats. A bulky man with a military moustache – his hat was of checked tweed with a fishing fly stuck into the band – handed her a piece of paper. 'We have a warrant to search your premises,' he said. The men clattered up the stairs, moving closely in a pack. There were only five of them, but their size and noisiness created the impression that there were many more.

At the same time Caroline's maid, Evelyn, who had a room halfway up the stairs, was entertaining church friends – three men and two women. When the Special Branch pushed open the door and discovered this, they immediately herded all the Africans into a van, thinking it was a political meeting.

At that moment, Fred came out of the living room and onto the landing. 'Good evening, Mr Carneson,' the tweed-hatted man said in a jovial voice.

'Good evening,' muttered Fred.

In the flat below, Sarah was still sitting at the desk, writing lists of things to buy for Mount Pleasant. The door of the flat opened and the head of the Special Branch peered around the doorway, looked at her, grinned and said, 'Well, look who we have here.'

On the landing was a bookcase. The man confiscated many of Caroline's books, including James Joyce's *Ulysses* – not actually a banned book but, according to Caroline, 'always removed in raids because of its reputation as titillatingly dirty'.

Fred, Sarah, Amy and Gillian were all arrested. They were taken home to pack pyjamas and toiletries before being taken to prison, where they were charged the next day. Amy thought that they would be detained for a long time under the ninety-day law. She started to pack, filling an enormous trunk. The security police had to carry it between two of them to the car and into the prison. In their cell, Sarah and Gillian were very worried, as Amy did not turn up. Three hours later, when she joined them in the cell, they discovered that it had taken an hour just to do a list of contents of the trunk.

Sarah, Amy and Gillian were all put in one cell. 'The warders were shrieking and screaming at us,' Sarah said. 'We decided to whisper to each other so that the warders would have to stop to listen to what we were saying. We used to call them the bitches with the dangling keys.' Some prostitutes were occupying the adjoining cell and Sarah, Amy and Gillian invited the prostitutes to join them. Sarah suggested to Gillian and Amy that they sit on the changes of clothes they had brought in case of theft. 'You are too cynical about people,' said Gillian. Amy agreed. The next morning, when they had to appear before the magistrate, Amy and Gillian appeared in the clothes they had been wearing the previous day. Sarah was the only one in clean clothes: the prostitutes had taken everything else.

In the meantime, Caroline had her first meeting with Himie Bernadt, our dedicated lawyer who was looking after the others who had been arrested the previous evening. It took Caroline and Himie some time to convince the security police that the black people who had been arrested had been attending a church meeting rather than a political meeting. Fred and Sarah and the others were remanded on charges of breaking their banning orders.

At one point during the trial, Caroline, recounting the evening's events, said to the court, 'I offered Mr Carneson a nightcap.'

'A *what*?' said the uncomprehending Afrikaans magistrate.

'A drink, Your Worship,' the lawyer explained.

Caroline insisted that the accused had all been in different rooms. The prosecutor suggested that her friendships with the accused had influenced her testimony. Standing in the witness box in her smart suit and blue straw hat, she protested in a tone of passionate indignation, 'But that would be *perjury*!' The magistrate looked at her and then sat down.

Amy was amused: 'Caroline bamboozled them at the trial. They couldn't make out what room anyone was in.' The case was dismissed.

Although that particular case had its humorous elements and my parents were not convicted, the security police were even more determined to leave no stone unturned in their efforts to get Fred and Sarah into prison.

Soon after this, Fred realised that it would be only a short time before he was arrested again. He left Mount Pleasant early one morning and went into permanent hiding in St Mungo Court. He was almost completely isolated in his cramped flat. He did what he could, but spent long, lonely nights waiting for the knock on the door that he knew was coming. He spent hours thinking about his family, the horrors of the war and comrades who had been tortured and died in jail. He knew that when he was picked up, more of his close comrades would also be arrested and interrogated.

On one occasion during this dark time, he asked one of his female comrades to spend the night with him. She refused. I was shocked to hear this, but soon realised that he was so frightened and alone that he must have felt desperate. I knew, though, that he would never admit it. I went every day to South Africa House in London to read the news. It was a terrifying shock – but not a surprise – when, on 8 December 1965, the dreaded phone call came asking me to return to Cape Town because my father had been taken into custody.

The two years that followed were a nightmare. My father was tortured, kept in solitary confinement for thirteen months and then imprisoned with the other political prisoners in Pretoria Central Prison. My sister had a breakdown and the security police made life so impossible for my mother, brother and sister that, one by one, they were forced to leave the country. My mother was the last to leave to begin a new life, exiled in a strange country as a stateless citizen.

PART THREE

Journey into Exile

1968–1991

They smashed his spirit,
Ruined sour earth, molecules of anger and resentment
What is the song that touches this generation?
The years spent in prison,
sunlight illuminating each object in the dark.
Ruined sour earth, molecules of anger and resentment
The years spent in prison,
sunlight illuminating each object in the dark,
his smile that recognises we are one with this beautiful earth.
Where is that in me?
Why no joy? Just grief.
His smile that recognises we are one with this beautiful earth.
I saw him after he had been tortured
Why no joy? Just grief.
What is the song that touches this generation?
I saw him after he had been tortured
They smashed his spirit, but it sprang up like crushed grass.

– Lynn Carneson

28

Dislocated

Sarah left Cape Town in September 1967 in a full blaze of spring flowers, but as she was frogmarched onto the SS *Vaal*, her heart was heavy. The memory of her last visit to Fred played through her mind like a broken record. She was deeply worried about Ruth and concerned about how she would manage in a strange country with no employment. She was bone-tired – so exhausted that she slept most of the voyage. When she woke up, she pined for her beloved country and husband. She had no idea if or when she would see them again.

My mother arrived during a gloomy and cold English autumn. All her children and a small group of comrades met her at Southampton. She first stayed with Esmé Goldberg, Denis Goldberg's wife, at 118 Hendon Way in London. It was bewildering to arrive in a grey city where it constantly rained and which, compared to Cape Town, was vast. Everything was unfamiliar: it was a challenge just to find her way around London, and she found the prospect of having to find work and a new home daunting.

In her first letter to Fred she wrote, 'Can't believe everything is so very different. Seen more people last three days than last three years. All send love to you and others.' She also managed to get a message through in code that Archie Sibeko, who had worked with Fred in MK, had arrived safely in London. During her first weekend in England I took my mother to visit John at his school. 'John looking very handsome, very adult,' she reported to Fred. 'Ate lunch in car. Too wet outside.'

One of the first people that Sarah saw in London was her old friend Blanche La Guma, who had been part of Sarah's underground cell in the fifties. They would become even closer in England because they could see each other whenever they wanted. When Sarah first arrived, Blanche took her by train to see Kew Gardens. They sat on the tube, nibbled sandwiches and talked together. While they were chatting, they passed a number of stations until they arrived at the same station that they had left from. They had taken the Circle Line, and had not realised that they were going round and round. They had a good laugh and eventually managed to find their way to Kew Gardens, where Sarah was amazed by how green everything was.

After a month, Sarah rented a flat in 6 West Hampstead Mews so that she and Ruth could live together. Ruth went to St Alfred's School, Hampstead, and my mother believed that London had been good for Ruth. She wrote to my father: 'Ruth already getting more out of life here. Can hold head up rather than being hounded. Thinks tubes most exciting. For first time is able to speak freely of you. Being here makes it less painful for her to accept your position.' Slowly my mother started to adjust to her new environment. 'London fantastic place,' she wrote to Fred, 'full of life and vitality. Vast world. Getting about takes some getting used to. Am learning to find my own way around the place fairly quickly.'

Sarah had a love–hate relationship with the weather, depending on temperature, sun and colour. When it didn't rain she thought autumn was beautiful. Although she talked about matters like the weather in her letters to Fred, she did not mention that Ruth had taken another overdose and was in hospital. Ruth had been pretending to be happy but in fact was struggling at school and felt alien and lonely in London.

> 17 October 1967
>
> Autumn London very lovely. Went for long walk Regent's Park, Pauline N., her lovely daughters and Ruth. Greens and browns very beautiful. Bird life most exciting. You will love walking in the parks of London … Spent one weekend country – Worcester. Countryside very beautiful. Trees something to see. Colours are breathtaking. Went to Wales, saw real castle – most of it gone but giving great feeling of history. Find it very exciting.
>
> All our love darling. Good luck with exams. Ever thinking of you.
> Sarah

My father studied and was continually writing exams on different subjects for a Bachelor of Arts degree, including history and economics. He also studied to be a chartered secretary. He wrote back to my mother whenever he was permitted. His letters were as important to her as hers were to him, bringing her news not only of him, but of their comrades in prison as well.

1 November 1967

Darling Sarah

Have permission buy records on account every two months. Go general pool so no guarantee we will get them. Have ordered Joan Baez with Miriam Makeba alternative.

Enjoyed your mum's visit. Looked remarkably fit. Gave me big kiss through glass on leaving, bless her heart.

Lovely warm feeling knowing you all enjoying life London. I want know details. What see on TV, what eating, what concerts, plays – and where. Mention places. Dave Kitson knows London well, can describe. Brings you closer to me. Think of all of you many times each day. Special session after supper. Spread mats, head on pillow, and just dream away, anticipating joys of reunion, pleasure of expressive love and emotion once more ... Summer rains begun. Get big kick from towering clouds, thunder, lightning. Pity no earth to give warm, heady rain scent.

Rain = mushrooms. Wonder if you'll find any London? Could do with big plateful right now.

Father Magennis, telling us of old parishioner, happened to say, 'And then he upped and died.' I couldn't resist remarking: 'What you really mean is that he died. You hoped he upped.' Thank heavens he has sense of humour.

When Kitson read your plaint re windows never opened, his comment was: 'What's she want to do? Heat up the whole of Hendon?' He also thinks you'll soon adjust.

So much want to say, so few words allowed. My love for you, for children, could flood over many, many pages, as broad and deep as the seas between us.

It was wonderful for me to have my mother, John and Ruth in the same country, after five years of being there alone. We saw as much of each other as we could. I was teaching English and drama and going out with Charles McGregor, whom I had met at a party in June 1966. He was interesting, wonderful company, very kind, well read and curious about what was going on in the world. He knew about South Africa and understood what I was going through. He had been educated at Oxford and I found him intellectually stimulating and full of energy. I fell in love with the blueness of his eyes. At the end of 1967 we got engaged. It caused quite a splash in the papers. At the time Charles's father, Kenneth McGregor C.B., was an eminent civil servant and a Labour councillor for Islington. He was interested to learn that Fred had also been a councillor, in Cape Town. His family was most welcoming, not just to me but to the rest of my family too. Charles's mother, Dorothy, helped my mother to find 19 Annington Road, East Finchley – the house that my mother eventually bought as her new home. Sarah thought that a stable home would give her, John and Ruth a chance to settle down. Unfortunately, her hopes for Ruth were not fulfilled.

Even though there was less tension and the intimidation from the security police had been left behind, Ruth continued to struggle to cope with life. On 2 October 1967, she took an overdose and slashed her wrists. She was admitted to Whittington Hospital in Highgate. I was overcome with grief and guilt, feeling that I had not taken enough care of her. She looked so fragile, with bandages on her arm, hugging her teddy bear. I was in a worse emotional state about Ruth than I had been on hearing that my father had been arrested. 'When I came to England,' Ruth told me years later, 'I had a total identity crisis. I lost all sense of self. There was no reference point. I was unfamiliar with the British social rules, I was still only fourteen and I had just come out of hospital after a major breakdown.' It was a terribly unsettling time for her, a complete upheaval. 'There was nothing familiar to measure myself against,' she said. 'There was a great big void of nothing that I could relate to. I felt nothing. It was much worse than being depressed: I couldn't see a way out. All I wanted to do was to die.'

Ruth was in and out of hospital for months, lurching from one crisis to another. Sarah was in a constant state of shock. On top of this, she had to find a job: she was short of money and I was not earning enough to support them. Luckily her first short-term job, like that of so many other South African political refugees, was with Joel Joffe, a member of the defence team in the Rivonia Trial and founder of Abbey Life, but after three months the hours and the travelling became too much, and she decided to find another job nearer to home so that she could be close to Ruth.

Between Ruth's stays in hospital, when it was summer, I took her on trips around England and France. She seemed to enjoy herself for short periods and then would withdraw into herself. Charles and I took her on a holiday to Spain, which she was able to enjoy for longer periods of time. In fact, both Ruth and I were entertained by Charles's outrage when we sat at an outdoor café and gossiped about the young girls walking past. Charles said it was unacceptable behaviour; Ruth told him not to be so English.

Charles persisted in a one-man campaign to try to get my father released. He persuaded people like Sir Eric Roll, Sir William Hayter and Lord Radcliffe-Maud to write letters to the South African ambassador. We did not expect anything would come of it but later, when Fred was eventually released, the fact that eminent, internationally known people were concerned about him played a large part in the government's decision to let him out of the country.

While my mother was trying to cope with Ruth and work, John was established in Leighton Park School. He had to work extremely hard to catch up with the other boys. We visited him every Sunday, and he always put on a brave face and was cheerful, full of jokes. Behind the façade, though, I could sense some of the same anxiety he had displayed in Cape Town. The last time he had been able to communicate with his father was one and a half years earlier, when Fred had been awaiting trial.

Weeks before his sixteenth birthday, John spent hours agonising about what to write in a letter to Fred. He sent his letter on his birthday, 9 August. The head warder, Mr Du Preez, received the letter on 15 August. He told Fred that a letter had arrived from John, but said: 'I won't allow you to read it because I don't like the contents.' The letter was returned to John, who was deeply upset. Fred wrote a complaint to the commanding officer:

> Not knowing the contents, I am unable to make any particular points in regard thereto, but I should like to place the following circumstances before you for your consideration. My son turned sixteen on the 9th of this month – he probably wrote the letter on his birthday – and I feel strongly that his age, immaturity and natural youthful strength of feeling should be given due weight in assessing the importance of what he has written and the manner in which he has expressed himself.
>
> As he is in England and therefore not in a position to visit me, letters are now the only means he has of opening his heart to me. Because of previous restrictions on correspondence and the need to discuss urgent family affairs with my wife, this is the first direct contact I have had with my son for almost two years. I am most anxious, therefore, to gauge at first hand his present attitude to life, to his studies and possible future career, so as to be in a position to give him whatever guidance may be necessary.
>
> Were the letter to be returned, I am certain that its rejection would come as a shock and a bitter disappointment to him and, in addition,

probably inhibit him, at this stage, from communicating properly with me in future letters.

I should very much appreciate it, therefore, if you would allow me to have the letter.

Du Preez was being vindictive. John had sent Fred a photograph of himself, and Du Preez objected to his long hair – not to the contents of the letter itself.

Fred kept on nagging the authorities to allow him to keep in contact with John until they permitted him to send a letter to John's head teacher, John Ounsted, and to receive one from him. Fred was extremely distressed that he was not allowed to play his proper role as a father. The letter he received from John Ounsted, however, helped him to picture what John's life was like and reassured him that John was all right.

Leighton Park School
Reading
Berkshire
England

24 October 1967

Dear Fred
I was very pleased to hear from you and am glad to have the opportunity to report to you about your son John, who is now halfway through his third term at school here.

In spite of the difficulties involved in settling down to life in a strange country and to an entirely different system of education, especially when changing schools in the middle of the school year, John settled in remarkably well and studied hard to earn sound grades at the end of the year in his public examination, the General Certificate of Education. During this term he is both beginning on more advanced work and taking Ordinary Level GCE also in physics and in chemistry, so he has a very full work programme.

It is John's intention to make a career in the field of biological sciences. It is early days yet to be sure whether this will come about, for he has not shown some of the early interests displayed by past boys who have become professional biologists. It is however a very reasonable aim for him, and we will watch how he develops.

Last spring term John played hockey and in the summer took part in summer athletics. This term he has played rugby football keenly, getting a try for his House 1st XV, in which he may possibly be going to play in the final game. He has also remained a very keen chess player, thoroughly deserving a place in the School 1st six. We have had matches this term with Eton College and with Abingdon School, and John has won his game in each of these.

John devotes a good deal of spare time to his work, and has had the bad luck not to be able to take part in all the organised evening activities he would like to, since several of his favourite interests all have their meetings on the same night. Photography is of course his first love.

During last year he took an active part in one of our social service projects, chopping firewood for delivery to disabled or old people in the neighbourhood who are unable to chop their own firewood.

John has made good friends at Leighton Park. He has been visiting the home of a nice boy called Andrew Lesser, and he gets on well with his study-mate.

We are all very pleased indeed to have John here among us, and I know that those who have made it possible will think it well worthwhile. John was delighted to learn that I had received a letter from you and had the opportunity to send you this report on him.

We are very pleased that John's mother and his younger sister are now in this country so that he can now enjoy more family life again. He is concerned to look after his mother and be 'a man about the house' and also to play his part in making a happy life for his younger sister.

Yours sincerely
John Ounsted

We had a conventional and very happy Christmas with Charles and his parents. They provided a sense of stability and normality. It could have been this or the fact that, apart from my father, we were all together again that helped Ruth slowly gain some confidence. She started painting and reading again, and it was during the Christmas period that she began to talk about writing something to Fred when it was her turn (we all took it in turns to write because the number of letters he could receive was at this time restricted). Until then it had been too difficult for her to write anything to Fred. So Ruth started drafting a letter to send to him. It was a painstaking process; she kept on asking me if what she wrote would be allowed, and she was insistent that he should not be upset by the problems she had had. She sent off the final draft on the day of his birthday – the first letter she had sent him in six months, since her arrival in London the previous July. Ruth addressed Fred with the nickname that we used to tease him with in Cape Town.

13 January 1968

Dear Mouldybaldy
Happy 21st birthday. Christmas with McGregors, food, wine plentiful. Presents – quantity plus quality, people much quality. Snow thick on ground, trees, powdery white icing sugar, tasteless and cold (indigestible).
    Television saw part of Bolshevik ballet, beautiful and exciting. Just finished reading *Gone with the Wind*. Not know whether to love or hate Rhett (hero), thought he'd like me better than Scarlet.
    School I approve, no uniform, call teachers by first names. Subjects – English, Spanish, biology, physics, art, hist., geog. Lynn and I have mutual crush on sexy headmaster.
    Lynn taking us birthday treat Royal Shakespeare Company twice – *Macbeth*, *Ghosts*. Exhibitions: Picasso sculptures, Cubist art and others. Roland (cousin) says yes, I've got artistic talent.
    Holidays – France, Lynn and I alone in car – ha ha. Incredible lorry cafés – loud-mouthed French and good food.
    Spain – hot long white sanded beaches. Village town crier, goats, pigs, well for water. Villa – view Pyrenees, own vineyard, plenty wine. Moorish, charming Othello-like host, artist friend of Lynn's. Friendly good Catalonian villages ... Beautiful drive through mountains to white-washed little port and beaches called Cadaques – home of Salvador Dali, ex-home Picasso. We saw Dali. Old man with handle-brush moustache. Surrounded by female starlets. Lynn and I didn't like them. Ate to heart's content – all sea foods: oysters, prawns, squids, delicious paella.
    Trip back – no money, taught Charles to nick grapes. Charles extremely nice, typical Scottish rooinek, scared of sun. Good brother-in-law.
    Travelled back train comfortably 1st class, filled our bellies with bread, butter, pâté and leftover liquor from Spain.

Fred was overjoyed to receive a letter from Ruth and to read that she was enjoying herself. Although no one had mentioned her difficulties to him, he spent many nights worrying about her and feeling guilty about having neglected her in the past. He was relieved to hear from her and to know that the family was safe, even though, as he told me later, the pain from knowing that he would not see us again for years was like a deep wound that never healed while he was in prison.

Ruth was starting to be able to enjoy life and was experiencing fewer setbacks. It seemed as if the family's fortune was slowly improving. Three days before Ruth wrote to Fred, Sarah answered an advertisement for administrative work at the *Morning Star*, a communist newspaper. She was surprised that people at the paper already knew of her and welcomed her warmly. She started work in the finance department doing cash flows and checking the accuracy of accounts. Sarah loved working for the *Morning Star*. Everyone she met at the paper was well informed and open to different opinions. It was the right environment for her: she remained there until she retired.

Not only did Sarah find a good job, but, in February, she, John and Ruth moved into their new home, 19 Annington Road. John, having finished school, had decided to study social sciences at a college in London, and Charles and I were getting married on 23 March. Sarah was happy to have both children back again, and glad to be involved in the joyful, celebratory planning for the wedding.

It was my parents' twenty-fifth wedding anniversary on 31 March, and Fred was acutely aware of these two important family occasions. His request to send two cables, one to me and one to Sarah, was refused, so he appealed to the prison authorities again, writing, 'On occasions such as these, of special significance, something more is surely called for from the head of the family. It is wholly inadequate for me to wish my daughter and her husband well for their wedding at second hand, as if one of the most important days in her life is worth no more than a few lines in a letter to a third person.' Fred's appeal was denied, and he was forced to 'deal with both matters in [his] ordinary "once-a-month" letter'.

Pretoria Central Prison
5 March 1968

Darling Sarah
You must be spinning like a top, what with moving into house, your job, preparations Lynn's wedding. Would be worried if not know your gift cope emergencies. Tell me about it.

Have done little else but think of you last few weeks. Thread a needle, and there you are. Light a cigarette, you're back again. Doesn't matter what I'm doing, you keep popping up. By the time the 31st and our 25th anniversary arrive I'll be in a fine state. Probably jump into one of the mailbags and get someone to post me off to you.

All day long I've been saying to myself: I'll take the whole 500 words to tell you what you mean to me. But words are such dead, dumb things. A touch, a glance, a smile – and all is said. One day that rich wordless language will be ours to use again. We'll surpass all the poets that ever were with one single touch of fingertips. Till then, I'll dream – dream of you and of our children, of our children's children and of all the quiet happiness that lies ahead.

Part of that happiness is with me now, thinking of Lynn and Charles. If only half my wishes for them came true, they will live in great joy all their lives long. Give them my love and my blessing ...

We were married in the Quaker Meeting House, filled with bright yellow daffodils, in Hampstead, London. In the spirit of the Quaker meeting, those who wished to say something were invited to speak. My mother read out a message from my father, who said that he and the other prisoners had toasted our wedding with a tin mug of coffee. There was a mixture of English and South African guests, including old South African comrades like Brian and Sonia Bunting and Albie Sachs. For the exiles, our comrades in prison were also present at the wedding, in spirit. Unfortunately my mother was not able to use many words to describe the event in detail to my father.

19 Annington Road
London N2
6 April 1968

Fred darling
Lynn looked stunning in red cloak and dress. Over hundred at ceremony. Many South Africans. All very moving and little sad because your absence. At ceremony people able to stand up and express thoughts. Many thoughts for you in SA. John and Ruth wonderful hosts.

My house not unlike Ryde Villa only smaller. Pocket-handkerchief garden. 12 rose bushes, 2 yellow broom. Mass varied yellow and blue flowers and shrubs. Small but colourful. Made few hundred on devaluation, spent it on edge-to-edge carpets, off-peak heating, built-in cupboards and new fridge bought before budget. House walking distance East Finchley tube. Back of police station, Fortis Green Road. Five minutes' walk Cherry Tree Woods. On direct bus route to Ruth's school. But takes me hour to get to Notting Hill Gate for work. Now working until 4.00 p.m. More relaxed, not so tired, but not so much money. Work more varied. Interesting.

Television limited use. Book reading still necessary. Reading books English background to try understand locals. 25th wedding anniversary. Family dinner. Drank toast to you, us and family.

Schools on holiday one month. John washing bottles etc. for funds. Ruth making bookshelf for 'little room'. Enjoys woodwork. Will send some of her paintings as soon as more organised. Spend Saturdays cleaning house, laundry and shopping. Try to manage show if possible. John better than Ruth housework. Food strictly budgeted. Will have to start eating like the English and will probably all put on weight. Hope to go up to the cottage Worcestershire over Easter. Will try to get back Sunday night so can join marchers Monday. Longing for country and fresh air and SUN. Spring freezing.

It appeared as though my mother, John and Ruth were beginning to settle down and make a life for themselves in London, but I was wrong. Ruth seemed to be better for longer intervals, and there were times when she seemed to be healthy and normal: she enjoyed having John and his friends around, when Sarah would make big pots of pasta or a rice dish to feed everyone. They would sit and watch black-and-white television. For Ruth it was even more fun during a power workers' strike, when there were frequent electricity cuts that forced them to sit in the dark, in candlelight.

Ruth's emotional stability did not last long. In May 1968, she started running away from home and then from hospital. I dreaded the frequent midnight phone calls to tell me that Ruth had gone again. We would phone all the hospitals and police stations, waiting for her to turn up, fearful it would be in a morgue. She used to accept lifts from strange truck drivers but, to our relief, nothing terrible happened to her. Police up and down Britain, who knew her well by this stage, used to phone us and bring her home. She was again in and out of hospital, and the doctors started putting her in a locked ward. Even this measure didn't stop her from running away. Sarah would visit her in hospital at night, after her long days at work.

Ruth wouldn't talk to her so she just sat calmly at Ruth's bedside simply to be with her.

At first, as in the hospital in Cape Town, the psychiatrist did not believe Ruth or my mother when they talked about what had happened in South Africa. It was only after I brought press cuttings and booklets about South Africa that the doctors took us seriously. They might have believed us sooner if they had seen the behaviour of my mother, Ruth and me at a dinner party around that time: hearing the doorbell ring loudly, we instinctively reacted as if the security police were ringing the bell. So deep was our conditioning that we all found ourselves outside, hiding behind a large tree, having independently fled out the back door. We looked at each other in astonishment: 'What are *you* doing here?' We fell about laughing and sheepishly went back into the house.

It took a full two years for Ruth to recover enough to lead a normal life. She told me later, 'I made a conscious decision to give life a chance. The last time I ran away I was sent to a terrible mental institution called Friern Hospital. The people there were long-termers and in an awful state. I thought to myself, "I'm still here, unfortunately. I'm not mad, just badly behaved. Where am I going from here? Am I going to make a career of being loony?" I took one look at that hospital and decided to accept that I was alive, here to stay, and had better make the best of it.'

Once Ruth had recovered fully, my mother could take more pleasure in her new life. She began to enjoy her freedom, her home, spending time with friends and exploring London. Because she had no transport, Mary Turok used to take her shopping on Saturdays.

Sarah was fed up with members of the SACP in London. She felt that they were not doing enough for those comrades in exile who were struggling and believed that she had been given no emotional or financial support. When Sonia Bunting did eventually visit, Sarah was furious, as Sonia started telling her what furniture she should buy and what colour to paint the house. 'You have no business interfering with other people's lives. I will do what I want,' Sarah said, although Sonia was probably just trying to be helpful.

My mother was by nature independent and she was learning to assert her independence in a climate where 'women's liberation' was a hot topic. As a newly-wed, this was also an issue for me. Most of the time I enjoyed being married, but I found that my role and status had changed. Suddenly people were treating me as if I was just a 'wife' and not a person in my own

The family in England on the way to Heathrow Airport to meet Fred after a separation of over eight years, 1972

WEST LONDON OBSERVER Friday, October 27, 1972

'We're prepared for armed struggle' says anti-apartheid man

ANTI APARTHEID supporters in South Africa were aiming to isolate white racialists — and hit them hard. If this meant armed struggle, West London Anti-Apartheid Group were told, then they were prepared for that.

The speaker was Mr. Fred Carneson, a South African and a former political prisoner in the country. He was one of three speakers who addressed the group on the subject of "Political Prisoners in South Africa."

The meeting was held in a church hall in Faraday Road, North Kensington.

Said Mr. Carneson: "Conditions in our country are explosive and a seemingly quiet situation could burst into flames."

He added: "We are aiming to isolate the hard core fascist element of whites and then hit them as hard as we can. And if that means armed struggle, then that is what we are preparing our country for."

Earlier, Mr. Carneson described the plight of black political prisoners in South Africa as "living in hell," and vividly related incidents of brutality.

Mr. Carneson said there was a constant, unavoidable undercurrent of violence and brutality towards black political prisoners from warders and their fellow prisoners.

"There is no rest," he said. "I can tell you that it is hell to be a political prisoner and to be black in South Africa."

Discrimination, he said, was carried to ridiculous lengths and he gave as an example the case of white prisoners who were given large towels and black prisoners who were given towels no larger than face-cloths.

Said Mr. Carneson: "The South African political prisoners are among the finest patriots the country has ever seen."

He said there could be no political solution in South Africa as long as political prisoners were held.

"Until these people are released," he said, "there is absolutely no hope whatsoever of a solution, at any rate a peaceful solution."

It was not easy to be reunited after eight years: Fred and Sarah had many strong arguments before settling down to living with each other again, 1973

A few months after Fred arrived in England, he took up his old role as political activist

A happy Lynn with son Simon, London, 1974

Fred, Shanti Naidoo and Hugh Lewin in London, where the struggle continued for the release of political prisoners, 1973

Fred was chair of the UK Anti-Apartheid Trade Union Committee for fourteen years and was instrumental in persuading the UK unions to campaign against apartheid. From left to right: Bruce Sanderson, Fred, Cate Clarke, Des Starrs and Roy Hutchinson, 1983

Fred working at the office with a comrade in London, c. 1981

Despite many gruelling years of imprisonment, Fred, pictured here at Lynn's house in London, 1975, was able to regain some of his former sparkle

Mr and Mrs John Carneson, just married, 1984

Sarah relaxing on the rooftop patio at Lynn's house, London, 1985

Fred, with Sarah, tells baby Busi Carneson that he 'could eat her, she is so beautiful', Morogoro, Tanzania, 1986

Family pub dinner in London, 1989. From left to right: Omri, Adam, Fred, Sarah, Lynn, Simon, Ruth and John Simmons

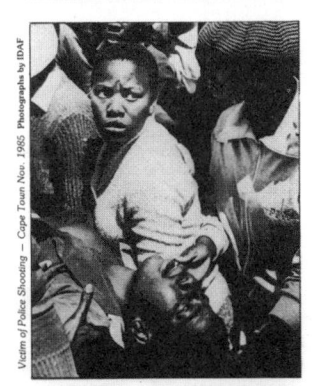

An excited Ruth and Sarah at an ANC conference in London, 1991, waiting to find out whether the negotiations were successful so that they could return home to South Africa

Protest pamphlet distributed by the ANC and the Anti-Apartheid Movement in England

Nearly home: Fred and Mendi Msimang, the ANC London representative, at Fred and Sarah's farewell party, London, 1991

AFRICAN NATIONAL CONGRESS
P.O.Box 38 28 Penton Street London N1 9PR United Kingdom
Telephone: 071 - 837 2012 Telex: 299555 Fax: 071 - 278 2736

ANC THE YEAR OF PEOPLE'S ACTION FOR A DEMOCRATIC SOUTH AFRICA

The Chairperson
African National Congress
Western Cape Region
NBS Building
George Street
Athlone, P.O. Box 2306
Cape Town

13 May 1991

MM/280/zr

Dear Comrade

This is to advise that two stalwarts of the Movement Comrades Fred and Sarah Carneson will be arriving in Cape Town on a South African Airways flight on 19 May 1991 at 10.05 hours.

Please ensure appropriate reception and integration into your structures.

Amandla!   Matla!

MENDI MSIMANG
Chief Representative
ANC MISSION: UK AND IRELAND

Mendi Msimang's letter asking comrades to welcome Fred and Sarah home when they arrived in Cape Town in 1991

Cape Argus 25/5/91

Fred and Sarah have come home

DENNIS CRUYWAGEN
Political Staff

BANNED, JAILED, EXILED... BUT LOVE WON

THE chemistry between them is alive and visible. It is clear that the emotional strands binding the souls of Fred and Sarah Carneson is not infatuation but the real thing — LOVE.

It has to be. What else would have insulated and protected them at a time when the government was hellbent on purging the country of communists, black nationalists, left-wingers and all other people who openly opposed their policies?

How, but for the power of love and their firm belief that their struggle was just, could they have triumphed over banning orders, detention, prison — in Fred's case — and a four-year separation?

But the political wheel has turned and the government appears to have abandoned its witch-hunt. The unbanning of organisations such as the South African Communist Party has made it possible for Fred and Sarah Carneson to return home.

Unlike some other returnees, Fred and Sarah are not in the prime of their lives armed with degrees or about to wade into employment.

No, they, like many other pioneers of the struggle, have long passed the stage where they could have been called young Turks.

Fred is 71 and Freda's 74.

So why did they return when they could have continued their lives as pensioners in Britain far away from the turmoil?

Determined

"We were determined to come back and join our people who struggled here. We are in our own country and want to live and fight here. We want to help build a genuine non-racial democracy where there will be peace and freedom for all," Fred said.

Not so long ago did he not think that this would be pos-

sible. After living as a fugitive, he was arrested in December 1965, charged with sabotage, for being a member of Umkhonto we Sizwe and the Communist Party, and being in possession of explosives.

"The only charges which stuck were membership of the party and for being in possession of the SA Communist."

He was sentenced to five years and nine months, serving the first 15 months at Pollsmoor Prison.

"Apart from being interrogated by the security branch, this was the hardest part of prison for me. I was isolated from the rest of the prison."

Next stop was Pretoria Local Prison where he completed his incarceration.

Birthday party

Sarah, meanwhile, was raising their children.

"I was too busy earning a living for myself and my family to really think about my difficulties. I was not alone — so many others were jailed at the time."

A banning order, her second restricted her to Cape Town between 1965 and 1970.

"I had to get permission to visit my children's schools.

Once she was arrested for taking her 13-year-old daughter to a birthday party.

In 1968 she decided to go into exile. "The security police were harassing my children. My youngest daughter couldn't cope with her father being jailed and the security police

visiting our house so frequently."

A consultation with Fred and others involved with progressive organisations followed. The response was unanimous: Go.

She left on an exit permit. But the state was not finished with her, remanding her of her banning order and ordering her to leave for the harbour on the day when she was due to sail.

"I knew I wouldn't be seeing Fred for the next four years. I was very disturbed, leaving a country I loved and a husband whom I loved. When I left Cape Town I wept because I didn't think I would see it again."

Neighbours' bedroom bugged

LONDON. — A shocked young mother found her bedroom was being secretly bugged because of a neighbours' feud. Police were called after the 25-year-old spotted a bore-hole linked to a microphone behind a wardrobe at her home. The neighbour, who faces civil action for eavesdropping, told po-

Six months after arriving in London she applied for permission to visit Fred. "I never got a reply."

Her departure was a relief for Fred. "I knew that Sarah was vulnerable. I was relieved when she left. It took one worry off my mind. Sarah was tough enough to take anything they threw at her, but I was worried about the kids."

Not worried

Not seeing her for the next four years did not worry him, he said.

"There was little sense of loss ... we were that close. I knew she was there. It did not matter if she was in London. We did not feel apart."

Fred was freed in 1972. His application to remain in South Africa for two weeks to see his family and wind up his affairs was refused.

"They told me that if I would be put under 24 hours' house arrest if I did not leave the country within 24 hours."

Security police made sure he left by following him from Pretoria to Johannesburg, where he had lunch with a relative, and then to Jan Smuts airport.

He went to prison with a Standard 8 certificate and left with a BA degree, majoring in economics and history.

Fred and Sarah have no income, but small British state pensions. "I'll try to find a job here. I was in the army for 5½ years in the last war. I don't know if there's a pension due to me."

lice: "I just wanted to know what the old hag was saying about me."

The woman said: "I'm disgusted. He's sick in the head prying on people's bedroom privacy. I blush to think what he might have overheard." — Weekend Argus Foreign Service

New beginnings in South Africa for Fred and Sarah

A happy greeting: Fred with Nelson Mandela at ANC conference in Durban, 1991

Sarah, Mandela and others, ANC Durban conference, 1991, where, for Sarah, 'it was such a joy to meet old friends after so long'

Walking from Muizenberg to Kalk Bay was a favourite walk of Fred's and Sarah's, 1991

When Ruth returned to Cape Town for a visit in 1991, Fred and Sarah took her to the places they loved. Here they are enjoying the beach at Fish Hoek

When Fred was ANC representative for the Cape Regional and Metropolitan Council during the interim government, he often spoke out against corruption in the Cape, 1993

Fred remembering the dead and grieving over loss of life as he points out names during a war memorial trip to Monte Sole, Italy, 1995

Fred and Sarah in 1994: 'The last twenty years were the happiest of our marriage'

Vote Fred Carneson

Diep River, Plumstead, Constantia (Ward S2)

Let's make it happen where we live.

Fred's ANC campaign pamphlet, 1996

NELSON MANDELA

15 September 2000

Mrs Serah Carneson and Family
CAPE TOWN

Dear Serah,

Graça and I wish to join the many thousands of colleagues, friends, comrades, and people from all walks of life in expressing our deepest sympathy to you, and to all members of the family on the death of our Comrade Fred.

We recall with appreciation Fred's significant contribution during the various phases of our long walk to freedom and democracy. We remember him as a dynamic activist and leader in the national liberation movement; a soldier in the fight against Nazism; a member of the Cape Provincial Council; an accused in the Treason Trial; a political prisoner and a husband and father.

During his long life he never wavered, nor slowed down in his commitment to the cause of freedom. All of us have reason to be proud of Fred's exemplary contribution.

Graça and I wish you and your family strength during this period of bereavement. Please be assured that you are all in our thoughts.

Yours sincerely

N R Mandela

Letter of condolence from Nelson Mandela and Graça Machel to Sarah, after Fred's death, 2000

A family picture, 2006. Bottom row, from left to right: Lynn Carneson, Siba de Wet, Sarah Carneson, Calsi Minaar and Nontombi Katangana. Second row: Margaret Painsley, Ntombi Carneson, John Carneson, Ruth Carneson, Simon McGregor, Lionel Snell, Busisiwe Carneson and Pamela de Wet. Top row: Jacques de Wet. Photo taken by Ricardo Minaar right. I was expected to serve food, clear up afterwards and keep quiet because I was an under-educated, uncultured South African female! When I discussed this with my mother and Ruth, I discovered that I was not alone in trying to work out my identity as a woman. We all thought that we had moved to a free country where men and women were supposed to be treated as equals; we were surprised to find that this was not usually the case.

Ruth was stridently feminist. My mother warned my father to expect differences in attitudes when he joined us in England. My father was in principle pro–women's liberation, but in fact still had conservative Catholic values about a woman's place in the home. He did his best to respond to my mother's comments about the subject:

> Shan't be astonished at new youth & women's attitudes. The odd book, article, youth supplement have helped keep us more or less abreast of what is happening in that respect. Be interesting to experience it at first hand. Have considerable sympathy with Women's Lib. movement, & particularly with their fight against the demeaning of women as mere sex symbols in adverts, pin-ups, beauty contests, etc. The emancipation of women is far from complete in our society, so good luck to those who are currently speaking out, even if we don't go with all their views.
>
> What do you do about the housework now that you're out working all day? Do you get a char in occasionally to help out, or what? Sweeping, dusting, polishing, scrubbing hold no terrors for me – but don't let that statement give you too many ideas!

I was also a serious feminist and wrote to my father suggesting that he start changing his 'old-fashioned' attitude towards women. I was not impressed by his response.

> Your eloquent, passionate protest against the subordinate role for women in our society was very moving. Spent last two evenings drafting and then destroying comments on the problem. Decided in the end that subject much too complicated (and maybe too delicate) to tackle effectively by letter. The possibility of misunderstanding is too great. When I am free, we can discuss it in person, at leisure and at length. There are no easy or complete solutions under the present set-up, but spelling the problem out in itself helps to relieve some of the strain and

sometimes points to potential remedies. All I can do at present is to hold thumbs and hope that you won't explode into little pieces before I get there.

When we discussed women's liberation with John, he wasn't interested – but he was certainly interested in girls. 'Have sweet girl Reading, but London birds better,' he wrote to my father. 'Reading is biggest dump ... Needed rest – Saturday school dance – passionate girl exhausted me – hate sweaty sticky girls.' After a few months in London he met Jenny, the daughter of my mother's old friend Pauline Naidoo. They went out for a number of years and together explored England, parts of Europe and Ireland, from which they returned with a much-adored black-and-white sheepdog called Kerry, who loved going to pubs and drinking beer.

The next few years shifted into a routine of working, studying, travelling and going to the theatre, concerts and exhibitions. Our activities were all described in as much detail as possible to my father, but it was extremely difficult to let him know what was happening with the struggle. My mother was travelling the country educating people – mainly university students and lecturers – about apartheid and encouraging them to join the anti-apartheid movement and support the ANC, ideologically and financially. By then we had all joined the ANC: membership had been opened to whites in 1969. When she could, my mother helped in the ANC's London office, and I continued to collect press cuttings about South Africa for ANC news briefings. Because of the censorship of news in South Africa, it was difficult to find out what was really happening. Often I found snippets of news in papers from all over the world rather than from the country itself. What news there was was a constant reminder of how things were getting worse in South Africa – more arrests, tortures and deaths in prison and an increased number of young white men being conscripted to fight Umkhonto we Sizwe and the 'communist threat' on South African borders. We were grateful that John was not among them.

29

My Stars Are Trapped

My sky is all entangled in a web of criss-crossed steel
My stars are trapped within a net of squares and dimmed too soon
My window wire-meshed makes a mockery of the moon.
Within my cell my thoughts turn slow on time's trimmed wheel
And dwell amazed upon these bars that hold us far apart,
And nights remembered lay a magic spell upon this wandering heart.
— FRED CARNESON, PRETORIA LOCAL PRISON, 1969

WHILE WE WERE getting on with life in London, my father was stuck in prison with nothing to look forward to but years of waiting. We could only imagine what it was like for him. He was never allowed to talk or write about his prison conditions: I discovered only later what his life was really like from his prison mates or from his large exercise books, in which he kept carbon copies of all the letters he wrote. He never stopped protesting vigorously, either about the prison conditions or about letters that were censored or that he did not receive. The authorities were constantly trying to make things difficult for him and other prisoners, and Fred frequently sent written complaints to the commanding officer about things like the poor condition of the mailbags they were expected to sew and the guard dog's uninterrupted barking.

Apart from visitors, sending and receiving letters to keep connected was of utmost importance to Fred. He waited every month to receive one 500-word letter, which kept him going for the next few weeks. The authorities continued to take great pleasure in censoring letters, withholding them from him and sometimes confiscating photos and cards. One of the things that he was not allowed to keep was the wedding invitation I sent him. He was so upset that they censored a significant portion of the letter he wrote to us protesting about it. A part of that letter that we were permitted to see read, 'Saw Lynn's wedding invitation, but not permitted to keep. Did not know at time counted for 50 words, unfortunately. Enjoyed photos: eager see others Ida bringing. Have kept one Lynn, Ruth in dining room. Makes lovely splash colour my locker.'

The authorities continued to return or censor all our letters, especially those from John: they knew how important Fred's son was to him and how devastated he was when contact with John was curtailed. In February 1968, Fred wrote a letter questioning the censorship of an 'innocuous' letter of John's.

> Sir,
> Several phrases were deleted from a letter handed to me on the 20th February. The letter was written by my son, John, a sixteen-year-old schoolboy. You may remember that, on a previous occasion, a letter from my son was challenged but subsequently given to me without any deletions. That letter proved, in fact, to be completely innocuous.
>
> From the general content of the letter at present under discussion, it is difficult for me to imagine what my son could possibly have said which justified censorship. The passages read as follows: 'Have sweet girl Reading, but London birds better – Reading is biggest dump. Enjoyed holidays, although somewhat lethargic' – (approximately 8 or 9 words deleted).
>
> The other passage reads: 'Am great fan of Hendrix – wild brilliant electric guitarist – drives me crazy. School group played him – broke window hall! (250 watts sound). Group played modified hymn religious worship!' (Approximately eleven words deleted.)
>
> I should appreciate it, Sir, if you would satisfy yourself as to the nature of the passages deleted, with a view to ascertaining whether the deletions were in fact justified. If you find that they are not justified, I should further appreciate it if I could be given the gist of what my son said.

From time to time, for no reason at all, the authorities decided to reduce the number of letters political prisoners were allowed to receive. My father found the limited communication from us difficult. 'Went through spell several weeks when could do nothing but think of you and children,' he wrote. 'Know shouldn't worry, but do. Can't get enough news. This lack adequate contact family's hardest burden for us.' In 1969, Fred wrote to Mr Senn of the International Red Cross, stating that letters had been reduced from one a month to one every three months, which contravened laws regarding prisoners. Depriving them of contact with their families was just one of many ways the authorities tried to undermine the morale of the prisoners.

Fred's morale when he joined the other political prisoners in Pretoria after having been tortured and then confined in solitary for over thirteen months was very low. His reputation, however, arrived in prison long before he did via a trail of legendary stories about this fighting spirit that had galvanised the Cape with his commitment and temper. It was therefore a shock when Fred arrived at Pretoria Prison a subdued man, one who was unused to speaking to people and terribly ashamed about having broken under interrogation. It was painful for the other political prisoners to witness his condition. He had lost his self-confidence and often doubted his own resolve. Sometimes he was overly dogmatic. The other prisoners didn't know how to handle him as they were trying to cope themselves, but felt that they should be gentle with him because he was so fragile. In the past he would automatically have been on the Prisoners' Committee, but he didn't take up a formal position of responsibility until the last period of his imprisonment. Looking back, fellow inmate Denis Goldberg felt that 'we should have tried to restore his confidence much earlier. In retrospect, life is so full of regrets.'

Fred was not always easy to live with. He would try to bum precious cigarettes off other prisoners because he couldn't make his own ration last. This irritated them. There was a roster for doing the evening meal, which was at 3.30 p.m. One evening it was Fred's turn but he decided to take his coffee and cigarette and lie out in the last of the warmth while others washed up. Denis was furious and told him so. Fred responded, 'I'm going to enjoy my time in the sun.' Fuming, Denis reprimanded him, saying, 'You shouldn't do that while you are on duty.' The next morning Rowley Arenstein told Denis that Fred was extremely upset. Denis replied that Fred had to set a good example because he was a leader. Defending Fred, Rowley told Denis that Fred had been exhausted because he was unable to sleep. Denis then went to Fred and said, 'I am not apologising for my criticism, but for the rudeness. I have rolled some cigarettes. Would you like them?' Fred took them, and peace between the two prisoners was restored.

Because of his heavy smoking, Fred used to cough all night and keep his cellmates awake. Bram Fischer took Fred aside and told him that he was being inconsiderate; he had to stop smoking for the sake of the other prisoners. Listening to him, Fred undertook a huge personal struggle and eventually gave up smoking – to the relief of the other prisoners.

Fred gradually regained his strength – and also his humour. Fortunately, by that time, because of international pressure, the prison officials had been ordered to exercise more care with political prisoners. As Fred regained his confidence, he started being cheeky and getting away with it. Inmate Hugh Lewin was amused by Fred's extensive and witty swearing vocabulary. At Fred's memorial in 2000, he remembered, 'He would shatter the apparent calm of the exercise yard to the delight and entertainment of his watching comrades. The constant battles between Fred and the awful head warder, Barney John du Preez, were explosive, loud and very funny, especially as they usually ended with Freddie in the ascendant, laughing that cunning laugh of his through the side of his mouth while Du Preez stormed in blind fury down the corridor, defeated and speechless. That was Fred's spirit; it did so much to carry us through those horrible years.'

There was another side to Fred unfamiliar to those prisoners who came from outside the Western Cape: he was a focused scholar and he took his family very seriously. As Louis Baker wrote to us when he was released from prison:

> I shared a cell with your father. I had known him before as a tough, hard-swearing bloke with a heart of gold. I now found quite a scholar and I envisaged him addressing a learned Oxford audience in good old Fred language. He was, when I left, taking things in his stride and looking forward tremendously to meeting his family again in England. Of course, the family now includes Charles. Yours was the first wedding of a child of an inmate and we all adopted you as our own. We all celebrated the occasion with coffee and some home-made eats and vowed that Charles would cherish you or else!
>
> Fred never stops talking about his beloved Cape Town and his delightful home there but, knowing his wife, is sure his new home in England will be just as happy. He realises that he is a lucky man to have such a family as his and I know his family is as fortunate in having him in it – of course it depends on whether you are all prepared to forge a peaceful existence once he arrives.

For Fred, small things were immensely significant. He wanted to know everything – what it was like on holiday for Charles, Ruth and me in

Spain and for John in Italy, and a minute-by-minute account of what Sarah was doing. So many things we took for granted were luxuries for him, including oranges:

> Dear Lynn
> Am now 'C' group. No additional privileges, but brings me nearer 'B' group. Two oranges per day last ten days. Fresh taste, scent, wonderful change. Temporary surplus, but hope develop regular feature diet. Long for information, ordinary doings, lives all my family, friends.
> We still are battling right to news. Under consideration. Cut off from events, though prisoners in other prisons get regularly. No reason given. Perhaps reckon ignorance is bliss!
> Another visit Red Cross representative. Fine man. Everyone delighted his interest – also with slab chocolate he brought. Unexpected, not normally permitted treat. Made mine last four days, letting every block melt fraction by tiny fraction in mouth. Mmmmm! Take little bites, otherwise dull routine existence.
> Constant apprehension re loved ones great strain on prisoners: feeling so much happier knowing Mum now able relax from tension, live normal life.

Little treats did not last long. Years and years of being deprived of liberty and loved ones in an extremely hostile environment dominated everything else. One of the greatest punishments, as hinted at in the above letter, was not being allowed any news of the outside world. When former prisoner Norman Levy was released in 1968, he came to see me and described how cut off prisoners felt from the world beyond prison walls. He wrote a report on the news situation, stressing the prisoners' 'mental castration' that resulted from the denial of access to information from the outside world:

> At the Pretoria Local gaol there were no news broadcasts; no daily or weekly newspapers; no magazines or journals containing articles of news value. The receipt of news of any kind was prohibited. Relatives were forbidden to discuss news items of local or international interest at visits and if they attempted to ignore this prohibition, they were threatened with the termination of their visits. Relatives were also prevented from writing about domestic and overseas news as these items were simply censored from their letters …

> The truth is that the policy of the South African Prisons Department (which reflects the attitude of the Commissioner of Prisons and the members of the Cabinet) is to demoralise and isolate political prisoners by deliberately denying them news and news-services: to apply a form of mental castration which will make them unfit to re-enter the world from which they have been isolated for so long. As such, prison policy towards political prisoners in South Africa is neither enlightened nor constructive but unashamedly cruel.

I sent the report to my contacts at Amnesty International and the Red Cross. They took up the matter, but, in spite of many complaints directed at the prisons, by the time my father was released in 1972, the situation remained the same.

Although deprived of outside news, the prisoners took great joy in the news they did receive: that of their families and friends. Letters were treasured and shared by all the prisoners. Visits, as always, were also very important and, while they were sometimes cancelled for no apparent reason, Fred counted the minutes to them: they lifted his periods of depression immensely. Most of the time visits were divided between my aunt Ida, her husband Leo and her children William and Zoë. My mother's brother Solly also visited and occasionally even my maternal grandmother went to see her son-in-law. My father's sisters and brothers, mainly Anthony and his wife Hester, and Hilda, also used to visit him regularly.

Occasionally Fred received unexpected visitors. One of them was Omer Rubin, son of Ralph, my mother's nephew. Ralph found an account of the 1969 visit in a private memoir written by Omer before he died in a sailing accident in 2003.

> Wednesday was visiting day at the Fort in Pretoria, and my uncle, Fred, was allowed one visitor every month for one hour. I was the visitor this July.
>
> I arrived at the gate of the prison with my travel documents as identification and was allowed in by a white police guard dressed in khaki uniform. He said, 'This place is easy to get into but hard to get out of,' maybe implying that I should not get involved in the struggle against apartheid while visiting South Africa.
>
> Uncle Fred was waiting for me in a stone-built room with a small barred window and a warden who was standing in the background. He was very excited and emotional and he gave me a hug and kiss and told

me that he was studying by correspondence to be a company secretary. He also was learning to be a carpenter.

We were watched by a warden to make sure that nothing illegal was done during the visit. Too soon my visit with Fred came to an end. He was happy to see me, for the only contact that he had had with the outside world was his monthly visits with Aunt Sarah's brother Solly and her sister Ida, who were taking turns. He only got one letter a month from his family which was heavily edited by the prison authorities. He missed terribly Sarah, Lynn, John and Ruthie who were in London.

As time passed, Fred found it increasingly difficult to cope with the long periods of incarceration.

2 January 1970

Saturday night, and we're all feeling more restless than usual. Memories of past gaddings about, no doubt. Habit dies hard even in subconscious. And yet I don't feel like going anywhere, even if I could. Perhaps I'm just getting old or perhaps even contemplation of pleasure sours in this place. Find out soon enough in a couple years' time. Forgive me if my letters seem a bit thin; the deadening routine of our days tends to leave us in a state of suspended animation, except for occasional and brief bursts of temper or irritation. Taking everything into consideration, however, our tiny community bears up wonderfully well under its almost complete isolation … No monk in a cloister longs for heaven as much as I long to be home again. Scarce an hour passes without all of you, and that includes Charles, popping into my thoughts.

In London, we did not realise how very hard it was for my father not to have face-to-face contact with us until I received a letter from Ivan Schermbrucker, who had just been released.

Johannesburg
South Africa
17 May 1970

Please forgive me for not writing sooner, but I have been so busy trying to get myself into some sort of order, and having Jill [Ivan's wife] here for a week, we naturally spent that time trying to get to know each other again.

There is one thing that I do feel VERY strongly about, and this is it. I feel very strongly that if it is possible your mother should come out to see Fred as soon as possible. I am told that possibly some sort of Guarantee may be necessary in Sarah's case – if it is deemed necessary that she obtain such a Guarantee, then for goodness' sake let her set about trying to get it immediately. If it will take a long time to get a Guarantee, then I suggest that YOU come in the meantime to see Fred. Will you treat this matter as priority number one?

Fred, like others, had a hard, hard time: the tough ninety-day period, followed by over a year in what was apparently also almost complete isolation had a devastating effect on his nerves. How any fellows survived this sort of ordeal I don't know, and I don't think that they did either.

It has taken Fred long years to recover. I am very pleased however to tell you that when I left prison he was in better shape than he had been for a long time. But it must be borne in mind that as the numbers are getting fewer and fewer, the stresses and strains among the prisoners is going to grow, NOT diminish. With the smaller numbers there, the isolation is growing, and that is deadly. During the last four or five months the already strict censorship has even been increased, and has reached intolerable proportions. Whole pages have once again just been disappearing. It just seems so absolutely senseless. Closer attention than ever must be paid to each prisoner, love and affection expressed through letters, reassurances that they are not forgotten, and above all the importance of visits.

Lynn, honey, if there is anything, just anything that I can do for you and yours just let me know, as long as it does not contravene my bans, etc. 'cause I think that I've had enough.

All my love to you, Ruth, John and your hubby,

Ivan

My mother immediately applied for permission to visit my father but was told that if she re-entered South Africa she would be arrested. We decided that I would take the risk and go instead, using my married name.

I arrived on 9 December 1970 and stayed with Aunt Ida in Johannesburg. It was strange to be back in South Africa, in an unfamiliar town, after having been away from the country for eight years. Ida managed to obtain permission for me to have an ordinary visit as well as a special visit, each an hour long.

My aunt drove me to the prison, where I was led through endless cream-coloured passages to the visiting room. The room was subdivided by two wire-mesh walls into three areas. In the first section I sat at a table with a policeman behind me; in the middle of the room – between my father and me – stood another policeman. There were mesh screens dividing both my father and me from the second policeman. Beyond the two mesh walls and the second policeman, at the other end of the room, sat my father at a table, a policeman standing behind him. We were separated by two wire-mesh screens, two tables and a policeman – yet it was still a relief to see him looking sprightly and well with a new, full set of teeth.

All we were allowed to talk about was family, travel and shows. He asked me questions about John, Ruth and my mother and I talked as fast as I could about how well they were, how busy they were and about a visit to see *Hamlet* at Stratford-Upon-Avon. He talked about his studies and visits from his and my mother's family. Then, for no reason at all, the authorities decided to cut the visit short. Half an hour was over too quickly. We had just started to connect with each other.

The second visit was better. I had managed to get the officials to agree to a 'contact visit' – we sat on either side of a table and held hands. We were also allowed to hug when I left. When I said goodbye I tried to hold back the tears that were running down my cheeks. He turned away so that I could not see his face as he walked back to his cell.

The visits were worth the risk, not just for him, but also for me. I had almost forgotten what he looked like.

Pretoria Local Prison
17 December 1970

Lynn's visit turned Xmas & New Year into sheer delight for me. Just knowing that she was somewhere under the same sky gave me a wonderful feeling of being with the family again. Hard to believe, now, that her last visit was only a week ago. She has grown into a most attractive & assured young woman, with the old Lynn zest for life still very much in evidence – I'm positively basking in paternal pride & egotism ...

While you're slipping and sliding on those ice-bound streets, I'm sweating in nothing but a pair of shorts, constantly brushing away insects which persist in mistaking my shiny bald head for some exotic irresistible lamp. Much rather be under those blankets you mentioned – that's a

warmth I'd certainly revel in. The heat beat me last night. Retired with
letter unfinished. Cooler this evening. Lovely rain. Spent ten minutes at
window, just watching it pelting down.

I imagine I'll find exploring London fascinating for quite a while after
my homecoming. If my resolution holds firm, intend to get up at the
crack of dawn & watch the city awaken. But not too often!

Heard that Bram lost one of his children recently. Please convey my
sympathy. [Bram Fischer's son Paul died not long after his wife Molly
died in a car crash. Fred could not directly contact the family but was
very concerned for them. Bram was devastated.] Also thank them – & the
others – for their good wishes, which are heartily appreciated.

Love to the children & a special husband/lover's embrace for your
own dear self.

The year 1971 was insufferable for Fred. The closer he was to being released,
the longer the waiting felt – and he did not even know if he would be
given an exit permit. 'Unlike Ruth, I'm not yet counting the days,' he wrote,
'though I'm watching the weeks slip away with quiet satisfaction. Permit
myself to dream more often now, but still ration myself to keep the present
bearable. The long haul is not quite over yet.' By April he could no longer
contain his eagerness:

13 April 1971

Saw film, *The Magus*, on Friday. Confusing, though some good scenes of
London. Watched with great interest. London looks an exciting city, full
of characters. As you once remarked, anything seems to go there – minis,
midis & what-have-you. Camera focused (too briefly) on rear of one
mini-clad lass, moving with a jiggle on a bright spring morning. Almost
reconciled me to the thought of that abominable weather. London will
only be the dressing at my real banquet – home. And that's wherever you
are, whether it's a shanty town, an igloo village in the Artic – or a flat
rock overlooking the ocean, with warm sun, warm hearts & warm blood
setting the sparkles on the wild sea waves dancing ever more joyously.

After that flight into fancy, I'm stuck. Look around the cell for
inspiration, but precious little. Pair of socks, one underpants, two
somewhat tattered khaki handkerchiefs (all washed two hours ago),
draped to dry on the grille; no inspiration there, only the thought that I'll
have to wash them again soon. Bookshelf & books – a reminder that my

eyes are no longer what they used to be ... Cupboard – coffee ... I'll break for a cup & see if that will help ... No. It didn't. My mind's washed cleaner than my socks.

Don't mention food to me. Keep alive on the stuff here, but derive small pleasure from it. Dream of a great heaped plate of steaming rice, splashed with tasty gravy, and full of titbits. Also of some of that famous English roast beef.

Letters were still censored, including one from Charles reassuring Fred that it would not be difficult for him to get a job when he came out, even though he was a communist.

> You won't have at all the same difficulties in the UK about getting a job as you did in SA. For a start, you will be an unknown here: you leave public life and re-enter private life the moment you land here. The only people who have heard of you are the SA exiles and *perhaps a very few students of SA politics & history. Further, there is a general feeling that the term 'communist' was used with deplorable looseness in SA ... Even if it were known that your SA sobriquet was 'Carneson the Communist', it wouldn't necessarily cause deep anxiety.* [Italics censored]

As time drew nearer to my father's release, we all started allowing ourselves to believe that it could happen. There was always the danger that he might be re-arrested under the 180-day law.

The Ministry of Justice debated whether or not Fred should be allowed to leave. On 21 December 1971, a paper was issued arguing for and against his departure, excerpts of which appear below.

> **Arguments against allowing Carneson to leave the country**
> The Commissioner of Prisons reported that it is clear that Carneson still has not changed his viewpoint.
>
> Kompol recommends that Carneson be restricted after his release under Group (b) and that he not be allowed to leave the Republic. His wife, Sarah Carneson, also a listed communist, left the Republic on 6 September 1967 with an exit permit and is in England active with unfriendly activities against the Republic. She owns a house that is also a meeting place of expatriate communists and ANC members. Kompol predicts that Carneson's presence will undoubtedly empower the expatriate and communist elements.

Arguments for why Carneson should be allowed to leave the country
His wife and three children are in England and in case he be prevented from joining them, there would certainly be very strong criticism and the Republic would be accused of being a 'Berlin Wall' between family members. It must also not be forgotten that his wife is still involved with critical activities against the Republic and it is felt that the refusal of an exit permit would only fire her on to increase her activities. During 1968 Sir Eric Roll, a former under-secretary of the British Department of Economic Affairs, campaigned for the release of Carneson. Amnesty International also had similar campaigns. If Carneson is restricted, this will cause that attention be focused on him again and he will get the publicity that his kind are always craving.

All in all, the Department recommends that the application for an exit permit not be refused on the condition that Carneson leaves immediately upon his release.

On 30 December 1971, the Minister of Justice approved a recommendation by the Department of Justice to allow Fred an exit permit. From that moment, we counted the days to his release, knowing that it would probably happen.

Pretoria Central Prison
6 January 1972

Sarah darling
Your letter took no time at all to reach me – a good start for the New Year. My thoughts turn more and more insistently to liberty and home, but I'm still not altogether convinced that it's not all just some pleasant dream.

Departure: It's important that we don't get our lines crossed in this connection. Have you already committed yourself to any particular airline? If not, please hold options open. If yes, then I must know full details well before end of this month. Details must include route, as this may possibly affect the types of inoculations required. Time is now much too short for generalisations – you must give me precise information about airline, times departure, arrival, route and all the rest of it.

I'm due out Thurs Feb 24th, but a lot will depend on how much is buttoned up before my release and just how early I'm let out on Thursday.

What would I like for my first meal? Anything! I'll probably be much too excited to notice what I'm eating. Weep tears of joy into the soup, and sprinkle the same over the next course too.

Another few weeks and we shall be able to dispense with all these words on paper. Fifty-one days, to be exact. Start to live again as a man should live – free.

* * *

1 January 1972

Fred my love

A happy New Year to you. I wish for you that this will be the happiest year you have known. I know how sad you will be to leave South Africa, but the life that waits for you here will be as rich and as full as you wish to make it. You will arrive here in time to see in the spring. To me it is the most exciting time of the year. When I first saw Kew I promised myself the joy of bringing you there. I know you will love it as much as I do. We shall also go to Kenwood; it's about an hour's walk from the house and in the summer they have concerts there. The idea is to take a packed supper, sit on the grass and enjoy music. Do not do anything to delay your homecoming. Our need for you is great and we have waited a long time for you.

Shall take week's leave from work and will buy clothes with you – after wearing a uniform for five years, nine months you should be allowed your own choice. It will be fun seeing your reactions to the new fashions. Mong the chocolate-brown Burmese cat is helping to write this letter by sitting on the top half of the pad.

December very busy time. Wish I could have shared Xmas with you.

* * *

9 February 1972

Sarah love

Expect to take delivery of one very weary and almost certainly disorientated husband on Friday 25th. Unless the plane is late, you'll have to be up very early and I hope, for your sake, that it's not too cold.

Ida brought me some smart 'going out' clothes. I tried on the trousers and the jacket this morning. The jacket fits as if made to measure. The trousers are perfect in the length, but a bit too tight in the crotch, around the waist and, I suspect, across the backside as well. I'm not certain if this is the new style or the effect of my expanding waistline. However, they'll serve well enough to get me out of the front door and that's the main thing for the moment. Spent most of yesterday evening writing sentences then scratching them out as soon as written. Seems so much easier to wait until we are together, when we can talk our heads off. I find I can't concentrate now for more than a few minutes at a time. Much too restless. By the time I'm released I won't need that jumbo jet. I'll take off like a rocket, all on my own, like Superman.

The waiting will soon be over.

* * *

18 February 1972

Fred my love
Welcome to freedom. I shall be thinking of you on the 24th, standing outside the prison gates, filling your lungs with air that smells so very differently to the air you have been breathing for so long. Of course you will be very tired when you arrive, so our plans are for you to have all the sleep you want and then to go walking on our heath, and to see people and do things as soon as you feel ready to do so. The only thing the family insists on is that we have you all to ourselves for the first weekend you are home.

The coal miners' strike has resulted in worse power cuts than we had last year; so far the only discomfort we have suffered is not having lights and having to depend on candles, which are now being sold at black-market prices, so I am asking Ida to get some candles for you to bring over.

We have a mass of paper cuttings and journals for you to read, so that you can catch up on things.

Soon we shall be able to talk of so many things.

Your ever loving wife,
Sarah

30

Freedom Is Not Always Easy

The wind of change is blowing through this continent.
— HAROLD MACMILLAN, 1960

AFTER NEARLY SEVEN years in prison, my father was released on 24 February 1972. It had been a long haul: arrest and torture before being charged, a gruelling trial and then a prison sentence of five years and nine months. A total of thirteen months before and after the trial had been spent in solitary confinement. Even after his release the security police made life difficult for him by saying that he could not leave the country because his papers were not in order. He had anticipated this, however, and both he and my mother had arranged for lawyers to back him up, with the help of Fred's family, Hilda, Aggie and Hester, his sister-in-law, who were there to see him off.

The excitement leading up to my father's release was more intense than that of a Rugby World Cup final. He was going to arrive early in the morning of 25 February, the middle of winter. We hardly slept the night before and the whole family was at Heathrow Airport an hour before his flight arrived. Just the family met him there, ready with a bottle of champagne and glasses. There was a hold-up at the airport: the prison authorities in South Africa had failed to give Fred a health clearance, so he had to get it at Heathrow. We waited for three hours.

We all drank the champagne when he arrived, standing in a circle around him just outside the passenger exit gate. It was his first taste of alcohol in seven years. The airport reunion was slightly awkward. After such a long absence my mother was overwhelmed with joy, but his presence also felt quite unreal to her. Seeing him arrive in summer clothes in the middle of a grey, cold drizzling winter was disconcerting and, as I hugged him, I draped a coat over his shoulders. I was aware of how long he had been locked away and that we had all changed; at the same time, though, he was still my familiar dad. Although I knew he would rather be in South Africa, I hoped that he would like London. As we drove through the City to Annington Road, we passed through Eaton Square, one of the most expensive areas of London. The houses were terraced and my father asked, 'Are these the slums we are going through?' He was used to detached houses in South Africa. I realised how strange London would be to him and how much he had to adjust to – not only to freedom but also to a new country and living environment. He was very excited and almost childlike when he arrived at the house. Everything he did he was doing for the first time in seven years – opening cupboards and doors; switching lights on and off; rushing out of the front door; crossing a road. He had never seen a television set. Things like miniskirts, discos, bistros and duvets were totally new to him.

After my father's arrival in London, there was a short honeymoon period where we joyously celebrated being together again. All the old comrades came to say hello, and Fred was elated and always joking. There were times, however, when he became withdrawn. Ben Turok was shocked when he first saw my father in London. 'He was a tired man,' he commented. 'He had taken a lot of punishment and it showed. He was not as ebullient as before. I think he lost some of his former sparkle. In fact, he was overwhelmed and totally confused. He had been locked up for years with practically no news of the outside world.'

One day my father asked me, 'What is this thing, an MCP?' He told me that he had opened the front door to an attractive young woman who had shouted at him, 'Don't be an MCP!' I told him that an MCP was a 'male chauvinist pig'. 'A what?' he said. I had to explain the detailed history of the woman's liberation movement in England. He would turn and gape with amazement when he saw women wearing miniskirts walk past. I suggested that, even though he thought they were beautiful, he should not stare at young women with his mouth open or he would be called not only an MCP but a DOM – a dirty old man. He laughed, reminding me that he was catching up on a lot of lost time: 'No harm in looking.'

Two weeks after my father's arrival, he proudly showed off the carpentry skills he had learnt in prison by making a pine double bed for him and my mother. He spent hours and hours reading piles of newspapers and journals, some Italian, French and Russian, exclaiming about the comprehensive news coverage that you could get in Europe. He also spent a lot of time in front of the television. It took him three weeks to get out of the house to start exploring London. His first trip on the London Underground astounded him. He was amazed, asking me in wonderment, 'Are you sure it's safe to be so far under the earth? What a marvellous feat of engineering!' When the train stopped and the voice said 'Mind the gap', he leapt off the train before the sliding doors closed, like a small child.

It was not easy for him. He was trying hard to take up his position as head of the family and to adjust to normal life outside prison walls. During the first few months I would be talking to him about ordinary domestic things and he would suddenly stare into space, his face completely blank, as if he were not there at all. Sometimes this would last for up to twenty minutes at a time. Apparently he had also done this when he came out of solitary confinement. We were all very worried. Perhaps therapy or counselling would have helped, but at that time things like that were not readily available. It took about four months before it became easier for him to be fully present with us. He still woke up at five every morning, surprised at the lack of light and dark skies.

In April, the beginning of spring, Sarah took Fred to Paris. 'I promised Fred that after his release we would do Paris in the spring,' she said to us. My mother funded the trip with £250 that had been sent by Bram Fischer's lawyers. A letter dated 16 February 1972 had arrived informing her that Bram had won a Lenin Peace Prize in 1966 and that he wanted some of the money he had won to go to her. 'He particularly asked ... that you be sent this money as a small token of his admiration for you – for how, throughout these many years, you have, with single courage and strength, stood by Fred and nurtured your family. The money, he says, is for you personally, to do with as you like – either to splash before Fred arrives or to ensure that you can have a good holiday together when he does arrive. It comes with Bram's warmest love and admiration, together with that of everybody at Pretoria Local.' My father was tearful when he read the letter.

My parents arrived in Paris at about four o'clock in the afternoon. Exhausted, they fell into a deep sleep, waking at 3.00 a.m. Later that day they went walking until they were tired, and spent many days getting onto the first bus they saw and sitting until it went to its destination and returned to the place they had left from. Their best day in France was at Versailles, where they sat on the grass and enjoyed a picnic of fresh French bread, Brie and a bottle of good red wine. They came back delighted, saying that they had had a wonderful time. That trip, however, marked the end of the honeymoon period.

When my parents returned from Paris, Sarah told Fred that he had to find a job. 'I'm tired of you sitting on your backside every day while I go out to work,' she complained. 'I can't keep supporting you forever.' He found a job at an insurance company, where his boss, Michael, underpaid and bullied him and kept threatening to sack him. Sarah told Fred that Michael's behaviour was unacceptable and that Fred should tell him to stop it, so Fred, in a typical flare of temper, shouted at his boss. Michael suddenly began to behave himself. Fred found working in a strange environment and travelling by tube every day a strain after the regimented life in prison, and he was often tired and irritable.

It soon became obvious that there was considerable tension between my parents. They argued and fought constantly. I later asked my mother what it was that they fought about. 'It could be anything,' she replied. 'Anything would set him off and he would go scarlet and lose his temper. One day I was cooking spaghetti Bolognese and he helped himself to some, picking up the salt. I warned him, telling him to taste it before he put salt on. He ignored me and poured salt all over the food. He couldn't eat it, so he threw all the plates at the wall and smashed them. It was a terrible mess. But he never, ever touched me. He knew that if he lifted a finger to me, I would throw him out.'

One day Mary Turok came to collect Sarah to take her to the market. When she came in through the front door, she saw a huge hole in the passage wall. Mary asked what had happened, and Sarah told her that they had had a row; my father had torn a heavy central-heating panel off the wall and thrown it down the stairs. Seeing the expression on Mary's face, my mother decided that they should limit their arguments to Saturday mornings. From then on, while they were cleaning the house, they used to scream and shout at each other until the clock struck midday. This was the signal for them to stop their arguments and go off amicably around the corner to the pub for lunch.

At one stage, early on, they refused to talk to each other for almost three months. Although I was sorry for them, I found them quite amusing; they were behaving like teenagers who were having a tempestuous love affair. At the time I was in hospital with sarcoidosis. When they came to visit me, they sat on opposite sides of the bed and refused to speak to each other. 'Tell Sarah that I need to go to the doctor. I have bad headaches,' Fred would say. Sarah would reply, 'Tell Fred that I gave him the phone number of the doctor and that he must phone and make an appointment himself.' I would repeat these messages in a totally exaggerated way and we would all laugh. They would go off looking ashamed – but both were too stubborn to make peace. A small thing had triggered off their refusal to talk to each other. They had both been at an ANC meeting, when my father had told Sarah to go into the kitchen with the other women to make the tea. My mother had replied that if he wanted tea he could go and make it himself. Sarah was not altogether surprised that things were difficult: 'We had lived different lives for many years. We had to get used to the fact that each of us had changed. We had to get to know each other almost from the beginning again. We had huge problems trying to understand what the other thought. We had a lot to sort out, and I didn't really realise how confused and in what a bad state he was in when he first came to London.'

Things started to improve slowly after Fred found himself a better and more suitable job. On the merits of his outstanding qualifications as a chartered secretary, he had been offered a job in the administrative division of the National Union of Teachers (NUT). He enjoyed working there immensely, and remained there until 1985.

One day, when I visited my parents, I was astonished to see them laughing together about a joke my father had heard. He had his arm around Sarah and was teasing her like old times. I asked them what had prompted their sudden reconciliation. As company secretary for the NUT, my father had had to go all over Britain to various conferences. He had recently been to a conference in Jersey that had lasted from a Thursday to a Saturday. On the first evening, he had phoned Sarah and said, 'I am with all these strange people that I don't know. I feel so lonely. Please can you come?'

Sarah got on the next plane and stayed with him during the conference. They spent a wonderful weekend together in Jersey, which cemented their new relationship. 'That's when we got close to each other again,' Sarah told me. Fred had hired a car and they had gone exploring. While out one day some ducks had found them. 'We were standing looking at the view and I felt something pecking at my trousers. When we looked down, there were these ducks making a big fuss around us. They walked forward, looked back at us, walked forward again and then walked back to us quacking loudly. I told Fred that I thought they wanted us to follow them. We followed the ducks down a path, and at the end of the path was a café. The café owner said, "Oh, the ducks have brought you. They are always bringing people because they know they'll get fed." We had tea there with fresh scones, cream and jam and threw the crumbs to the ducks to pay them for their effort.'

As their relationship improved, my parents were able to talk more freely to each other. It was comforting to be able to share the problems involved in having two teenage children. Fred helped my mother to deal with the lame-dog friends Ruth brought home. 'There was this American drop-out who stank, and who had a dog that smelt like rotting fish,' Fred remembered. 'He never washed his clothes and used to air his socks on a tree. He said that he was a Vietnam War resister. He always came at meal times to scrounge so eventually we asked him to read a newspaper while we ate. Ruth told me that I was mean, but I was simply firm.' Fred checked up on the 'resister' and discovered that he wasn't in fact an anti-war campaigner, but just a bum who had run away from his father. 'Here was this stinking man and stinking dog,' recounted Fred. 'I asked him if he was working. He said, "No, I don't approve of the system." So I said, "Then you won't approve of us disapproving of you. Go and have a bath, get a job and then come back." I told Ruth that she could do better than that. What she said to me was just as strong as the smell of the dog!'

Fred missed his prison comrades terribly. 'In conditions like that you get very close to people, you know,' he would say sadly. The first thing he did when he arrived in London was see Denis Goldberg's wife, Esmé. We took a photo of Esmé, and Fred and I sent it to Denis. A kind warder showed it to Denis, but told him that he couldn't keep it, as no photos of former prisoners were allowed. Fred had arranged for me to write 500 words a month to Denis under my married name. 'It will be a pity for you to get out of the habit!' he said to me. Denis and I wrote letters to each other for twelve years. I used to share my problems with him and he would give me well-considered, wise advice. My father taught me to write about news in code. Occasionally we got it right. More often than not, though, the prisoners at the other end got it wrong. On one occasion, I wrote Denis a letter about Greek-island hopping and my visits to the theatre. From this, Denis and the other prisoners concluded that student uprisings were taking place in the Western Cape – when in fact I had simply been writing about island hopping and the theatre.

Fred spent hours writing letters to comrades who were in exile, particularly to those who were finding it difficult. Moses Kotane, a lifelong communist and ANC leader, was in Moscow. He hated the cold and, because he did not speak Russian, felt even more isolated. Fred and Sarah went to see him in Moscow in 1974 when he was terminally ill in hospital. His last letter arrived a week after he died. His final words to them were, 'I feel so lonely.'

As soon as Fred settled down, it did not take him long to become politically active again. He teamed up with Brian Bunting and other members of the South African Communist Party. Although he was not uncritical of the Soviet Union, he still believed that it was important to toe the Party line and reluctantly agreed to the expulsion of those who criticised it. Ben Turok was one of the people who was expelled. He and Mary were dissatisfied with how the Party was operating, and Ben had spent some money in good faith through an organisation in Canada – but without asking permission. Brian Bunting saw to it that he was not only expelled from the SACP, but could not join the Communist Party in England. 'I was extremely upset,' Ben said. 'I was a total outcast. I was disgusted and terribly depressed.' He talked to Fred about it and, while Fred understood Ben's point of view, he explained to Ben that he couldn't do much. It was too important for him to maintain his own links with the Party.

Life settled into a routine for Fred and Sarah. Because they were both working, they could afford to buy a second-hand car, in which they loved exploring the English countryside. They walked in the country almost every Sunday, and lived a life filled with work, marriage and companionship, family and, of course, continued activism.

31

The Struggle Continues

Anti-apartheid activities took up almost all of my parents' spare time. The struggle in South Africa, armed and civil, was intensifying: there were more personal, media and organisational bannings and restrictions; there were thousands of arrests, tortures and deaths in detention; and there were clashes between people armed with stones and petrol bombs and the police, who were armed with batons, bullets, tear gas and whips. Hundreds of thousands of black people were forcibly removed to areas where there was no food or work, and activists were being systematically assassinated by what was believed to be a covert section of the extreme right wing of the South African Police.

Strikers grew in numbers, and there was continuous social unrest and mass demonstrations, indicating the increasing opposition inside the country. Black schoolchildren began to protest against being schooled in Afrikaans and were arrested, tortured and shot down. In 1976, Soweto schoolchildren staged a revolt that turned into an uprising in which hundreds were killed and thousands injured. Black students boycotted lectures and increased violence caused more schools and colleges to close down.

Thousands of MK cadres were being trained in the Soviet Union, Mozambique and Tanzania in the mid-seventies. Bombings of police stations, installations and other targeted buildings were escalating. The South African Bureau of State Security (BOSS) adopted new schemes to allow the government to take even more draconian measures, including attacks on activists and exiles all over the world.

Not a day went by when we did not think of friends who were still in jail or working underground. Sarah used to send comrades like our beloved Dora Tamana money when she could. Dora would write back to my mother via her sister, who was also in exile, to tell us how she was doing. Fred and Sarah often had meetings at their home and at those of other exiles. Most of us met once a year for the ANC bazaar at the Camden Town Hall to raise money. It was a little like the old community again, but in a different country, with many missing.

Fred and Sarah were active on multiple fronts. Both worked in the ANC office, campaigning for sanctions against South Africa, helping to organise speakers for mass demonstrations against the apartheid regime, planning fund-raising events and playing a prominent part in group rallies. I helped when I could, and we all took part in demonstrations and vigils outside South Africa House. I continued to collect press cuttings for ANC news briefings that went into the ANC journal *Sechaba*.

Fred also kept the books for the London office of the ANC. From the time I started working, I donated 10 per cent of my salary to the ANC. One day Fred came to me and told me that I was donating far too much, and that he was worried that some of my hard-earned money was being used as 'unnecessary expenses'. I was upset by this but decided to continue with the donations as money was badly needed for the struggle and I hoped that most of it would find its way into the right hands. It was not an appropriate time to make a fuss.

During that period, we met a number of young black MK militant activists who were in exile in London or passing through. Many of them were wary of white people, despite the fact that a number of white people were heavily involved in the struggle. All of these young militants had pseudonyms so that their real identities remained concealed, and many were given temporary but legitimate jobs as a cover. Bongi, one of these people, met Fred and Sarah in London when she was working for the South African Congress of Trade Unions but was still involved in MK activities. She realised that Fred and Sarah were very different from average white South Africans: they treated everyone as equals. Bongi was touched when at an ANC fund-raising meeting they suggested that the comrades sell their own unneeded belongings. She felt that 'they were more like black Africans, truly part of the face and identity of the struggle. Because of this, young black people listened to their political thinking and advice with great respect.'

Fred became the international representative of the South African Communist Party. In that role he raised large sums of money from Communist Parties all over the world, not only for the SACP but also for the ANC. Wolfie Kodesh, another sterling activist, said, 'Fred was very quiet about it but we knew how much he did.' As international representative Fred was able to use his knowledge of languages; he was asked to represent the Party at conferences and other functions in France, Spain, Portugal and Outer Mongolia, and he relished these exciting travel opportunities.

One evening my parents were coming to my house in London for dinner. Fred phoned and asked if we could provide supper for one more person from Mongolia – a communist country at the time. He arrived with the Mongolian ambassador – an extremely elegant gentleman wearing the latest Italian cashmere woollen suit. It was winter and extremely cold, so my father said, 'Comrade, why don't you invite the driver to join us?' My father rushed out to the street and brought in a very burly, short, wild-looking man. Pulling out a chair for him, he said, 'Comrade, come and sit with us. Here is your chair.' My father was completely oblivious to the fact that both the ambassador and the chauffeur were acutely embarrassed by this. Fred's firm belief in the equal value of all workers meant that he treated everyone in the same way, regardless of rank. It did not occur to him that any communists might think differently.

In October 1973, Fred was elected onto the Executive Committee of the Anti-Apartheid Movement. Mike Terry was Executive Secretary. For over fifteen years, every month, twice a month, they went to Anti-Apartheid Movement Executive meetings and Trade Union Committee meetings. Afterwards, they, together with Vella Pillay, another exiled South African, would take the Northern Line back to East Finchley. Mike treasured these meetings, but often he emerged from a meeting angry and frustrated by the way the discussion had gone. 'It was Fred's calm words that often helped me to put problems into perspective,' he later said.

Fred was also chairman of the Anti-Apartheid Trade Union Committee. He worked hard over many years to build up trust, credibility and confidence with the British Trade Union Movement. At first many unions were resistant to applying economic sanctions to South Africa. At most early meetings there were more apologies than people present, but Fred was not deterred. He was always willing to explain the South African trade union situation to interested unionists. He worked closely with Lord Bob Hughes, a Labour MP and well-known trade unionist who was then Chair of the Anti-Apartheid Movement Executive Committee. Bob appreciated Fred's attitude that all South Africans should be free to share in the riches of that wonderful country. Although most of the time Fred was positive and cheerful, he confided to Bob that he survived exile only because of the immense love that Sarah and his children gave him. Bob told us that he had been very moved when Fred said to him, 'The binding of my family keeps me going at times when I am almost at the point of despair.'

Fred and Sarah were so politically active that it was difficult to believe they also had to hold down full-time jobs. Fred seldom brought his politics into his work and he had a reputation among his colleagues for being highly professional. He was remembered by his staff for his terrible sense of humour and love of playing practical jokes – like putting whoopee cushions on their chairs and then laughing like a hyena when they unwittingly sat down.

On April Fool's Day one year, Fred's secretaries decided to get their own back. Every day for lunch Fred ate a tin of fruit salad while sitting at his desk, so, mischievously, they found a tin of baked beans that was the same size and swapped its label with that of Fred's tin of fruit. At lunch time, Fred took out the tin, opened it and, when he saw baked beans instead of fruit, picked it up and left the room without saying a word. He marched to Marks & Spencer, where he had bought the fruit salad, and complained. The mortified staff apologised profusely and compensated him by giving him two tins of fruit salad. On his return to the office, he put the two tins on his desk and told his secretaries what had happened. They fell about laughing. My father indignantly exclaimed, 'I don't know what you think is so funny about this.' They then explained the joke to a reddening Fred – he had been well and truly fooled.

Sarah continued to work for the *Morning Star*. She became 'Mother of the Chapel', the equivalent of shop steward, and fought for better wages and working conditions, which meant that she could do what she most loved – organising. People frequently used to go to her with their personal or marital problems and often went away feeling better, armed with good common-sense suggestions. She was always cheerful but could be stubborn and tenacious as well. At the *Morning Star* she met and became great friends with Joe Berry, a co-worker, and his wife. The Berrys became travelling companions of Fred and Sarah's, and they spent happy holidays together, going with them to countries in the Soviet Bloc. Joe constantly nagged Fred and Sarah to write their autobiographies, to which Sarah would reply, 'I'm too busy living for the future to be wasting time on the past.'

The birth of my son, Simon, on 12 August 1973, was one of the happiest times of my life and, for a short time, of my marriage. My parents were delighted. They used to take Simon for walks on Hampstead Heath, which was close to where I lived, but Simon loved being at home and would kick up a terrible fuss when they took him out. My mother joked, 'Fred, he takes after you; he is so active.' My father laughed, 'I hope that doesn't mean he has inherited some of my worst characteristics!'

At the time I was halfway through an MPhil about the value of drama in education, and I used to walk around the house or on Hampstead Heath talking to Simon about my ideas for my thesis. He would look at me as if he understood and then he'd chuckle and throw his toys out of the pram.

Unfortunately, my happiness was short-lived. On a grey, icy day in November, when Simon was four months old, I found Charles's diary on my desk. Curiosity got the better of me and I was shocked to find out that my husband was not satisfied with our relationship and that something was terribly wrong with our marriage. I was devastated. From then on I was in tears most of the time and was very worried that my deep distress was affecting our baby. Charles and I decided that we would give the marriage eighteen months before agreeing on a divorce. He had enough time to bond deeply with Simon before his publishing company, Longman, sent him to Nigeria on a two-year contract.

My parents did their best to help. My mother was able to make me laugh when one Saturday morning she phoned and said, 'When I got out of the bath this morning, the whole house smelt of manure. I looked out of the window and there was a huge heap of manure in the front garden! A man had come by with a horse and cart saying that he was selling good garden manure. Fred bought the whole cartload.' Everything was full of manure. For weeks, goodwill was spread in gardens all over my parents' neighbourhood.

Fred was often too preoccupied to remember things like anniversaries and presents. He would remember at the last moment that it was Sarah's birthday and exclaim at the office, 'Oh my God, it's my wife's birthday.' He would buy a bunch of flowers on his way home. Sometimes, regardless of whether it was Sarah's birthday or not, he would surprise her. He knew she loved mangoes, but in London they were exorbitantly expensive. One day, he got his secretary to decorate a box and put two beautifully wrapped mangoes in it. He presented it to my mother with a flourish: she was delighted. His everyday surprises and acts of love more than made up for his forgetfulness about birthdays and anniversaries.

In September 1974, I was offered directorship of the Schools Council Drama Project, a three-year contract to explore what children learnt through drama. I found a nanny for Simon and, because I was director, I was able to work flexible hours so that I could be with him as much as possible.

That same year, when my parents came to visit one day, they looked very happy and excited. 'What's the good news?' I asked. Fred had received an embossed letter from the Soviet Union. It was an invitation to Fred and Sarah from the Soviet government, asking them to come on holiday in the USSR as VIPs. They were thrilled, and accepted enthusiastically. The first place they visited was an opulent health spa, where, to their puzzlement, a doctor was available to look after the guests. After a while, they realised why this had been organised. On the first evening at the 'health' spa, they sat down to a sumptuous meal that started with caviar and champagne and continued with multiple courses. In between each course an official stood up and made a speech, ending with a toast, after which he downed a full glass of vodka. Sarah, who seldom drank, had to be carried home. 'That was what the doctor was really for,' they agreed ruefully. On the same holiday they both took the opportunity to have a full medical check-up. A gynaecologist discovered that a number of things were wrong with Sarah. After the doctors had presented her with various options, including surgery, Sarah decided that, as she had lived with the problems for so long, she could go on doing so for another week or two before dealing with them when she got back to London. She refused their offer to operate on her and continued with her holiday.

Fred and Sarah also visited other Eastern Bloc countries – East Germany and Romania. On arrival at their hotel in Romania, they decided to go exploring, forgetting to ask the name and address of the hotel. Later, when they realised that they were hopelessly lost, they found a young policeman who understood a little English. They explained who they were and what their situation was, and the policeman said, 'Follow me.' After half an hour, he deposited them at the hotel. Sarah, her experience of policemen overwhelmingly negative, was surprised by his farewell gesture: 'He kissed my hand – the first time I have ever been kissed by a policeman.'

The next morning they came down for breakfast and saw a jar of chillies on the table. Fred tried one. He said nothing but quickly drank two glasses of water. Joe Berry, who was also an official guest, asked my father whether he recommended the chillies. 'They're excellent,' said Fred. 'Try one.' Joe put one in his mouth and chewed. His eyes immediately started to stream: he cried for half an hour. Choking and weeping, he told Fred that he would get him back. Fred laughed until both of them were crying with mirth.

My parents could not understand Romanian customs and practices. One day they went for a long walk on the beachfront. They passed the men's section: they were all nude. They passed the women's section: they were all nude. The family section was also all nude. In their swimming costumes, Fred and Sarah felt over-dressed. Later, they were taken to a health spa, where they took off their clothes and covered themselves with mud before using the separate entrances designated for men and women to the dam, where they met in the middle. By this time, the mud had washed off. Sarah was puzzled, recalling the nude beach scenes they had witnessed: 'Why separate entrances?' she wondered.

Both of them loved exploring communist countries together. They were joyfully making up for the many years that they had been separated, when they had been prevented from travelling wherever they wanted.

While Fred and Sarah were exploring different parts of the world, Ruth had met Ed Suleiman, who lived with his mother, Julie, around the corner from where Ruth, Sarah and Fred lived in Annington Road. Although Ed had been born in England, his parents were Turkish and, while they were not strict observers of Islam, they had a Muslim background. Ed and Ruth struck up a friendship that developed into a partnership. Ruth moved in with Ed, and on 7 March 1975 Omri, Ruth's first son, was born. Fred, Sarah and Julie were pacing up and down in Julie's living room from five o'clock in the morning until mid-afternoon, when Omri arrived. Ruth was very calm throughout the birth, and Sarah was extremely proud of her, saying, 'You're just like a peasant, giving birth like that!' When Fred came home from work the next day, he brought Ruth a big bunch of flowers; he had already bought everyone at work a cream cake to celebrate.

When Ruth was strong enough, she, Ed and Omri went north to Sunderland, where Ed was studying. They lived there for a couple of years, during which time Adam, Ruth's younger son, was born, on 31 March 1977. Ed was very busy with his studies, so Ruth had to take care of the babies largely by herself. Fred and Sarah tried to visit her as much as possible, but to stay in contact Ruth would go out in the freezing rain with a handful of coins to phone them from a phone booth. When Ruth and Ed came back from Sunderland, they lived with Fred and Sarah for about six months. Ed was a community organiser. As my parents only had two bedrooms, Ruth and her family stayed in one of the bedrooms. The house was somewhat crowded, but Fred and Sarah didn't mind; they really enjoyed the children: Omri was a lively toddler and Adam a noisy little baby. That year a happy and chaotic Muslim–atheist Christmas took place and Julie's little dog ate the turkey.

In September 1977, the drama project I was working on came to an end. Our book *Learning Through Drama* was the culmination of hours of discussion all over the country. It was a great success. I was able to spend time with Simon, who was three at the time and asking 'why' about everything. One evening I was reading him a book called *Mr Happy* when he asked me, 'Mum, what is the mind?' I tried to explain, but he said, 'No, that's the brain; what's the mind?' Simon and I used to take frequent walks on Hampstead Heath, sometimes with his friends. I would watch them rushing from swings or splashing in the bright-blue paddling pool. But Simon missed Charles and it broke my heart when Charles came back to visit and Simon would put our hands together, trying to get us to hold hands again.

When my marriage broke down, I went for counselling and group therapy for two years before I finally got divorced in 1980, after having been married for twelve years. I also learnt a technique called co-counselling, which enabled two people not trained in psychology to help each other work through their problems. I co-counselled with a man whose marriage was also breaking up. This helped both of us deal with difficult issues and regain much lost self-confidence. I found the world of therapy and personal growth enriching and it led me to a deeper understanding of myself and others. At the time, I was waking up most mornings feeling extremely sad and anxious. In 1978, I went to see a psychotherapist called Mavis Klein. She listened and said, 'Have you ever spoken to your parents?'

'You mean actually talk to them face to face?'

'Yes,' she confirmed. She suggested that I write a list of events in my past when I had felt scared or lonely and share them with my parents.

My parents had invited me for supper that night. I said, 'I've got something to share with you.' I read out my list. Both parents were speechless, and then we all burst into tears. We sat on their settee and they put their arms around me. My mother said, 'If we had considered the suffering that we were causing you children, we could never have done what we did.' Both of my parents then told me that, after Ruth had broken down, they had had sleepless nights, plagued with guilt over how much their children had suffered. They knew, though, that unless they fought apartheid, our lives would not have been secure either. I told them that I understood, and that I would not have wanted them to do things differently.

A heavy burden had been lifted from me, as I had been able to share some of my pain with my parents. That evening, I felt emotionally closer to them than I had ever felt before. I went home with a sense that I had been deeply acknowledged. All of us had been able to talk for the first time about the terrible emotional stress we had all been through.

For years after that, Fred and Sarah spent an enormous amount of time babysitting and helping Ruth, John and me take care of our children. They put themselves out to such an extent that, three years after this event, John, Ruth and I all felt, 'They must stop now. They have done enough. We must tell them that they have done enough.' Something had been healed and completed for all of us.

32

Unsafe in a Safe Place

ONE DAY, IN 1981, when Fred and Sarah arrived at the ANC office, they saw a boy aged about eighteen slumped at a table with his hands on his head. 'What's the matter?' Sarah asked, approaching him, but he could not answer; he just shook his head. 'Are you worried about your family back home?' He nodded. 'You know, we know what it is like, from our own children.' Fred put his arms around the boy and Sarah gave him a glass of water. 'Any time you want to talk about things, you can come and see us.' For the young in exile, the ANC was not just a political party; it was a very big family, and Fred and Sarah often acted like foster-parents to young South Africans who had no family in London. Like many other exiled groups, we were a close-knit community. Although ANC units were scattered all over London, almost everyone knew everyone else, especially as we held fund-raising parties at each other's houses and congregated at important meetings. Most exiles also found their way at some point to the ANC's London office at 63 Rathbone Street in Islington.

At branch meetings, Fred and Sarah taught the young generation the theory and history of the struggle and why, for South Africa, negotiations were more appropriate than a revolution if civil war was to be avoided. At such meetings they explained why it was crucial that the Party and the ANC continued to bring all races together to bring about change. They reminded the comrades that white workers had played a prominent part in the formation of the SACP. It was important that a new South Africa should be a non-racist multiracial society where people lived in peace and harmony with each other.

Because of his Treason Trial, MK and prison background, Fred held a high status with the young black people based in London. Sarah was also deeply respected, viewed as a strong person who could stand up and fight in her own right. Her young comrades in London described her as 'a small, short lady with a big heart and a big brain'. She made sure that the struggle of women – the triple oppression of those who were female, black and working class – was never forgotten, bringing it up at almost every meeting.

In the early eighties Fred met and worked closely with a young black militant named George Johannes. George and Fred worked at a Communist Party office at Inkululeko publishers in Archway. They used to express their views on the role of the working class and the unions, and the theoretical differences and similarities between the ANC and the CP. Fred believed that, although the working class was the leading force, in South Africa's struggle for democracy it would be the alliances between white and black and rich and poor that would strengthen the working class for political change.

When Fred and George sat over cups of coffee, they discovered that they had quite a few things in common. Like Fred's father Anthony, George's father had been a railway labourer. They had both been brought up as Catholics, at which Fred had a good laugh and said, 'You know, Catholics make the best communists.'

'Why?' George asked, curious.

'Because Catholics have the Jesuit in them,' replied Fred.

George nodded, agreeing: 'I understand what you mean.'

We were aware that the South African security police were working undercover in cities that harboured active exiles. These agents followed people around, trying to find out what they were up to. It is not surprising, then, that when Fred recruited George into the SACP, it was done covertly. One day Fred phoned George and said, 'I need to talk to you. It's very important; you have to come now.'

George immediately left to meet Fred at a designated bench in Highgate, looking to the right and to the left and behind him to establish if he was being followed. When they met up, Fred said to him: 'You've been accepted into the Communist Party. You are going to be on probation.'

'For how long?' George asked.

'Until you are no longer on probation,' Fred replied with a smile.

Our halcyon days of feeling safe in London were coming to an end: things were growing tense in the British capital. In addition to their activities in London, we knew that BOSS was assassinating activists in other countries. Nevertheless, it came as a terrible shock in 1982 when we heard that Ruth First, prominent political activist and writer who had been a reporter at the *Guardian* and *New Age* and was married to Joe Slovo, had been killed by a letter bomb in Maputo. When I was a child, my father used to take me to visit the Slovos in Johannesburg whenever he was collecting money for the paper. Ruth would allow me to totter around in her high-heeled shoes – she loved Italian shoes and had a large collection. Because of her, I developed a love of Italian shoes myself. I thought Ruth was very beautiful; I wished that I would grow up to look like her. I was horrified when Albie Sachs described how, after the bomb, 'her body and legs were intact but her elegant, strong face was blotted out'. My father was devastated by her death, but became even more determined to 'stop those bastards as soon as possible'.

In February 1982, Mendi Msimang, the ANC London representative, called a meeting. He told us that Scotland Yard had got hold of a list of leaders targeted for assassination in London and that family members could also be targeted. Both of my parents were on the list as 'Enemies of the Apartheid State'. Mendi briefed us to check all letters in case there were letter bombs and, if anything seemed suspicious, we were to notify the police. We were also told to be extremely careful about who came to the front door. By that stage I was running a business from home, so this proved a real challenge, especially as my English staff did not understand why, suddenly, I had to check all the mail, including junk mail.

On 14 March, after working hard over the weekend to make placards and leaflets in preparation for a big anti-apartheid march during the Commonwealth Conference – 'Free Political Prisoners', 'Sanctions Against Apartheid Really Work', 'Say No to Torture in South Africa' – about 130 of us stood in the drizzle outside the ANC office in Rathbone Street, Islington, with our banners and ANC flags. We started moving off, toyi-toying and chanting 'Free Nelson Mandela'. We had just arrived at Hyde Park to join a massive anti-apartheid rally when we heard a loud explosion from somewhere nearby. About half an hour later we were told that there had been a bomb and the ANC office in Islington had been ripped apart. If there had been people inside or on the street in front of it, they would not have survived. Shocked, we realised that we would have to be even more vigilant. It was terrifying to think that, had we left just half an hour later, most of us might not be alive today.

The violence of the South African regime had spread overseas – even to a relatively safe city like London. Our secret ANC ward meetings were organised by word of mouth, and many of us, including me, were nervous all the time. Fred and Sarah made it clear that we should not be blackmailed or intimidated by the oppressive Nationalist regime. We should remember why we were in the struggle. 'We must never give up,' they told us. 'We must continue irrespective of what the regime is doing. Apartheid will fail and we must never stop fighting for what is right.'

I had my own reasons for refusing to give up. Writing letters to Denis Goldberg every month was a constant reminder for me that there were political prisoners still suffering in jail. Writing these letters was not always easy. At the time I felt that my own life was pretty boring and tedious, consisting of nothing but work and household chores. Spending time with Simon and sometimes his friends in the evenings was precious to me – a favourite television show of ours was the science-fiction series *Doctor Who*. I wrote to Denis and asked him if I was boring him with my mundane life. I told him that I felt so guilty because I was free while he was not. 'Please don't feel guilty because I'm here and you're there,' he wrote back. 'To hear from you is to make it easier for me. Really 'n truly, it is a privilege to share, however vicariously, in your life. The ups and the downs are equally important to me.'

Like a few other prisoners, Denis was, after so many years of captivity, offered a reprieve – something that was among the early signs of change in the government. Denis thought very hard about it. Using 'divorce' as a code, he wrote to me asking about negotiations for his release. The letter was primarily for my father and Brian Bunting, as Denis wanted their opinions and blessings to leave prison. My father discussed it with other members of the South African Communist Party and gave me a reply: 'Under no circumstances should he agree to his release. It would serve the cause better if he remained in prison.'

My father said that he was very sorry for Denis, who had had a hard time. 'You need to understand that one person's suffering can not be compared with the suffering of the masses,' he told me when I challenged the decision of the SACP committee for its being unnecessarily heartless. I demanded a reason for wanting to keep him in prison and said to them, 'He has already been there for almost half his life!' Fred gave me an explanation: the problem was that the guys in prison had no idea of what was happening in South Africa, or abroad, at the time. The Nationalist government was beginning negotiations with the ANC, and the ANC was determined to get what it wanted. Nelson Mandela had also been offered a release but had refused to leave prison unless certain national demands were met. This approach was adopted as ANC policy for all political prisoners. My father was unhappy about the situation with Denis and couldn't sleep for many nights, hoping that Denis understood that this was not just my father and Brian's decision. I was torn. On the one hand I desperately wanted Denis to have his freedom. On the other, I understood the strategic reasons for their view that he should not leave just yet.

Denis wrote back the following month, again using the metaphor of my divorce.

Pretoria Central Prison
17 October 1984

Your wish to do something about the term(s) of your settlement yet not to do anything contrary to your principles can, I see, create a dilemma. It seems to me that principles, while individually stable, exist in a hierarchy of values/norms. To meet practical situations everyone, but everyone (alone or together), rearranges that value hierarchy. Dilemmas and disputes thus arise over the question of which value is to have priority in a given situation (which must also be related to its wider context).

There is a widely held belief in an alternative approach to your situation, i.e. other than the one you describe. That widely held opinion appears to contradict your conclusion. This appearance, in my opinion, arises from your postulating the 'wrong' value as the absolute term against which all others are to be measured.

The real question I believe is what you want to do with your life and how you can best contribute to achieving the goals you think are most important. More concretely, it seems to me, what is important is not the making of an approach to having the terms of your divorce settlement revised, but the manner or content of your approach. I believe that such an approach can satisfy your needs without requiring you to sacrifice your future independence of spirit and your commitments, while (hopefully) enabling you to get on with the things that are important (like your PhD; like preparing for an interesting job where you can be useful (we discussed this)).

Indeed it does seem possible to satisfy the bureaucratic requirements of an official process without landing in a bind. We do it all the time. And doing it doesn't confer legitimacy on the dominant elements of the situation which they do not already de facto possess, and need not negate your own values. I always find writing about value systems a most complicated task, because in offering my views (which I know are not idiosyncratic) they need to be qualified by expressions such as 'if I were in your position', 'if I were you', etc. (lest they seem too categorical).

The conclusion I come to is that if we could meet we could sort out the issues quite easily, I think, and end up as one.

Unfortunately this meeting of minds was not to be. Denis made his own decision and agreed to be released. He felt strongly that the fact that he was going to be released did not mean that he had changed his political views.

Denis was let out of prison on 28 February 1985. He flew straight to London to be with his wife, Esmé. There he met with Brian and my father and tried to explain his position. He was unsuccessful, however. 'I ran up against the whole Committee,' he said. 'They refused to discuss my views.' Fred was very upset as he was extremely fond of Denis. They had travelled a long way together. I was furious about Brian and my father's attitude, especially as I did not think that they explained their position adequately to Denis.

Fred threw himself even harder into his political work. He was still travelling the world to raise money. In 1988, Fred and George Johannes went to a fund-raising event in Paris just after Dulcie September, ANC representative in Paris, had been assassinated. Both Fred and Sarah had attended the funeral in Paris the previous week. At the funeral, Sarah had looked around and commented to Fred, 'There are so many police around that all the police in Paris must be here.' Fred said ruefully, 'It would have been better if, when she died, just one policeman had been present to stop her being killed.' After the funeral, Fred stayed on in Paris to lead the London delegation of the SACP to the annual carnival organised by the French Communist Party. He also gave some of the leading speeches. It was an opportunity to raise funds and Fred and George helped to operate the joint ANC and SACP stall. George later commented, 'It was interesting to see how Fred was with members of the Communist Party in France. He behaved as if we were coming to a broader family and he spoke to them in fluent French, which he'd learnt during the war.' The French were fascinated to find a white rather than a black South African – who spoke their language – campaigning for freedom.

By then, South African trade unions had grown in size and strength. As Chair of the Anti-Apartheid Trade Union Committee, Fred chaired many discussions on how British unions could best relate to the South African trade unions. He and Errol Stanley went to trade union and Labour Party conferences to make sure that the Labour Party and the unions continued to support the struggle. Fred was also on the ANC Political Regional Committee, the executive working committee that managed all ANC branches. Because of the many senior veterans who were living there, London was the biggest regional centre at the time. Both Fred and Sarah were on the Political Prisoners' Committee. It was a time of increased activity, with people coming and going and a strong sense of allegiance among London-based members.

By this stage – 1989 – there were many signs that the apartheid regime was in serious trouble and could not last much longer. People started to dream that a different South Africa might be possible. Regular ANC seminars were held all over the world; in London we held intense discussions about issues such as the interpretation of the Freedom Charter and how it could work in practice. But we had no idea whether formal negotiations were actually going to take place or, if they did take place, whether they would work.

When Fred led discussions he spoke freely and passionately, without the aid of written prompts. Pallo Jordan, who attended some of the meetings where Fred facilitated discussions, later remembered:

> In his usual fashion, Fred was very tough and vigorous and just went down the Freedom Charter list. The third clause, 'Mineral wealth belongs to the people', and the fourth clause about the land had both been bones of contention, especially from those who were anti-communists. Fred said, 'Hang on, people might think these are radical clauses. If you disaggregate the economy, this is not so radical.' He pointed to large corporations that were then under the Nationalists and pointed out that there was a huge chunk of the economy – part of the big white monopolies – that were already nationalised. It gave people pause to think a bit. He also reminded people that if something was state-owned, it didn't always work for the benefit of the people. He argued that the control of big monopolies stifled the private entrepreneur. I remember him comparing Anglo to the big corporations in Britain. They all spread their nets wide by controlling a number of related processes within the countries in which they operated. What also startled people were his proposals related to land-settlement patterns. He said one had to break up white-only areas so that they could not plot against a

democratic government ... Not only was [Fred] privy to the thinking of the framework of the Freedom Charter, he had also had time in prison to think. He was very methodical. He didn't just accept and take things for granted.

33

Time to Travel

Parallel to all of this activity, Pamela Ramsden and I were building up our consulting company, which specialised in assessing and developing the quality of decision-making at the top of companies. We were both single mothers looking after our young sons. When we had spare time, we attended courses on personal growth, particularly if an element of spiritual development was involved. In 1982, we landed up in Interlaken, Switzerland, at a Magic Rainbow Ceremony, a conference convened by Native Americans for all the religious orders to come together to pray for world peace. The conference marked the beginning of my fascination with Native American teachings: I very much respected the Native Americans' relationship with nature and their belief that the centre of their world was spirit and heart rather than materialism and thought. While I was there, I met Harvey and Diane Swiftdeer. I felt at home with this couple, who reminded me of the compassionate warmth of my parents' African comrades. A six-year spiritual journey led me into a relationship with Black Elk, a Lakota leader, who on numerous visits to the States educated me in the Native American teachings that were to influence the course of my life.

In February 1984 I was asked to hold a Pipe Ceremony and to play a game that I had devised based on these teachings called the 'Inner Quest Game' with a group of people in Gloucestershire, England. I held a 'sweat lodge' in a field owned by the parents of one of the participants, Lionel Snell, who found Jerusalem artichokes under a bush, cooked the most delicious soup for us, and won my heart. I thought to myself, if a man was so in touch with nature that he could find artichokes under bushes, he could survive anywhere. Lionel lived in a magical Cotswold stone cottage situated between three little rivers and a small waterfall. It was filled with the relaxing sound of water, and I was delighted when he invited me to stay that April. Shortly after that we started going out together. It was only years later that he told me that the artichokes had escaped from his vegetable garden, but I didn't mind.

While I was beginning a new relationship, my brother John was preparing to get married. He wrote to say that he and his partner Ntombi, with whom he was living in Tanzania, had decided to marry. Ntombi was a young ANC activist who had escaped from South Africa when she was a teenager and had made her way to Tanzania by walking and hitchhiking to the Solomon Mahlangu Freedom College, the ANC school for black South African children in Morogoro. The college was also a meeting place for activists working in various parts of Africa. Ntombi was sent to Cuba, where she learnt Spanish and was taught to cook and cater for large numbers of people. When she returned, she was in charge of catering for 2 000 people at the college, where she and John then met.

My parents were delighted. My mother was happy because John had found someone he loved, and my father was extremely pleased not only because his son was happy, but because Ntombi was a Zulu and the marriage was a symbol of the non-racist society that he was striving for.

John and Ntombi got married in the Camden Town registry office in London. Ntombi wore her traditional dress, and the registry office was full of friends – young ANC activists and other members of the exiled community. When the ceremony was over, John and Ntombi sat down to wait for the marriage certificate to be presented to them. The registrar said, 'Will Mrs Carneson stand up.' My mother promptly rose from her seat. The registrar looked puzzled, and everyone started to laugh. Ntombi stood up as the older Mrs Carneson sheepishly sat down. The reception was a joyful occasion and the newly-weds returned to Tanzania with the blessings and good wishes of all. Meanwhile, Fred and Sarah were preparing for a holiday of a lifetime.

Sarah had retired from the *Morning Star* and, in 1985, at the age of 65, Fred retired from the National Union of Teachers. At his retirement party people were very tearful, saying that they would miss him dearly. For the first time in their lives, my parents had time on their hands and Sarah's family clubbed together to send them on a round-the-world voyage. They planned to visit relatives and friends in a number of countries, including Europe, Australia, Canada and America. While they were gone, they lent their house to a young MK couple who had been given permission to marry. Bongi, the MK activist who my parents had met while she was working and studying in England, was engaged to Mazolo Mafu, an MK commander in Kampala. They had been given permission by the ANC to marry in London.

Before they left, Fred and Sarah welcomed Bongi and Mazolo and showed them around the house. According to African tradition, they were not allowed to stay together before they married, so Bongi slept downstairs while Mazolo slept upstairs, next door to my parents. They had no money, so my mother helped Bongi to prepare the reception at my parents' house. Among those who attended were Mendi Msimang, Manto Tshabalala-Msimang, Brian Bunting and Adelaide Tambo. For security purposes they married under other pseudonyms. Although Bongi was used to living in England and working and socialising with white people, Mazolo was much more wary. He mistrusted whites, but as Fred and Sarah invited him in as part of the family and made him feel at home, he 'forgot that they were white'.

While Bongi and Mazolo were enjoying their honeymoon at 19 Annington Road, my parents were exploring the world. They received visas for America, but were worried that they would be forbidden entrance because of their communist involvement. They queued in the 'aliens' line in New York to get to passport control and, when there, were questioned thoroughly by the immigration officers after they had filled in the forms stating that they were members of the Communist Party – two elderly people in their mid-seventies. 'Have you ever been in prison?' the officer asked.

'Yes.'

'Have you ever been a communist?'

'Yes.'

There was much consternation – most people said 'no' as a matter of course. Eventually they were asked, 'Are you plotting to bring down the US government?' My father looked seriously at the man as if he were considering it and then replied with a big smile, 'What? In two weeks?!'

The passport officer waved them through, saying, 'Enjoy your stay in America. I hope that you will be convinced that we are the best country in the world.' My parents told him that they'd let him know – after they had been right around the world.

When they returned from their world voyage in 1986, nothing had been resolved in South Africa. International outrage was escalating and sanctions against South Africa were widespread across the globe. The country was going bankrupt. In spite of some concessions by the government and offers to release political prisoners, the whole country was in turmoil. There was fear that the massacre that had occurred in 1985 at a funeral procession in Uitenhage, when the police had opened fire on a number of unarmed mourners, would be repeated and that public executions would get worse.

By then, the ANC had headquarters in London, New York and Lusaka and had assumed the key role for any future government of South Africa. They were holding fruitful meetings with the Congress of South African Trade Unions (COSATU), by then a very powerful force in South Africa with a membership of over 500 000 people. The forces of opposition to apartheid were flexing their muscles.

While international negotiations were being held in 1985 and 1986, there was little to do but wait. Fred and Sarah decided to go to the Solomon Mahlangu Freedom College at Morogoro in Tanzania to visit John and Ntombi and their newborn grandchild Busisiwe – Blessing. I was slightly nervous about Fred and Sarah's safety in Tanzania after John wrote that one of his friends had been fishing by a river when a hippo was chased by some men towards him. The hippo bit him in the back and he died immediately. The men had had no idea that there was anyone in the hippo's way. But this story, of course, did not stop Fred and Sarah. The trip was a moving experience for them, not only because they were seeing John, Ntombi and their first granddaughter, Busi, but also because they were back in Africa with old and new comrades. They were very taken with what they saw at the college, especially in terms of what was happening with the education of the youth.

Fred's notes expressed how deeply moved he was to be back on African soil:

Solomon Mahlangu School
Mazimbu, Morogoro
Tanzania

25 July 1986

Arrived at Mazimbu at about quarter to eight. Taken straight to John and Ntombi's house and first sight of Busi, tied African-fashion on her mother's back. A beautiful baby, plump, happy, friendly, very well advanced for her four months of age. House cool and comfortable and well run. Mazimbu complex bigger and more spread out than expected. Single-storey houses arranged in units. Lots of activity with everyone with more work than they can cope with. Children a delight. Warm and friendly. Am told many have psychological problems, arising from traumatic experiences: fathers and mothers elsewhere and in some cases coming from families who were massacred. Many old comrades there. Tearful experience seeing them again.

Africa. Africa. Africa. Space, scents, sights, sounds. Crows, stars, distant mountains, birds, dust, sun and heat. Tanzanians, and gossip about old comrades.

Morogoro, poverty, backwardness, but everywhere good humour. The warmth of human kinship, tolerance, respect for human dignity. Stocks in shops reflect poverty of country and people. Glorified trading stores. Bank crowded with customers – be interesting to know who banks and average bank account. Market animated and colourful. Fruit, vegetables, dried fish, little mounds of peanuts, naartjies, oranges, beans. Beans, nuts, pulses sold by litre tin.

Mazimbu well supplied with food. Ntombi makes maximum use of what is available at any time. Pawpaw, bread, rice, pumpkin. Good cooking, more to eat than they used to eat in London. Farm – maize, sorghum, beans, pigs, goats, cattle, chickens. Find weather pleasant. Cool in mornings and evenings and also during early part of day, especially when rain clouds about. Mazimbians feel cold, but temperature-wise for us, more like a changeable English summer.

Ntombi good linguist, can speak Swahili – has excellent rapport with locals. Thoroughly African – a matriarch in the making. Warm, generous, shrewd, practical, innate and instinctive feel for human relationships. Wonderful mother. John – overworked and overworks. Responsible, conscientious, sees funny side of life, but serious when occasion requires.

Women's Day 9th Aug. Ruth Mompati symbolic march. Masai attending. Soviet and African guests from women's organisations – speeches – multicultural event in evening.

Sarah gets malaria – Dr Pepe, a Cuban doctor, treated her; injections, anti-nausea pills – hefty dose chloroquine. Responds to treatment – up and about on second day. Proof of effectiveness of prophylactics.

Sarah was amused by how crazy Fred was about his granddaughter. 'Fred loved Busi,' she said. 'The first time he pushed the pram, he went down the street. Busi screamed extremely loudly; everyone could hear her. Fred started running with the pram back to the house. At the same time Ntombi, hearing Busi scream, ran towards him. They collided!' When Fred took Busi for walks, he carried her in his arms and said, 'Oh, you are so delicious. I could eat you – eat you up.' One day, when Fred, Sarah and Busi were out walking, two tiny children took one look at Fred and ran off shrieking. 'What's the matter?' Sarah asked, catching up to them. 'That man eats babies,' they replied earnestly. Recounting the incident, Sarah said, 'The only way to reassure them was to spend what felt like hours getting them to pour sand onto Fred's hand, emptying the sand and starting over again until they lost their fear.'

It did not take Fred long to get up to mischief with some of his old comrades. At the school, the ANC security unit was somewhat feared, and there was a strict curfew at night. Fred and Marius Schoon, a younger man who had been in prison with Fred, shared a bottle of whisky one evening. John had warned Fred to be back in time, and grew increasingly nervous when curfew arrived and Fred wasn't home. Long after curfew, Fred and Marius walked past the security house. A security officer came out. 'What are you doing? There is a curfew here,' he said sternly. Fred and Marius, merry after a bottle of whisky, started tiptoeing past in a comic fashion, putting a finger to their lips and whispering loudly, 'Ssssshhhhh, we're scared, very scared', and then chuckling heartily. To John and Ntombi's great relief, they were ignored. By the time they had to leave, Fred and Sarah had made many new friends and reconnected with some old comrades. They were sorry to leave Morogoro; the trip had been a happy one.

While Fred and Sarah were in Tanzania, Ruth was having a tough time. She and Ed found living in London with small children in a tiny flat in a rough, crowded area difficult. Ed did community work; he worked long and irregular hours for little pay. As soon as the rent and transport were paid for, there was very little left over. The children had nowhere to play and they missed being close to nature. Ed and Ruth decided to move to Devon, near a small town called Totnes, to live in the country. Although they liked the town and the beautiful scenery, Ed was unemployed. They had no money and lived in a tiny caravan, which provided very little space for four of them. Ed went out most nights to the nearest pub, leaving Ruth in the cramped caravan to look after her two children on her own. She was terribly lonely. They lived there for four long months until the autumn of 1987, when they split up.

Ruth returned to London to live closer to my parents. While Omri was at school and Ruth worked as a trained nursery nurse in a nursery school to earn a living, Sarah looked after Adam when his schoolday ended. She would fuss over him and feed him his favourite food, which at that time was fish fingers.

That year, John and Ntombi also returned to England. John took a teaching job while completing a PhD, and Ntombi signed up for a 'chef and catering' course in London. They stayed with my parents for a few months until they found their own place. Ntombi's behaviour initially drove Sarah mad: in traditional Zulu style she was respectful to our mother – 'she spent all her time cleaning the house, tidying up and waiting for me to give her instructions,' Sarah told me. After a while, Sarah realised that there was a cultural misunderstanding. She took Ntombi aside and told her that in her house that was not necessary.

Busi was then three and a half years old. She loved Fred, and later described her impressions of her grandparents:

> My partially bald, white-haired, rosy-cheeked, full-bellied grandpa spoilt me a lot. He called me 'Queen of Sheba' and made breakfast and dinner times eventful by constructing real-looking buildings from place mats and serviettes. We also loved a gross but funny, squishy toy version of Margaret Thatcher that belonged to Lynn's dog, Seamus. When you squeezed it, it made a funny face and squeaked. My grandpa always had either a coffee, wine or cheesy smell around him. With a schoolboy grin he told me, 'Stinka, get that thumb out of your mouth.' His food always tasted better than mine, so I would sit on his knee and eat his breakfast. I got a great appreciation of cheese from him, especially Brie.
>
> Granny used to push me in my stroller through the streets near her house, and on Hampstead Heath. She would call me 'Busikins' or 'Sweetie pie'. She used to make delicious sweet-and-sour pork that I loved.

During weekends Fred and Sarah loved having the family over. They delighted in providing delicious meals, often in their garden, and enjoyed playing with the children. There were always friends and visitors coming and going and joining in family life, including old comrades like Wolfie Kodesh, who used to sit in the garden and gossip with my parents, all of them dreaming about returning to South Africa while the children ran up and down the grass.

34

Nearly There

Fred, Sarah and their comrades were beginning to talk of return but did not know exactly when it would happen. What with effective sanctions, disinvestments, an oil crisis and the escalating cost of defence, South Africa was virtually bankrupt and in considerable debt. The National Party was split, the extreme right-wing faction wanting more draconian measures and the moderates arguing for reforms of the system. Business leaders were calling for the democratisation of the country, the freeing up of labour and the repeal of extreme laws. There was considerable pressure on the Nationalist government to negotiate with the ANC. In 1986, several reforms took place, including the repeal of the Blacks (Urban Areas) Consolidation Act, a cornerstone of the apartheid regime. At the same time, thousands of people had been arrested. The ANC and the Inkatha Freedom Party (IFP) were clashing violently, and there was large-scale civil unrest. The National Party still represented a tiny but powerful minority of the population. To offset reforms, P.W. Botha had bombed ANC bases in Zimbabwe, Botswana and Zambia. Almost all the political prisoners were still in jail, including Nelson Mandela and Walter Sisulu.

We had witnessed the liberation of Angola in 1974, Mozambique in 1975 and Zimbabwe in 1980. The writing was on the wall for South Africa: change was inevitable. There was intense debate about whether to negotiate or not, and under what conditions negotiations could take place. There was little confidence that the apartheid regime and its advocates could be trusted: we believed that the government could be trying to lure leaders back into South Africa to arrest or assassinate them.

In July 1987, an independent white delegation – mainly Afrikaners who wanted an end to apartheid – led by former opposition leader Frederik van Zyl Slabbert, then co-director of the extra-parliamentary Institute for a Democratic Alternative for South Africa (IDASA), met with the executive committee of the ANC in exile, including Thabo Mbeki, in Dakar. The talks were invaluable, opening a dialogue between the regime and the liberation movement. For all who attended, just being there was extremely dangerous. Yet this did not deter anti-apartheid whites of the regime from meeting the ANC in Leverkusen the following year. Further talks about negotiations took place, while in London we held meetings and discussions almost every day, always waiting for news of what was happening. It seemed, once again, that the country was on the brink of a very bloody civil war.

Comrades continued to be assassinated and attacked all over the world. At an ANC branch meeting in North London, we were deeply distressed to hear that our old family friend and comrade, Albie Sachs, had been seriously wounded by a car bomb in Maputo. His right arm had been blown off and he had extensive injuries to his face and the rest of his body. He was flown to London for treatment and I went with my parents to the hospital to find out how he was. He had had a terrible time, both physically and emotionally, and it took a long time for him to recover. Fortunately, he was helped through the recovery process by a young woman called Vanessa, who was later to become his wife.

International pressure against apartheid escalated with an International Labour Organisation tripartite conference in Harare, with representatives from various governments, the United Nations, the Organisation of African Unity (OAU) and a number of national liberation movements.

The turning point came in 1989. On 4 July, Nelson Mandela, who was then imprisoned at Victor Verster Prison near Paarl, met President P.W. Botha to discuss opening negotiations. P.W. Botha – still fundamentally committed to apartheid ideals – was replaced at the next election by F.W. de Klerk, who, despite his initial reputation as a conservative, believed that changes were necessary and moved decisively towards negotiations to end the political deadlock. In August the OAU's ad hoc committee on southern Africa, consisting of several heads of state, adopted and issued the Harare Declaration. It laid out what conditions were needed for sanctions to be lifted and for South Africa to be restored to the comity of nations. This was adopted by the UN General Assembly. Mandela refused to leave prison until the conditions were met. De Klerk and Mandela met in December to finalise arrangements. On 2 February 1990, De Klerk announced at the opening of Parliament that all banned organisations, including the ANC and the SACP, were unbanned. Political prisoners were to be released, executions suspended, restrictions on media reporting removed and all remaining apartheid laws revoked. There would be a new constitution based on universal suffrage, and Nelson Mandela would be released immediately and unconditionally.

When we heard the news, we were at a large ANC meeting. We were stunned. After an initial sense of disbelief there was huge relief that civil war had been averted. It was only when we saw the release of Nelson Mandela on 11 February that we allowed ourselves to feel cautiously victorious. Getting into bed with former, possibly current, enemies was not easy. Even so, change was in. In addition, Mandela had inspired the world: from being the symbol of injustice, South Africa became a shining beacon of hope.

We had always hoped, but never expected, to see South Africa again. Now it really seemed that this might be possible: for Fred and Sarah, the dream of a free South Africa looked as if it might well be coming true. Their other dream – that communism, led by the USSR, would save the world – was shattered: the Berlin Wall had been broken down and the Soviet Union had collapsed. In January 1990 Joe Slovo published his pamphlet 'Has Socialism Failed?'. This was during Gorbachev's period of 'Perestroika', a programme of reforms aimed at combating corruption and the abuse of privilege by the political classes, encouraging greater press freedom and allowing dissent. The unrest in the Soviet Union came to the surface and many people complained about Soviet officials who had abused their power. There were numerous debates about whether socialism was still valid and a legitimate force for change.

The South African Communist Party decided that it was more important to focus on change in South Africa than be deterred by what was happening in the Soviet Bloc. The Party had to find its own national character and the form of socialism that was appropriate to the South African situation. Fred and Sarah were too excited by the changes that were taking place in South Africa and the prospect of going home to be utterly devastated. They had expected the collapse of the Soviet Union for some time, so, although it was sad for them, it was not a great surprise.

Progress in South Africa did not go smoothly. We still feared that the Nationalist government would not share power with the ANC without bloodshed, so we did not let our hopes get too high in case they were dashed. Yet we were beginning to fantasise about what old, familiar and much-loved places might be like and how wonderful it would be to reunite with friends and surviving comrades. We were all very keen to return, although I could not go back immediately as my son was still at school and my business was flourishing.

Violence was still occurring – the Sebokeng massacre had set back a meeting between the two parties by a month – yet the political process was under way. In May 1990, the two teams met as equals for the first time at Groote Schuur mansion in Cape Town, where the ANC proposed the establishment of an interim government and peaceful resolution was agreed on. At that landmark meeting, the white leaders realised that their 'enemies' were not only educated, serious and good-humoured people, but, remarkably, were determined to build bridges with their oppressors and fill the vast racial and cultural gulf. The comrades, desperate to return to South Africa, were told to wait. ANC officials kept saying, 'Wait, let's see what is happening.' No one was allowed back to South Africa before the ANC knew that it was reasonably safe to return. We read about the meeting in news briefings and *Sechaba*, and discussed it at ANC meetings. Although we were cautiously optimistic, we knew that the country was still unstable.

When the ANC finally announced that it was possible to return, Fred and Sarah immediately applied for permission to go. They were excited but also worried, as were many other exiles, that things might revert to the way they were; that the Nationalist government was fooling them into returning.

In 1991, there was a major ANC conference in London. Nelson and the beautiful Winnie Mandela, Jacob Zuma, Thabo Mbeki, Albertina Sisulu and many other activists from all over the world were there. I sat next to my parents, Ruth and Simon. It was a time for celebration, victory and hope, a time for reuniting with long-absent comrades. The ANC anthem 'Nkosi Sikelel' iAfrika' was about to become our national anthem. We sang and danced and cheered; we were triumphantly nearing the end of our struggle.

Before my parents returned to South Africa in 1991, they had a farewell party at Ruth's house at 118 Stapleton Hall Road, Haringey. Many South Africans and English comrades and friends were there to see them off. George Johannes was deeply moved: 'The joy! That memory of them hugging each other – of two elderly people going back on a new honeymoon, going back to an old haunt of theirs, where their ultimate love was a love of the people, the country and a love of the struggle that had been won. I remember how happy they were – they couldn't wait to go. They wanted to be back in the struggle in the country with the people.'

PART FOUR

Rainbow Days

1991–2010

One day, perhaps, we shall be able to lead an ordinary, normal life, with no fears in the background to nag at our simple joys, no danger to cast its shadow on our pleasures.

– Fred Carneson, written in solitary confinement, 6 February 1966

35

A Warm Welcome

My parents arrived back in Cape Town on the morning of 19 May 1991. By then they could not wait to see their beloved Table Mountain, framed by a tabletop cloud and clear blue skies. Unfortunately, it was raining on the day they arrived – sheets and sheets of cold rain. In fact, it rained solidly for two weeks. They didn't care.

Much to their amazement and delight, when they got off the plane they were greeted by a large reception of old friends and young people who were waving flags and posters saying 'Welcome Home'. 'It gave us a wonderful warm feeling of comradeship,' they said. 'It was marvellous to see young people we had never even met in our lives before welcoming us home. It was one of the best experiences in our lives. It was a very emotional experience; it left us almost speechless. It was wonderful to be among our own people again – a warm homecoming.'

Athol and Bubbles Thorn invited my parents to stay with them. Athol, who had been a director at *New Age* many years earlier, had advised them to get some sleep on the plane because he and Bubbles had arranged a tea party that day for all their old comrades still in Cape Town. 'It was very emotional,' Sarah said. 'After all those years of house arrest, prison and exile, it was wonderful to be united with old friends.' Among their friends were Basil and Norma Jaffe, our family doctor and his wife, and the Yengeni and Tsolekile families, who lived in Langa and had helped to sell the *Guardian* and *New Age* in the fifties and sixties. For Fred, 'it felt like being home again'.

Fred and Sarah spent their first two weeks in Cape Town visiting favourite haunts that had been forbidden them when they were banned, especially the False Bay coast on the Indian Ocean. Their old comrade Wolfie Kodesh took them for long walks along the beach from Muizenberg to Fish Hoek. They revisited the colourful fishing village of Kalk Bay where they used to fish and discovered that the fishing harbour had hardly changed:

the fishwives were still there, shouting at each other and gutting fresh yellowtail and kingklip that my parents took home to braai for lunch. They went to Seaforth – with its lawns and boulders – where they used to picnic often when we were small. Now there were black and white schoolchildren rushing into the water together. 'It was a thrill seeing them,' they remembered. 'We saw in reality one of the things we fought for.'

Fred and Sarah were invited, as veterans, to the first legal ANC conference in Durban, where they met many more people they knew. It was the first time they heard Thabo Mbeki speak publicly. They reunited with his father, Govan Mbeki, who had worked with my father during the days of the *Guardian*. At the conference they also saw Nelson Mandela and Walter Sisulu, comrades of old. The atmosphere was exhilarating, triumphant and joyful. They threw themselves passionately into lengthy discussions about the constitutional, structural and strategic basis of the new government and about the ongoing negotiations with the Nationalist government. Relations with the government were extremely uncomfortable, distrust and anger on both sides threatening peaceful resolution.

After being with the Thorns for a few months, they stayed with Amy Thornton (née Reitstein), who had been in prison with Sarah in 1960. Fred was on a high – no place was as good as Cape Town. They wanted to settle down as quickly as they could, and Amy was amazed by how fast they moved. 'They went out and bought a flat, a car and furniture, all in one day,' she exclaimed.

What had happened was that they asked Jack Barnett, their architect friend who had witnessed their wedding, to help them. Jack found them a flat they liked in Plumstead – 204 Primrose Park. He checked it out from an architectural point of view and advised them that it was very sound and a bargain. They bought it on the spot. My parents were relieved to have their own home again. Fred loved it because there was a huge tree that danced in the wind in front of their lounge, and an excellent view of Table Mountain. He enjoyed sipping a chilled glass of dry white wine at sunset, sighing loudly with contentment as he watched the mountain for as long as he wanted. The flat was just across the road from the railway station – on the line between Cape Town and Simon's Town. Although the train clattered past, they were near reliable transport should they need it.

Before Fred and Sarah bought a car, they travelled by crowded minibus taxi with the local black people. They were always the only whites and were certainly not the youngest people in the bus. One day the taxi was going so fast and was so packed that when it jolted, Sarah landed on someone's lap. They were terrified. When the taxi eventually came to a stop, Fred said to the driver, 'Mate, I suggest that you take a pilot's licence to fly this thing.' The driver and everyone in the taxi laughed, and both Fred and Sarah got out with great relief. Fred was amazed by Cape Town driving. 'If you want to know how crazy Cape Town is, just go in one of those taxis,' he said. 'Cape drivers are mad. Absolutely reckless. They don't indicate, they don't stop and they overtake on the inside lane. You have to be a genius to drive safely on these roads!'

Fred was exuberant but he was also aware that there were considerable challenges ahead. In his journal of the time he wrote:

> Although we have won the battle we have not won the war. The country is not yet stable. There are still pockets of violence both from the extreme right and black factions in different parts of the country. It is a bloody miracle that we have not had civil war.
>
> After a long struggle, we are at the end of Nationalist oppression and the beginning of a free South Africa. We have come a long way and there is a long way to go. The plight of the poor is still terrible. At least many people will have better conditions – water and electricity and jobs. Blacks will have opportunities to take positions of power. But not everyone cares about the plight of the majority. Those people who are jumping on the gravy train and getting rich quick are not helping the progress of this country. We always knew that the first phase would be the development of a black middle class. We have to deal with unemployment. That is a huge problem. We may have to work out a different relationship between the ANC and the Communist Party. The ANC is a multi-class, broad-based organisation representing many different groups, and will take over a well-developed capitalist economy. There will be a lot of negotiating to make sure that what is done is for the advance of the working people. Although we have analysed the Freedom Charter step by step, the extent to which the Freedom Charter will be implemented will have to be thought out and argued very carefully.
>
> We are at the beginning of a new stage in our country where for the first time all our people have a chance in life. And the mood here is vibrant, joyful. People just want to get on with building a new South Africa, so there is a lot of work to be done.

From 1991, Fred served as Western Cape treasurer for the South African Communist Party. He found himself working with old and new comrades. He and Brian Bunting were back working together in Cape Town, and Chris Hani, whom Fred knew from early MK days, was a frequent visitor to my parents' house. Chris was considered a great leader, a hero, highly charismatic and certainly a contender for a leadership position in the government of a democratic South Africa. He had a huge following, and Sarah admired him greatly, believing him to be very intelligent and very human, with a tremendous sense of responsibility. Chris and Fred would sit for hours sharing past experiences.

Fred and Sarah were also active members of the ANC Wynberg branch. In England, everyone had been punctual. My parents would turn up on time to Wynberg meetings only to be frustrated when people arrived late or the 'com didn't pitch'. They refused to accept that people had transport problems. 'Then you must change the time we meet,' they argued. During the meetings, Fred would impatiently listen to some of the comrades who liked to take the stage and talk endlessly. He and Sarah wanted to focus on clear goals, values, principles and practical ideas. Sarah believed in being 'to the point', while Fred was more analytical and sought the broader context. They brought rigour and discipline to the meetings, which were sadly lacking in both. Fred explained, 'In the past, there was a small number of us so we could focus on the rationale behind our actions. Now we are dealing with many people who have not had that background.'

My parents' political activities did not stop them from having an active social life or enjoying the beauty of nature. They loved having parties at 204 Primrose Park, where there was a mood of optimism and high hopes. Bongi Mafu, Mazolo's wife, remembered, 'Fred used to tell very naughty jokes. I laughed until I cried.'

As often as they could, they would walk through Kirstenbosch – one of the loveliest botanical gardens in the world. It was a joy to see the plants growing and at sunset to watch the brightly coloured sugarbirds and malachite sunbirds settling on the huge yellow and orange proteas to sip nectar.

They couldn't wait for Ruth to visit them in Cape Town. Like me, she was impatient to get back to see what the city was like. She was the first to visit and came on her own, as both her sons decided to remain in London. This was the beginning of a love affair with Cape Town, which led to Ruth moving to the city for good in 1997. When she arrived at the airport on that first trip, Fred and Sarah were there to give her a warm welcome. Fred was so excited that he wanted to take her everywhere to see all the sights immediately. 'It was like he had built Table Mountain himself, single-handedly, every rock, bit by bit,' Ruth laughed. 'They treated me like an absolute princess. They totally spoilt me, wined and dined me. They gave me anything I liked and fed me non-stop.' After her arrival in South Africa, my parents wrote to me to catch me up on all their news. By then I was looking forward to visiting Cape Town myself. It would be my first trip back in thirty years.

204 Primrose Park
Exeter Road
Plumstead
7800

4 November 1991

Dearest Lynn

It was wonderful welcoming Ruth back to Cape Town and already we are all three finding it difficult to believe that she has been here for only three full days. Apart from the seasonal winds, the weather has been fine so we have been able to show Ruth quite a bit of Cape Town, though we have not yet had time to explore the city itself. A swim at Muizenberg (for Ruth only!); a run along Boyes Drive; an arts and craft fair at Constantia Village; a look-in at the Constantia shopping mall; a marvellous morning at the Cape Town Waterfront; an evening stroll and huge ice creams on the promenade at Sea Point; a trip down memory lane to Mount Pleasant; a visit to Auntie Bella; and a swim in 'our' swimming pool at the bottom of the garden.

It is now 4.45 a.m., sixteen days after I started this letter – that will give you some idea of just how busy we have been. Busy with what, is another question! Time does fly along at a merry pace, especially when one is rushing here, there and everywhere.

At present we are starting on day three of a five-day stay at Jack and Naomi Barnett's Simon's Town cottage. Very comfortable, with a luxuriant garden, a magnificent view and within fairly easy walking distance to the sea shore, providing one is walking downhill. Bit of an uphill slog coming back, but then one can always hop into the car and be on the beach within three or four minutes.

Ruth has put on a few pounds since she arrived and is looking all the better for it. She is having a marvellous break.

Mum and I are both keeping well and keeping fit with quite a bit of walking in between the shopping. We've joined the Botanical Society, so Kirstenbosch is ours whenever we feel like a stroll or just a quiet, meditative sit and look. Balm for the soul, as you'll discover for yourself.

Much love to you and Simon and a pat on the head for Seamus. Greetings to all our mutual friends.

Dad

From Mum
A few words from me although Dad has given you all the news. We are looking forward to your visit and taking you on a sightseeing trip. It is very beautiful here, but there are many unhappy problems which I don't think will be solved in the near future. I find I have to readjust my thinking and my way of life. On the one hand I do not have the freedom of movement here that I had in London, on the other hand life is more interesting and exciting here and of course very much more beautiful. It is taking time to unpack all our things and settle down, and we have been taking time off to enjoy ourselves.

We all send much love to you and Simon.

One day, my parents and Ruth went into Cape Town by train. Ruth wanted to talk politics. Fred, who was looking out of the train at the mountain, said, unusually, 'I don't want to talk about politics now. I want to start the "Look Party".'

'What is the "Look Party"?' asked Ruth with interest.

'Be Quiet and Look at the View!' replied Fred.

They never stopped pointing out to Ruth the progress that had been made – no more 'Whites Only' benches, trains, restaurants, beaches or schools; children of all colours playing together in the playground. 'This is what we fought for,' they said with pleasure.

They took Ruth to meetings in a rough informal settlement. Held in a hall with no electricity, lit by candles, made of corrugated iron, and bergies wandering in and out, it was a dangerous place to be, but they were fearless. The meetings always started with a prayer. At one meeting they asked Sarah, who was an atheist, to bless the meeting, which she did. Fred and Sarah also took Ruth to a number of political functions, including the

SACP conference in Salt River, where Chris Hani was the key speaker. He received a rousing welcome. Unlike in the past, the conference was completely mixed racially. Ruth was overwhelmed: 'It was truly African. People were singing "Nkosi Sikelel' iAfrika" and the atmosphere was vibrant. Then and only then did I feel, "Now I have come home."'

Sarah worked at the ANC Cape Town office in Salt River with Willie Hofmeyr, Reggie September and Johnny de Lange. They were organising an ANC 'People's Parliament' march on 24 January 1992 and expected 50 000 people to be there. One of Sarah's jobs was to issue money for petrol and travelling expenses for people who were leafleteering over all the townships. The atmosphere was one of tremendous activity and euphoria, but Sarah also reminded people to be careful with the money they were allocating. She urged them to write down everything and get receipts, or 'the money will find feet of its own and run away'.

After thirty years away, I arrived back in Cape Town for a holiday on 24 January 1992, my birthday. Until four days before I left, I did not know if I would be granted permission to return to Cape Town. When my lawyer Justin Hardcastle phoned to say I could go, I still did not believe it. After so many years of exile, I could go back!

On the plane I was so excited I could hardly sleep. A slight fear still lingered: had it really changed? Would they let me in? Would they arrest me for past activities? At the passport office in Cape Town the man read my special letter explaining why I had no South African passport and stating that I was a South African citizen, and he casually let me in.

My parents and Ruth met me at the barrier with a large bunch of brilliant pink, blue and orange flowers. Table Mountain shone purple in the background against a sheet of blue, blue sky. 'Happy birthday. Welcome home,' it seemed to say. Hugs and tears and hugs and tears again, the place so familiar and so like a dream. My father asked me if I would like to go into town after unpacking, as the mass demonstration that they had helped organise for an alternative Parliament was taking place. We went by train. The stations were exactly as they had looked when I was a schoolgirl: small platforms; white ticket office; bright-red hibiscus bushes and people hanging out of the third-class coaches. When people saw us wearing ANC badges, they saluted us. My father told everyone that this was my first day back, to which they responded, '*Mayibuye*' – Welcome – with wide smiles from the heart. The difference was that on the train we all sat together, black, white, coloured and Indian.

The centre of Cape Town was packed. We found ourselves in a massive crowd of people chanting, marching and toyi-toying. They were jogging slowly in rows and rows to full-blooded freedom songs. People in the crowd found out that I was a 'returnee' and that it was my birthday. They sang to me: 'Happy returns. Many, many happy returns.' My mother looked overwhelmed and was squashed by the crowds, so she and my father moved out to the side and agreed to meet us later. Ruth and I, arms around each other, were swept forward and away by the singing, happy mass of people. The police were discreetly present in the distance. It was so different from the past.

We toyi-toyed right around the Grand Parade and back again, past buildings full of watching people, bright flower stalls and people hanging from trees. Ruth and I caught the eyes of two black women and together we danced to the rhythm. Heat and sweat did not matter. This, I felt, was where my heart and soul belonged. Then the long speeches and I was back to being eight again, remembering my father addressing large crowds on the same Parade.

We started looking for our parents, but the crowd was thick. Eventually we found my father, who was looking upset. 'We got mugged,' he told us. 'Ma is over there sitting next to one of the comrade representatives.'

'What happened?' we asked, shocked.

'We were waiting on the corner, keeping out of the demo, when a group of about twenty youths came running the opposite way – steamrolling, they call it. Before we knew what was happening they were frisking me and had Ma around the neck. They took my watch and my wallet. I was fighting them off when some young women surrounded Ma, protected her and pulled me in. One of the women fetched a steward who found us a place to sit.' They were quite shaken, but not surprised. 'There are so many poor people; it is inevitable,' my mother said. 'We must learn to be more vigilant in future. This is nothing compared to what we had to put up with in the past.'

Luckily neither of them was hurt. We decided to go home. Walking to the station, a number of people offered us their drinks. One man, who seemed drunk or stoned, asked my father to give him some money. My father apologised, 'No, I'm sorry, mate. I have nothing. I've just been mugged.' The man took several steps backwards, pointed to himself and asked, 'Was it me? Was it really me?' He opened his jacket with a flourish. There were hundreds of watches pinned to the inside. 'No,' said my father, looking at the watches. 'I don't recognise mine.'

'Have any one of these,' offered the man.

'No thanks!' said my father. 'Mine was a special one.'

'That's a relief,' the watch thief responded, and disappeared. We burst out laughing. I knew I was definitely home. Only in Cape Town could this happen.

In spite of the euphoria and optimism pervading the country, we all knew that there was serious unrest. Negotiations about power-sharing with the Nationalists were by no means over. Conflict between the Zulu nationalist IFP and the ANC, in alliance with the United Democratic Front (UDF), had cost thousands of lives, many by means of the infamous tyre 'necklace'. In April 1992, the Human Rights Commission stated that unprecedented violence was 'the result of forces working to destabilise the referendum and the peace process'. In May, CODESA – Convention for a Democratic South Africa – talks ended in deadlock, the Nationalist government refusing to agree to constitutional changes and De Klerk attacking the ANC for, among other things, retaining its arms caches and generally showing bad faith. The ANC threatened mass action. Civil unrest continued and, in June, almost fifty people were killed by suspected IFP extremists in their homes at Boipatong in a massacre – one incident among many in the widespread township violence threatening to consume the country. The following day, the ANC accused De Klerk and his government of complicity in the violence and of supporting the IFP in anti-ANC attacks. On 2 July 1992, De Klerk published a letter to Nelson Mandela accusing the ANC of stirring up violence, and made proposals about political change that were unacceptable to the ANC. Mandela responded scathingly. The struggle was not yet over. I was back in London working, and was very worried about the safety of my parents and their comrades. I knew that for them it was just an extension of years of struggle rather than something new.

In August a forty-eight-hour strike initiated by the metal workers began with programmes of mass action to demand early transition. The people were not going to give in, no matter what the cost. Then, on 7 September, Ronnie Kasrils led an ANC march to Bisho, the capital of the 'independent' homeland republic of Ciskei. The mini-state's troops opened fire on the ANC demonstrators and, in a terrible massacre, twenty-nine people died and two hundred were injured. Civil unrest was permeating the country and our hard-won peace was teetering on a knife edge. It was a nerve-wracking time.

Mandela, De Klerk and the other chief negotiators were determined, however, to prevent the negotiations from breaking down. Two weeks after the Bisho shooting they signed a transitional Record of Understanding committing them to a single, elected constitutional assembly that would ultimately approve the new constitution. The peace process, although stumbling, remained on track.

36

Turning Point

In March 1993, in spite of a highly charged atmosphere, John decided to return to South Africa with Ntombi and Busi, to the great delight of Fred and Sarah. He had found work as a lecturer at the University of Cape Town. Fred warned them that the situation was tense and they would have to learn to be tough. When they arrived, my parents fussed over them, driving them around, providing meals and taking care of Busi. On 10 April 1993, they were having tea together when Fred switched on the television to watch the news. What they heard stunned them. My father's close comrade Chris Hani had been assassinated. Fred was beside himself. 'The bloody idiots!' he shouted. 'After Mandela, he could have been the next president of South Africa. Those bastards knew what they were doing. This is a deliberate attempt to destabilise all our hard work.'

I was working in Philadelphia when Bongi Mafu phoned me. She was in a terrible state, saying that her husband Mazolo had just phoned her to tell her about the assassination. Mazolo was a good friend of Chris's and had been visiting him at the time. He had gone to buy some coffee from the shop, and when he came back, Chris was lying in a sea of blood with his young daughter looking on. Mazolo had told Bongi that he would phone back when he had taken the daughter to a neighbour who could look after her. I phoned my parents immediately. They were both very distressed. My father went straight away to see Chris's family.

The situation in South Africa became critical: people were extremely angry and many wanted to cancel the talks and go to war. People were being killed on trains and townships in large numbers, and there was much uncertainty about dates for the first election because of the high levels of violence. The whole country was rocked by shock and outrage at Chris Hani's assassination. Public anger was intense and sustained.

It took huge organisation and strength of mind for the ANC to contain what could have been an even more explosive situation. After Chris's death,

Nelson Mandela publicly appealed to the nation to maintain stability. The country listened, and the ANC emerged a lot stronger because of this. In June, after multiparty talks at Kempton Park, to everyone's relief there was agreement that the date fixed for the general elections would be 27 April 1994. On 18 November, the leaders involved in the negotiation process endorsed an interim constitution and an electoral bill. They also reached several agreements about what would happen in the transitional period when the ANC and the Nationalist government 'power-shared'.

Gradually things settled down. At the end of an exhausting year, we could all look forward to a more positive one ahead.

With the mandate set to prepare for the elections and interim power-sharing between the ANC and the Nationalists in place, Fred took his part in the negotiating forum, particularly regarding ways of alleviating poverty. He organised budgets to service a wider section of people and helped to set up non-racial boundaries in local government. He was nominated ANC staff representative on the transitional Cape Metropolitan Council and the Cape Regional Council. The last time he had been a councillor was in the late 1940s – at seventy-four, he had come full circle. He was also on the Reconstruction and Development Programme committee, a programme that attempted to put ailing South Africa on its feet.

Fred attended every meeting and took part in debates and arguments about health, affirmative action, control of the taxi wars and employer–employee relations. He initiated a motion on corruption that twice got delayed because someone had 'lost' the papers. Eventually, because of his persistence, the motion was accepted by the Cape Metropolitan Council, as was his motion on noise pollution. He was also outraged that some teachers came to school drunk, and campaigned to have them sacked on the spot. He believed passionately that banks and investment companies should lend money to the working class: 'How can they help themselves with no money? Those mean bastards who are refusing to lend money don't even know that it will benefit them in the long run,' he argued. 'I am already getting fed up with corrupt and lazy politicians. There are too many of them in this place.'

Both Fred and Sarah took part in discussions about change in the Wynberg Communist Party branch and their ANC branch. They were saddened that sections of the liberation movement had been seduced by power and wealth and felt that the chances of achieving the stipulations of the

Freedom Charter had receded. Any new government would have to be pragmatic to stand up to institutions such as the World Bank, they realised. The real challenge would be to deal with the tension between the global goals of materialism and the goals of development for the poor people in South Africa.

My parents threw themselves into preparations for the election. Sarah, a little seventy-eight-year-old white lady, went from door to door with members of the Wynberg ANC branch throughout Wynberg, including the non-white areas. She handed out leaflets and carried painted banners. People listened to her with astonishment: an elderly white woman campaigning for the ANC was an unexpected sight. Sarah and her comrades sat behind tables on pavements of busy Claremont to help people register to vote. They were determined that this election would be a great success.

In between campaigning, the Wynberg ANC branch planned several social outings. Kay and Mansoor Jaffer spent a lot of time with Fred and Sarah during these times. 'They knew how to have fun,' Kay remembered. 'Fred would clap people on the back and say, "Hello, mate, how are you?" Sarah had a walker, but she got up and danced, walker and all!'

37

The Dream Danced Awake

THE FIRST DEMOCRATIC election, held between 26 and 29 April 1994, was a major turning point for South Africa. To see people of all colours and backgrounds stand together all over the country in queues to vote, all talking and laughing, was a victory for all of those who had fought so valiantly for equality. For those of us who took part in the joyful end of the old and the beginning of the new, it was an experience that will never be forgotten.

The build-up to the election was intense. On 17 February, 10 300 observers were hired to monitor the election, for which nineteen political parties had registered. A national peacekeeping force was set up to reduce the risk of violence and sabotage. On 28 March, violent clashes between the IFP and ANC security guards occurred. After difficult negotiations, the IFP agreed to participate in the elections and political violence dropped dramatically. In addition to those voting in South Africa, South Africans all over the world, including me, were allowed to vote.

Fred and Sarah helped to organise and mobilise people to go to the polls – over the election period their car was constantly full of people who had no transport. They gave out voting numbers at a polling station in Plumstead and, when they had a tea break, they would walk around looking at row upon row of people queuing to vote. Some had queued throughout the night. Fred was ecstatic: 'The whole country, coloured, white and black, came out to vote,' he said delightedly. 'Everyone was friendly, happy and talking to each other regardless of colour or what political party they belonged to. There was no tension. People were able to go in and vote and come out without trouble.'

For Fred and Sarah, to see black people voting for the first time was a dream come true: 'The days of the election were the most important and exciting days of our lives. It was an outright triumph, like "Victory Day" in England when people partied in the streets to celebrate the end of the Second World War.'

Ntombi's mother, Nomvula, was visiting Fred and Sarah at the time. She sat and watched people streaming into the voting booths on TV. All she could do was weep for the three days of the election: it was the first time in her life that she had been able to vote, even though she was a grandmother. She felt that she had won her freedom.

I was at a conference in New York City in April 1994, so I went to vote in a large tent near Central Park. There was a small queue of people there. After my fingerprints had been taken for identification purposes and I had been issued my number, I went into the polling booth. There on the paper before me were a number of names, including the ANC's, next to a photograph of Nelson Mandela, waiting for my cross. I marked my choice and put my vote in the ballot box. It was also my first South African vote: I had been deprived of my citizenship when I left in 1962. As I came out of the tent, I burst into tears. I sat on a bench and cried and cried. An Afrikaans man, seeing my tears, approached me and said, 'I know, it's terrible. Don't be upset. One day *alles sal reg kom* (everything will come right).' I just looked at him, disbelieving, and went on crying. Eventually he wandered off.

As soon as my conference finished in New York, I flew back for three weeks to be with my parents, Ruth and John and his family. Given what we had all been through, it was a deeply important time both for the nation and for my family. We had pulled through; we had helped to achieve this momentous event in South African history.

At long last, the results were announced in all the papers all day, all night and all through the following day. It seemed to take ages as the votes were counted and re-counted. Apart from sleeping for a few hours, we sat patiently on my parents' beige settee, glued to the television screen. On 2 May 1994, the final results were announced: a landslide victory for the ANC!

> **JUBILANT CROWDS CELEBRATE**
> Thousands of excited ANC supporters clogged township streets from Gugulethu to Khayelitsha last night in a spontaneous celebration of their victory, Sapa reports ... Waving ANC campaign placards, jabbing fists into the air, shouting slogans and blocking traffic, they snaked through the dense mist which had descended on ill-lit streets ...
> 'We are free at last!' – *Argus*, Tuesday 3 May 1994

De Klerk handed over power to the new president, Nelson Mandela, saying, 'Just as we could not rule South Africa effectively without the support of the ANC and its supporters, no government will be able to rule effectively without the support of the people and the institutions that I represent. I enthusiastically pledge that support in the interest of working for national reconciliation and reconstruction.' Nelson Mandela, first black president of South Africa, accepted power. He did so with no bitterness: 'To the people of South Africa and the world who are watching: this is a joyous night for the human spirit. This is your victory too ... This is one of the most important moments in the life of our country. I stand before you filled with deep pride and joy – pride in the ordinary, humble people of this country.'

We all rushed out into Main Street Plumstead. A spontaneous motor cavalcade formed all the way through the suburbs to the Grand Parade in the centre of Cape Town. Cars were hooting; flags were waving; people were dancing on top of their cars. Five black bakers covered in flour rushed out and danced on the pavement. Everyone embraced each other as music and jubilant singing filled the air. I thought, 'We can never go back. Now we will either create or mess up our own future.'

Fred and Sarah were formally invited to attend President Mandela's inauguration. There they joined in the celebrations with so many of their comrades who had won freedom for the country. The repressive regime was gone. People were walking tall; South Africa was the icon of the world. In 1995 we won the Rugby World Cup tournament. The Truth and Reconciliation Commission was an inspiring model.

But the transition from 'struggle' to governing a complex and poverty-stricken country was, and still is, an enormous task. Most of the MPs were not experienced or equipped to take over offices of power. As is normal in the beginning stages of a new constitutional democracy and new systems of power, a mixture of positive and negative things occurred. Even today, many years later, South Africa is a *lekker gemors* – a delicious mess – and still has a long way to go. For Fred and Sarah, the 'new South Africa' would never be the same as the old and, although they had many concerns, there was no comparison with how terrible it had been. For them, it had been well worth it.

38

Reflections

AFTER THE GENERAL ELECTION of 1994, Fred and Sarah decided that they could take some time to rest and enjoy life before becoming active again. Fred was in his mid-seventies and Sarah nearly eighty. They wanted to make the most of what time they had left. The problem was that, for Fred, time to himself also meant that the pain from the past came back to haunt him. They had achieved victory, but he never forgot those comrades who had lost their lives to achieve a freedom that they never saw.

Fred became reflective. He got up at five o'clock every morning. Many times he would wake me up to see the sun rise over the mountains. Then he would start to worry and agonise over things. He still had bad dreams about comrades who had died in captivity, and he told me that he had not forgiven himself for cracking while under interrogation. Every time I said that this was not justified, he repeated the same thing. One morning after we had watched the sun rise, we were sitting sipping coffee and he brought out a letter for me to read. It was written by Bernie Gosschalk. After his first wife, Ruth, died, Bernie married Zelda, who was a journalist. She had expressed interest in writing my father's story to Bernie. Zelda was visiting Cape Town at that time, and Bernie had sent her a letter about Fred, whom he deeply respected. She passed it on to my father.

14 October 1994

Dear Zelda
This relates to Fred Carneson and your comment on the telephone about his negative feelings about himself. I don't know his feelings about himself. There are two whites in the Cape I respect above all: Denis Goldberg and Fred. I could also talk to you about Bennie Turok and, in a different way, about Winnie. But I'll keep with Fred. Had he been an African he would have been killed like Looksmart Ngudle, the spirit of

joy and life personified, beaten to death, probably in Caledon Square. I still grieve for him and remember that wonderful face. What a loss to South Africa. But back to Fred.

My memory is incomplete, but he was arrested around December 1965 and disappeared into the machine. From the time of his solo arrest, he was interrogated non-stop, not tortured in the way Africans were – none of us had that, and let us never forget it. He was tortured more subtly, just kept awake endlessly. He was also flown to the secret interrogation farm centre near Pretoria in their own Special Branch plane, still being kept awake: a tap on the knee, an 'offer' of a fag, but endlessly awake. Eventually he broke. Who doesn't? Fred was in such a bad state that he spent, I think, four days in an oxygen tent, close to death. He then spent 13 months in solitary, the longest a white person had had to endure.

Came stage two. They arrested a number of us, though we were not connected other than we knew Fred. They wanted me to take the witness stand to state that Fred had trained blacks in the Paarl mountains to go down to murder whites. I knew this was a downright lie and I made up my mind that come what may, I would not go into the witness stand to testify against Fred. That was my personal decision. I knew that it could mean prison for a minimum of five years and I feared that terribly, feared the separation from Ruth, who had been working with Fred. To force me, they told me things about her and said that they would bring her in too. I was worried stiff about the children. I knew the family were petrified, useless. I hoped that friends, Dot and Harry, Frieda and Helene, would look after them. But come what may, I was not going to be an instrument to convict the last guy that I would give evidence against. Don't forget, I had been in solitary at Kuils River, then Caledon Square, with the infamous Special Branch hovering around, fearsome, ruthless, destroyers of Africans. I did not know who had been taken in apart from Albie, because of his life-saving graffiti on the cell architrave. So for those five months, all I thought of was that appearance in court to testify against Fred. As I have said before, one cannot switch off the mind. That mental torture is actually the worst. No sleep. Fearful of every key in the lock.

As you now know, Ruth's courage, single-handed, got lawyers to point out that sleep deprivation was internationally illegal and that people suffering from sleep deprivation were not sane enough to testify in court.

I have never spoken to Fred about this. When I am in Cape Town, he will be one of the first people I will visit. He is the epitome of life, joy, hope, optimism, and truly a wonderful guy who gave everything for South Africa. There are very few of us who can say that.

If there were ever to be a pantheon of South African heroes, my one vote would go to Fred. He sacrificed everything. Very few of us whites can claim that. I'll see him; I'll tell him. It is a challenge to tell him, so that his self-esteem is high, that he is not distressed in his lonely hours. At 76 years of age, that is little enough for a friend to do. Sarah I know and she seems to have survived the trauma. I do not know how Lynn, Johnny and Ruth have taken it. Fred loved his children like no one else did. He poured his warmth and pride into them.

If you want to write a story, you won't find a much more inspiring one in the white 'sector' of the liberation movement. A challenge? You're safe on one count. Unlike so many people, Fred won't change now. Good luck with it.

Bernard

When Zelda gave Fred the letter, she said that it was a 'charged and emotional day'. She had been invited to lunch by Jack and Naomi Barnett at their house overlooking the sea in Simon's Town. She brought the letter with her to give to Fred. 'He was not at all what I'd expected,' she wrote afterwards. 'I'd thought he would be lean, rather gaunt and reasonably tall; instead in comes this wonderful Santa Claus clone – round rosy cheeks (he'd been for a swim with Jack, his daughter Lynn, and granddaughter Busi), comfortable tummy and just a little taller than myself. But what a lovely, warm man! When Jack introduced us I told him how much I'd been looking forward to meeting him. I sat next to Fred at lunch, manoeuvred it that way so we could talk: he told me he was back doing the same work that he did before, full of life and enthusiasm, full of wisdom, totally empty of bitterness. Coming back for him has been total justification of all that went before.'

After lunch Zelda asked Fred to come outside, where she gave him the letter. 'He was very, very moved as he read it (I was too, as I reread it over his shoulder) and it seemed to unlock some buried memory in him. He recalled the murders of Looksmart and two other men, and as he told of them, his voice faltered and a single tear rolled to the top of his cheek, where it stayed, quivering, like some precious jewel glinting in the sun. Of course, I had tears too, for him. I was unbearably conscious of his anguish. I don't think he could understand my closeness to him, but he felt it, I know, and appreciated it. I was so choked up I just wanted to come home, to be alone and howl like a wounded animal – for all of us. But with it all, Fred is a very happy man. For him, it was worth everything.'

While I was staying with my parents in 1995, I woke up at two in the morning to get a drink of water. There Fred was, at the table, totally engrossed in writing something. I went up to him to see what it was, and he covered up the notebook with his arms like a child stopping someone from seeing his homework.

It was only years later, looking through his papers, that I realised he was working on his autobiography. It was never completed. I came across some random notes and images written in 1994 that seemed to me to distil the essence of the key themes in his life.

Fred's Notes, 11 August 1994

Joe Berry gave me this notebook last Sunday after I had told him I intended writing a book. It was a gift which said more plainly than words: 'Stop talking about it: get on with the job!'

And that is what I am now doing in this, my first ever 'writer's notebook'. Only time will tell if I shall finish the job. Or, if I do finish, whether or not it has been worth the effort to anyone except myself.

Do I have a story to tell? I believe I have, but for that story to have any value it must also be the story of all who have gone into the making of it: my parents, my brothers and sisters, aunts and uncles, teachers, friends, colleagues and comrades, and my wife, my son and my daughters, and their children and partners! And my enemies, too, for they also enter the story. All the villains in the piece, but nonetheless human for all their villainy.

So, I have at least started the job. I shall make the start by getting all the materials and tools together, then measure and cut and finally polish.

On second thoughts, that might not be the right way to go about it. Better perhaps just to write and then get the facts later: the dates, the names, the events are all there when I need them. Or I hope so! I shall send Joe a photocopy of this first page of my notebook, as a thank you for telling me to get on with the job.

'When I give food to the poor they call me a saint. When I ask why the poor have no food, they call me a communist.'
– Brazilian Archbishop Helder Camara (*Morning Star*, 10 June 1994)

To a child the world is a wonder and delight, turmoil of imagination, of fears, a yearning for love, and a seeking for self. Darkness bursting into light.

The winter mornings are biting cold, sharp frost on the ground, a far cry from the breathless heat of summer.

Poverty. Vests and underpants. A refinement that only came much later in life.

Mud floors, karosses on the floor, goats tethered outside the shack, earthy smells, water from the well. A warmth over all. Wrestling young oxen to the ground.

People dying, dying, dying.

Why, when I dwell on my family, do my thoughts turn time and again to why my brother Joe killed himself. Could not bear the carnage.

Why human cruelty?

Fears oppressing

Frustrated angel

Sunlight

A rough sea of emotions, rising and falling with the tide of emotions

Piano notes dropping like sparks.

Galway Bay – the haunting tune, 'Have you ever been across to Robben Island / When the moon shines bright on Table Bay'.

Voices of condemned prisoners.

I can still remember my own version:

> *Have you ever been across the Bay to Robben Island?*
> *When it's just about the closing of the day*
> *You can sit and see the moon rise over Cape Town*
> *And see the sun go down on Table Bay.*
>
> *Have you ever been across to Robben Island?*
> *Where the warders they do curse and they do shout,*
> *And the convicts in the quarry pick and shovel*
> *And have no time to stand and gaze about.*
>
> *Have you ever been across to Robben Island?*
> *When the wind blows cold down corridors*

*And the convicts spread old tattered blankets
Upon the icy concrete floor.*

*Have you ever been across to Robben Island?
When memories of loved ones come to tease
And the sights of softly singing long-term prisoners
Go out and mingle with the ocean breeze.*

*Have you ever been across to Robben Island?
Where the dreams and hopes of men are kept alive
By the courage and the faith of freedom fighters
Who know the golden dawn will soon arrive.*

Here we are. The golden dawn has really arrived. Who knows what the future will bring? It can only be better than it was, however bumpy our progress may be.

I found many of these thoughts and feelings incredibly sad, but my father could turn grief into humour. I was not surprised when he sent a copy of the first page of his book to Joe Berry, who wrote back to Fred, 'I laughed and laughed till I nearly choked on breakfast. Good on yer, mate! It's true that in our lives, making history was more important than writing it – but there comes a time when that history-making needs to be recorded – as we saw it then and now – for the young 'uns who pick up the banner.'

Fred never completed his book and I did not see much of it. He felt that life was too short – he preferred to enjoy living, sipping wine, and spending time with friends and family, especially his grandchildren.

Sarah was also happy, especially because Johnny and his family were nearby. They used to take Busi for little walks, showing her the Egyptian geese on the lawn and watching her swim. They also spent many hours in their white Volkswagen exploring places they had never visited before. Sarah would pack a picnic lunch, put a cool bottle of wine in the boot, look at the map and stick a pin in it. If they liked the look of the place, they would just take off. Sometimes they would like it so much that they'd find a bed and breakfast and explore some more.

One day, they had a scare. Sarah took Ntombi, who was pregnant at the time, and Busi, to Cavendish Square in Claremont to get Busi's uniform for her new school. They went up the escalator and Sarah held on to the black hand rest, but her hand stuck. The escalator kept moving; she was trapped. The moving stairs pulled her and she scraped her legs badly – there was blood everywhere and she ended up in hospital, where she had to have a skin graft. Her body reacted against the anaesthetic, however, and she went blind for a short time. My father teased her once she had regained her sight, saying, 'You chose your timing well! You nearly missed seeing your grandson.' John and Ntombi's son, Sipho, was born on 24 December 1994.

Fred was in a terrible state while Sarah was in hospital. He would phone the hospital every hour to see how she was and then count the minutes to visiting hours. He was unable to concentrate, even on reading the newspapers, and tried to calm himself by making numerous cups of tea. He could not do enough to look after her when she came out. The accident brought home to him how much he loved and appreciated my mother. I found this entry in his notebook, dated 14 September 1994:

> I brought Sarah home from hospital this morning, still traumatised by the operation and woozy from the anaesthetic. At the hospital I helped her dress, pulling on her panties and her stockings, tying up her shoes. Now she lies sleeping in her own bed, lost in her own world, completely relaxed. I look on her and look and look, seeing and feeling with an ever-increasing intensity of love and recognition. What do I see? A mop of thinning grey hair, tiny eyelids, a snub nose, full lips relaxed. I look and look and my heart is filled with love and tenderness – and sorrow and guilt at all the hurt and grief I know I have caused her in the stormy years of our marriage.
>
> I think of the children she has borne, our two daughters and our son. What were her emotions as she carried them in her womb? Can I or any man ever hope to know or share the secrets of creating life? Oh, blessed indeed is the mother. There she sleeps; my mate, and I wish and wish and wish her well.

39

Late Life Love

Once Sarah had recovered from her skin-graft operation, she started to become restless. She was not used to living in a flat and missed not being able to go out into her own garden. For nearly two years she had been nagging Fred, 'We have been here long enough. I want to move to a house.' Fred's response had been either, 'Let's discuss this later; I'm busy', or, 'I don't want to talk about it'. He was happy and settled. Sarah badgered him for so long that eventually he agreed to look for a house. Once he had made the decision, he went out looking in earnest, and on the same day found a house in Kirstenhof, in the southern suburbs of Cape Town. He came back and said to my mother, 'Sarah, I have found just what you want.' And it was. They bought it straight away. I bought their flat from them so that I would have a base in Cape Town.

They moved to 49 St Joan's Road at the beginning of 1995. The house was a light, L-shaped single-storey with three bedrooms. The large sitting room had French doors that opened out onto a patio, which extended to a garden with a swimming pool. Round the back of the whitewashed house was a veranda covered with vines to provide shade, which would be perfect for eating outside. There was also plenty of space on the other side of the house, by the kitchen. Opposite the house was an area of green grass and trees, and nearby was a police training centre with beautiful grounds that were open to the public – and even had a pub to which residents were welcome on certain nights of the week, to Fred's delight.

The following five years were the happiest of their lives. Sarah felt that they had time for themselves: 'Those days were some of the best days of our marriage. You know, in the past we were too busy to really get to know each other. If we had an argument, we never had time to ask what the argument was really about. During those five years we were able to relax together in normal circumstances and to do things we really loved doing without any pressure or stress. It was wonderful.'

For Fred, aged seventy-five, 1995 was also important for another reason. He was invited to go to Bologna by Ronnie Kasrils, a member of the Communist Party and former Umkhonto we Sizwe commander. Fred remembered him as a young man in London, full of enthusiasm and coming to Party meetings wearing working men's chunky brown leather boots and an anorak.

When Ronnie Kasrils contacted Fred in 1995, he was Deputy Minister of Defence. He had been asked to take a deputation of South Africans to Bologna in Italy to commemorate the Second World War. He knew that old comrades like Fred, Wolfie Kodesh and Rusty Bernstein had fought in the battle of Monte Sole, near Bologna, so he phoned them and asked them to visit him at his office in Parliament. Fred entered Ronnie's palatial office beaming and saying, 'You've come up in the world! It's wonderful to have you in government here.' When Ronnie invited them to join the delegation, they said they would love to go; it was a great honour.

In the Battle of Monte Sole, Fred, Wolfie and Rusty had been with a small group of South Africans who fought along the length of Italy and then captured the steep hill – a victory that opened the way for the liberation of Bologna and of Italy. In 1995, they spent four days in Bologna. On the first day they were taken to the mountains near a sleepy village to lay wreaths in the cemetery where the South Africans were buried. The cemetery was beautifully kept and, as they waited, the old war veterans started wandering around, looking at names on the graves.

Ronnie found Fred at one of the graves, tears streaming down his face. He turned away from Ronnie and wept. Then, said Ronnie, 'he came back and put his arm around me. He had found the grave of an old friend, aged twenty-one.' Fred told Ronnie about the battle and the young man. 'What a terrible loss of a young life,' he grieved, shaking his head, his eyes still brimming with tears. 'Just think of the life he could have had if he had not been killed.' Ronnie was deeply moved: 'I saw in Fred such a wonderful compassionate human being, such depth and empathy about the loss of this youngster.' Fred's deep grief also affected Rusty and Wolfie. Rusty felt helpless; he didn't know what to do. Wolfie put his arm around Rusty and watched Fred, who was inconsolable. 'That old bugger,' Wolfie said. 'He cried for all of us; that's what he did.'

On the fifth day they went to the place where the South Africans had captured the Nazi positions, opening the hill for the Allies to advance. Rusty, Wolfie and Fred had been in the thick of the battle: they had pressed up the steep mountain with the Nazi machine guns firing at them. Fred remembered his sergeant, who on his own had attacked the Nazi machine-gun post to put it out of action. He was weeping again. For Ronnie, Fred's weeping 'was of the tears of life'.

The veterans then toured a place where people had been tortured and executed. In this village, between thirty and forty people had been butchered because of their support of the partisans. The old men sat in the tree-lined square and Fred described what had happened. As he looked around, he saw some elderly villagers watching him, and he started talking to them in fluent Italian. They embraced him and soon there was an excited crowd of Italians, old and young, listening to his story in their own language.

Ronnie felt that he could really understand why Fred had fought apartheid in South Africa: 'Fred fought fascism all his life because he knew it. He had a love of life, and went for life, going hammer and tongs. No quarter was given. At this place I saw the immense depth of humanity and feeling for fellow human beings that he possessed. He lived his deep love for people through his politics. I could not have seen this more poignantly than in that valley.'

When Fred came home, he could not stop talking about his trip. He threw himself straight back into his ANC and Communist Party work. He and Sarah were concerned to find that many of the values they believed in – including honesty, discipline, hard work, reading and homework before discussions, humility and selflessness – were sometimes missing among the new members. Sarah would argue, 'These virtues have stood the South African Communist Party and its allies in good stead over many years. We cannot afford to lose them.'

Both Fred and Sarah were irritated by the young generation: 'These people don't know what they are talking about. The buggers are just coasting, out for their own self-interests,' Fred complained. 'It drives me mad when they give lazy, flippant answers to complex and important issues.' Fred and Sarah never stopped arguing the value of honest, disciplined and rigorous political discussions and ideological debates: 'Comrades, you need to understand that practical work on the ground is only meaningful and effective when there is a foundation of political education and strategic thinking.' Both Fred and Sarah tried to persuade newer members at meetings to spend more time thinking.

They spent evenings teaching those who had no understanding of the theoretical basis of Marxism and showing them how to debate: they felt it was important to raise political consciousness and levels of thinking at meetings. They explained that in South Africa there was a difference between racial inequality and class, but as South Africa developed, class differences between the rich and the poor would become as important. Sarah would always ask the hard questions, even if it meant delaying the closure of meetings. She would not allow people to get away with mediocre, badly thought-out decisions.

Even in his seventies, Fred would muck in with everybody else, travelling to Johannesburg with the rank and file in very uncomfortable public transport and staying in basic hostels with comrades. For a young communist like Garth Strachan, Fred 'embodied the unselfish, humble revolutionary'.

In 1996, when Fred was seventy-six, he decided to retire. Yet after three months of retirement he got bored and became active again. He told Ronnie Kasrils, 'Most of our people don't understand the importance of Council. We need to train them. You have to know and understand the ropes. In a transforming situation, the officials will run rings around our people, including the mayor. We mustn't lose sight of the importance of establishing strong councils that fully represent the people's needs. Our people are new to this. They are starting from scratch.'

Although they were fairly active politically, Fred and Sarah spent as much time relaxing together as they could. They enjoyed giving parties and having braais. Sarah loved planning, organising and seeing that everything went smoothly. Fred enjoyed sitting with friends, talking and joking about the old days. He used to talk about the thief in the next-door cell with whom he had managed to communicate when he was in solitary confinement: 'That car thief,' he'd say, 'he was in solitary because he had a habit of escaping. I wish he could have taught me a thing or two!' Fred would chuckle and keep guests amused for hours. He and Sarah also loved to get into intense political discussions and talk with old comrades late into the night.

On 17 June 1996, Sarah had her eightieth birthday party at the house. It was the middle of winter, and the house was cosy, with a large fire. All the old Cape comrades and many of their children came. All Fred and Sarah's children and grandchildren had flown in from different places to be there. Fred stood with his arms around Sarah, beaming: everything had come together for them and they looked relaxed and happy. Fred was more of his old ebullient self and Sarah was less worried about money (they had both been given 'veterans' pensions in honour of the work they had done in the struggle).

After the party, they took themselves off to one of their favourite places – Avalon Springs in Montagu – to escape the rain and cold of Cape Town. Fred, who suffered from arthritis, basked in the comfort of steaming hot water while watching waterfalls tumbling from the red-gold rocks above. He and Sarah loved lying in the warm water at night, gazing at the myriad stars shining above them and competing with each other to see who could spot the greatest number of falling stars.

They enjoyed travelling and exploring South Africa, Namibia and other countries, and had two favourite places where they loved staying in the Western Cape. One was a cottage they frequently rented in the beautiful, and at that time unspoilt, Betty's Bay. Their old friends and comrades Basil and Norma Jaffe, Athol and Bubbles Thorn and the Richmans had houses there. They used to love walking along the beach, watching the sandpipers hopping along and the waves crashing on the white sand. When Lionel and I came to the Cape on holiday, we would go with them to the Harold Porter National Botanical Garden, which had a river and red disas tumbling down the mountain's rock faces. Lionel was so excited by the plants on the mountainside just above the cottage that he would wake up early and sit outside with my father talking about life and nature.

My parents took me on a number of their excursions, including to a charming English colonial village called Greyton. Many years ago the locals had started building a road across the mountain to McGregor, the next village, but had run out of money. Today this deeply rutted dirt track with shacks on either side is known as 'the road to nowhere'. My parents, then in their late seventies and early eighties, said, 'Let's see where it goes, anyway.' I was worried that the car would break down or that we would be hijacked, but they took no notice of my concerns: they went anyway and nothing happened to them.

Fred and Sarah were not worried about crime, but John, Ruth and I were concerned about their safety. John, who was living and working in King William's Town in the Eastern Cape at the time, was particularly anxious and regularly phoned early in the morning. One day, no one answered. He panicked and phoned Mansoor Jaffer to ask if he would check up on them. Mansoor told John, 'It's the morning of Eid; I'm going to mosque.' He was so worried, however, that he decided not to go to mosque. When he arrived at St Joan's Road, he rang the bell and heard Sarah's 'Hello?' from behind the door. Fred had taken someone to the airport early that morning, and Sarah had taken off her hearing aid. She had heard nothing, but burglars had stolen their TV and video player. The robbers came back for more a few months later, when Fred and Sarah were out. Irritated, they fortified the house by putting up an electric fence, and then decided to get on with their lives as usual. We were all extremely worried, but they were not too bothered. 'Well,' said Fred, 'they have taken most of our valuable possessions, so there is nothing more for them to take. They would be stupid to come back.'

One of my parents' greatest pleasures was when all the family came together over Christmas and for the first few weeks of January. We ate delicious meals prepared by Sarah under the grapevines, fat bunches of sweet green grapes above us. Amid the many jokes, bad puns and laughter, we loved arguing – all talking at the tops of our voices with great delight. Fred enjoyed his food and wine and would doze off, snoring thunderously, which is when we would creep away so that he could have his nap.

Fred loved having children around. He used to encourage Sipho to swim in their swimming pool by getting into the water with him and inventing ball games in the pool. Busi was then a young and very pretty teenager. 'I can't remember not being happy when I was around Grandpa,' she remembered. 'He loved to show me off to his friends and read my poems to them.' Sarah, who was always interested in what was happening to her family and friends, enjoyed playing Scrabble or Rummikub with anyone who wanted to play. She was also an enthusiastic gardener, liked going to the nursery to buy her favourite plants and had colourful flowers all year round.

Januaries were a good time for us: my father's birthday was on 13 January, Ruth's on 18 January and mine on 24 January. We always celebrated our birthdays together by driving out of Cape Town through the mountains to an excellent restaurant, La Petite Ferme, in Franschhoek, which was situated on the side of a mountain, overlooking vineyards. We established a tradition that we ordered all the desserts on the menu and passed them around so that we could all dig our spoons in and have a taste of each one. After lunch, we would spread the blankets we'd brought on the lawn below the restaurant. Everyone would fall asleep under the large oak trees and wake up refreshed for the journey back through the mountains to Cape Town.

On 14 November 1999, Lionel and I were married in England. I was fifty-five and Lionel was a year younger. We decided to have a second wedding in Cape Town and arranged it for 22 December. When we arrived at my parents' house, we were impressed by a large, colourful flower display on the sideboard. 'There is a history to that,' said my father. He told me that, the week before, he and my mother had appeared on TV on a programme about H.A. and Pauline Naidoo. A week later, the doorbell rang. There was a black man standing there with a huge bunch of flowers. Fred told him that he did not have any change to buy flowers. The man explained, 'No, I am not here to sell flowers, but to give them.' He had seen the TV programme and explained that he remembered Fred from thirty years back, when he had operated the machine at the printers that produced *New Age*. He had come to pay his respects. This man had come a long way, from Bonteheuwel in the Cape Flats, to bring the flowers. It had taken him almost half the day to travel to my parents' house in Kirstenhof. Fred was speechless, but opened the door wide. 'Come in, comrade. Let's have a cup of tea and talk about old times.' Sarah joined them with a plate of meat and vegetables. 'When was the last time you had a good meal?' she asked the man. They all sat down together and talked about the old days, and the flowers were put in a place of honour in their very best vase.

Lionel and I had our wedding reception at Suikerbossie in Hout Bay, on the side of the mountain with lawns overlooking the shimmering sea. It was large enough for 120 guests – family, friends and old comrades, some of whom had also been in exile. Seeing familiar faces from the past coming to bless our marriage made me realise for the first time in my life that, however young and small I had been growing up in South Africa, and however peripheral I was to their lives, I had been and still was, so many years later, part of that community of comrades who were still together after such difficult times. I realised how much I needed and loved them all. Albie Sachs gave the main speech, mentioning 'L.L.L.' – 'Late Life Love', and saying that he hoped I would persuade Lionel one day to come and live in Cape Town.

'Late Life Love' did not apply only to Lionel and me. It was such a good description of my parents and the blossoming and deepening of their love for each other after so many years of ordeal and separation. We did not know that our wedding reception was one of the last parties that both Fred and Sarah would attend together.

40

'Bella, Ciao'

Goodbye, Beautiful

I woke up one morning
O bella, ciao! Bella, ciao! Bella, ciao, ciao, ciao!
With a premonition of death.
Comrade, if I die,
When I die,
Bury me under the shade of the mountain
And on that mountain
That beautiful mountain
Will grow a flower, a little flower
The flower of liberty

— TRANSLATION OF 'BELLA, CIAO',
ITALIAN SECOND WORLD WAR SONG

MY FATHER CELEBRATED his eightieth birthday at a huge joint birthday party with Brian Bunting on 13 January 2000. They had been close friends and comrades for over sixty years. They had fought together for the liberation of South Africa and had lived to see the successful fruits of their efforts. All the family and over a hundred people were there. It was such a pleasure to see my father dancing joyfully with as many pretty women as he could. My mother, in spite of having to use a frame for balance, was also dancing happily when she was not chatting merrily with friends.

It was therefore a shock when I received the phone call in mid-2000 to say that my father was gravely ill. He had already visited his doctor, Charlie Miller, who had said that he feared it was a brain tumour, but that he would have to confirm after tests had been conducted. Fred asked Charlie if it was safe to go to Montagu for a holiday. Charlie replied, 'If you are going to die anyway, it doesn't matter where you die. So go and enjoy yourself.' Fred and Sarah had a wonderful holiday before Fred collapsed at the hotel.

I cancelled all my work and rushed to Cape Town, extremely anxious and sad. When it was confirmed that he had only two months left, we asked him how he would like to spend his time. We knew that he would gradually lose control of his limbs and that his speech would eventually go, so we took him to his favourite places, knowing that each walk was becoming more difficult for him and that it might be his last.

One of Fred's most loved places was Kirstenbosch, which was blazing with red-hot pokers and winter flowers. It took my father over an hour to walk along a short stretch of flower beds where bright-pink, yellow and dark-red daisy bushes were blooming. He looked intensely at every flower – the number of petals, the stamens, the stalks waving gently in the wind. It was as if he were trying to absorb the memory of each flower and each bush, and was saying goodbye to each petal.

At first Fred was able to walk and talk reasonably well. Then he became more and more unsteady on his feet and his speech started to slur. Still he wanted to live to the fullest and savour every moment that was left of his life. He attempted his favourite walks along the coast for as long as he could. One was from the beach at St James, with its little rock pool and colourful bathing huts, along the coast to Muizenberg, where the long white beach stretched for miles. He would go every day, resting on a bench by a thatched cottage to watch the waves crashing white on the ochre rocks, until he no longer had the strength. It was on one of these walks that he said to me, 'The best times of my life were with the family. The worst were the war and my interrogation. Can you write our story for us? We have been through so much; our story should not be forgotten.' That walk was one of the last times Fred saw his beloved sea. 'My tide is going out too swiftly,' he said.

I resented not spending every minute with my father, but I was working on a major project in Pennsylvania and running my company in London. For the next two months I had to commute between London, Philadelphia and Cape Town to see Fred and the rest of the family as often as possible. In addition to the jet lag, travelling in itself was exhausting. The second time I arrived back in Cape Town, my father had deteriorated considerably. Speech was difficult; he had had a couple more falls and could walk only slowly. But he wanted to keep going. We took him on another favourite walk – along the catwalk on Fish Hoek beach – to see the deep-blue and turquoise water and the flowers along the path. Although it was an effort for him, he got to Sunny Cove, the end of the walk, where he sat on a bench looking at the sea, purple mountains in the distance. He was so proud to have managed it: 'I don't need heaven,' he said very slowly. 'This is it.'

That was the last time. At home, he could still enjoy a cool glass of white wine, and we bought him only the best. When it was a warm day, we used to wheel him out onto the patio so that he could look at the garden and see the reflection of the clouds in the water of the swimming pool. John, Ntombi, Busi and Sipho were there. Five-year-old Sipho was very religious at the time and told my father that he would definitely go to heaven. We asked my father if he was enjoying the warmth of the sun on his back. He smiled and said, 'Jesus wants me for a sunbeam.' Sipho straight away responded, 'Of course he doesn't want you for a sunbeam. He wants you for an angel.'

Ronnie Kasrils, who was there at the time, said that Fred never lost his sense of humour: 'He was joking with me right to the day before he died.' The funniest joke for my father came from his doctor, Charlie Miller. Charlie was very fond of Fred and the whole family, and used to visit the house at least once a day to see if my father was comfortable. One day, he told Fred, 'Life is a sexually transmitted, terminal disease.' My father thought that this was hilarious; he repeated it to all his visitors.

Most of the time, however, he was struggling hard to cope, even though he put on a brave face. One day after supper, the phone rang. A very familiar voice was on the other end of the phone: 'This is Nelson speaking. Why did you not tell me that Fred was sick?' Mandela had taken time off from his presidential duties to talk to my father. They spoke on the phone for over twenty minutes, and Fred was very moved by what Mandela said, but he did not want to talk about it.

The last time that I came to see my father was in mid-winter. He was in a wheelchair and, although it was obvious that he was still thinking clearly, the sound that came out of his mouth was almost unintelligible. There was so much he wanted to say about what we needed to do for South Africa. A steady stream of comrades came and went and spent time with him. They would talk, he would respond and they would check that they understood. Luckily, most comprehended where he was coming from and could work out what he was trying to say. At dinner one evening, my father wanted to tell me something important. I knew it was likely to be political, so I guessed what it was and asked him to nod if I was right. What he wanted me to know was that he did not think that 'affirmative action' was working; he wanted me to help find other solutions.

In the evenings, because it was winter, my mother arranged for a fire to be set and we would sit around it with him, sipping whisky and eating caviar on biscuits. It was a sacred, quiet and beautiful time. My mother would be attentive to my father and my father would gaze at her with total adoration. Although I had come to give them support, I felt that I was being given a precious gift in spending that time with them. As he looked at the fire, my father told me, 'That is how I would like to go: first blazing like the logs, then gently burning, then glowing like the embers until they go out, one by one.' As death approached, he said, it would be like part of a poem he remembered: 'Like a ship, coming home from sea, to a safe harbour'. So much of his life had been far from safe.

I was with him the week before he died, and very much hoped that I would see him again. By that time we had arranged a hospital bed for him so that he could be propped up more comfortably. He also had round-the-clock nursing and his main concern was how to help make the nurses' work easier when they were shifting him. I sat beside his bed one day, holding his hand. He was able to look out into the garden. It was a warm day and the window was wide open. A white-and-yellow butterfly flew into the room, hovered over him and flew out again. I could see his eyes following the flight of the butterfly. I said to him, 'Dad, this may be the last time I see you, so I would like to say goodbye.' I told him how much I loved him and how much he meant to me. He just looked at me and said, 'No, I won't say goodbye. You will see me again. It's not goodbye.'

That was the last time I ever saw him alive.

When he was dying, everyone took turns to sit with him, even when he was sleeping or not conscious. My mother spent most of the evenings with him, but his children and especially his grandchildren also sat with him. This included my son Simon, Omri, Ruth's oldest son, and Adam, her younger son. Adam used to sit at his grandfather's bed strong, silent and sympathetic for long periods of time.

Up until his death, many friends and comrades came to pay their respects. Garth Strachan and Ronnie Kasrils saw Fred the day before he died. 'When we went to his bedside just before his death,' Garth said later, 'he whispered, "All passion spent." Both of us were overwhelmed with the feeling of a man who had given his life to the struggle without regret or malice. He had never sought out or been in the limelight or top leadership, but his qualities made him stand out among the very best.'

Wolfie Kodesh, Fred's old comrade who had been with him during the war and worked with him closely over the years, was with Fred when he died on 8 September 2000. 'He just looked as if he were going to sleep,' said Wolfie. 'He looked at peace.'

We were overwhelmed by the number and quality of condolences that came in from all over the world. The very first letter was from Nelson Mandela and his wife Graça.

Fred was cremated in Cape Town. The funeral was organised by the Communist Party and, although we were deeply grateful, the family had to fight for time to speak during the funeral. The hall was packed, and there were many speakers to pay him tribute. Unfortunately, due to food poisoning, I was not able to go to the more public memorial service in Gugulethu, where Fred was well known. The hall there was also packed, and my mother and John spoke. It was extremely lively with a lot of singing and toyi-toying. The Wynberg branches of the SACP and the ANC both said that they would call themselves the 'Fred Carneson Branch' and that there would be a Fred Carneson Day on the date of his death dedicated to demonstrating for a just cause. Although I had not been able to attend, I was very pleased to hear that he had been given a good send-off.

After the memorial service, I had to go back to work in London and America. I was very distressed to leave my mother on her own, even though I knew she would be well looked after by other members of the family and close friends. She told me that the nights were the worst, when she was left alone with her memories and had no Fred to argue with.

When I got back to London, the National Union of Teachers, where my father had worked for so many years, hosted a memorial service for him. Once again the hall was full of people and I was amazed by the extent of my father's activities in England. What was moving was the number of deep friendships that he had made and the many people who had missed him when he had returned to South Africa.

Of all the condolences that we received, I found the one from Wilton Mkwayi to be the most moving.

> To me Fred was like a big tree where I used to rest and have good discussions. Now the big tree has fallen and we should accept that Fred is gone. *Indoda yemadoda ihambile.* His death is a loss that will be irreplaceable.

If the *Guardian, Advance, People's World* and *New Age* newspapers were not published, perhaps a person like me couldn't have known Fred and worked with him. In 1956 when we were arrested for treason, the Big Tree was with us. We were both jailed in the sixties, me in Robben Island and Fred in Pretoria. Just when I was released, he was one of those to tell ex-prisoners what had happened outside of Robben Island.

The very day he died, we heard about Fred's death, even in my small village, and there were phone calls of sadness all over South Africa.

I am very sorry that I am unable to attend the funeral. It is frustrating that I cannot afford the fare.

Sala kahle, and know that we are mourning his death.

Yours in the struggle

Wilton Mkwayi

Epilogue: Was It Worth It?

I**N WRITING THIS** book I hope I have given a picture of what it was like to be white activists during the oppressive years of apartheid. For me, however, the story of Fred and Sarah goes far beyond politics. It is also a love story, and the story of how a marriage and a family can survive against all odds. As a family, we tried to lead as normal a life as possible, but it was difficult. In thinking about our story, I am haunted by two questions: Was the price that my parents and their children paid too high, and, in terms of the legacy they left, were the sacrifices worth it?

My parents' marriage was not easy. They were very different people and, when they were younger, they often argued. They lived apart for longer than they lived together, and much of their communication was through letters. Even so, their love and relationship grew and matured over time. Fred felt that the strength and quality of their marriage had probably derived from what they went through together. Although he found it difficult to express verbally, Fred really loved Sarah. 'Sarah was the safe harbour I could come home to time after time,' he told me. Although Sarah was often irritated by Fred, she enjoyed his sparkle, his sense of fun, his enthusiasm, his love of art and nature and, above all, his total commitment to the struggle. She claims that shared belief 'was the glue that kept us together. We knew that we could not survive unless we supported each other through thick and thin.' What also kept them going was a shared love of life, a sense of adventure and, importantly, a sense of humour. Fred and Sarah agreed that their last twenty years together were the best. These happy times were appreciated by all of their grandchildren, who remember 'sitting and eating as a family under the grapevine, Grandpa with a glass of wine, talking and waving his arms, Granny providing delicious food and helping us with our problems'.

It is impossible to separate their marriage from their political activities.

EPILOGUE

When asked whether, if they could have their time again, they would live the same way, both replied that they would. Fred smiled and said, 'Next time round, I would have been cleverer about not getting arrested.' He knew also that the struggle was by no means over, and he was streetwise about the current challenges facing South Africa. 'Greed, corruption and divisions between people are not new,' he responded when I asked him what he thought of the new South Africa. 'The class struggle is not a bed of roses. Once again, we have to build an army of conscious, selfless cadres to take the battles forward. There is no substitute for hard work and building unity in campaigns to improve the lives of working people.'

While Sarah is grateful that, after all she and other activists went through, apartheid was overthrown, she is not impressed by certain former comrades who 'now act only in their own self-interest'. At ninety-four, as she sits on her patio in her retirement village, she reflects: 'We need to learn from our successes, but also from our mistakes. In human terms we made some mistakes. Expelling people because they did not toe the party line was unacceptable. You shouldn't punish people because they disagree.' Looking at the bright array of flowers she planted in the small bed outside her room, she pauses to think and then continues: 'Also, at first, we judged people when they dropped out or left the country; we didn't realise at the time that some people knew how much they could or could not tackle. We thought they were cowards. It's only with hindsight that we realised some could cope better than others. By toeing the party line we failed to deal with the terrible atrocities carried out by Stalin and Soviet Russian imperialism. On the other hand, had we got involved in that, we might not have been able to focus on our main objective – the liberation of South Africa.'

There are few comrades left, but when they see each other they still enjoy discussing the issues of the day and setting the world to rights. My brother John observes that, for them, all their sacrifices were well worth it:

> They gained enormously in terms of the quality of their lives and thought. This quality was an intense reality, embedded in their many connections, social and intellectual, to vast social movements that spanned continents. Compare their rich lives to those of an average middle-class white South African family during apartheid. I think that the price for them was far more dreadful in terms of being trapped in the sterile culture and spiritual desert of a petty master race.

EPILOGUE

In retrospect, this may have been so. But there were times when it felt as if our difficulties would never end. For us as children, life was tough.

As a child, John experienced a terrible sense of isolation and anxiety. Much later, he wrote:

> My parents were a tiny island of resistance in the vast ocean of white hostility to us. We were isolated. I had my own psychological fractures and agonies that were unique to the children of white activists who were born in the 1950s and 1960s, the days of extreme apartheid. Being in the wrong place at the wrong time, or having a banned book in the house, could and did have dire consequences for them and for me and my sister. To protect us, they [Fred and Sarah] never spoke to me directly or in any detail about the struggle. I had to guess and work things out from vague fears and little clues, and I never grasped more than a tiny fraction of what was going on.

While growing up John was often confused and anxious. As an adult he strove to understand more through academic studies and discussion with various comrades. He felt that what he gained from his childhood was far greater than what he suffered. For John, our parents' activity was worth it:

> What they did do was to share with us in a myriad ways – without any equivocation – their general outlook, moral principles and abhorrence of racism and oppression. The books and music we had in the house gave me an outlook and motivation that set my moral and intellectual course and equipped me with a deeper understanding of society and history. As an adult I also committed to the struggle and the values I learnt as a child influence the choices that I still make today.

In spite of the terrible times my sister Ruth had in her teens, there is no doubt in her mind that she benefited from having parents like Fred and Sarah:

> The most important lesson my parents taught me is that change is possible. It is possible to have a vision of a better world and to make it happen. My parents taught me about courage; they were not afraid to take on the formidable might of the apartheid regime. They combined idealism and pragmatism. They worked hard and methodically and not

for personal gain, but to create a healthier society. To a large extent what they fought for over decades they achieved: a democratic, non-racial South Africa.

Was it worth it? I don't hesitate to say, yes, it was worth it. My parents brought me up to be human and to treat each and every person with respect and compassion. Childhood was not easy; I never had a sense of security or of feeling safe; at any time the house could be raided, my parents would disappear and I wouldn't know if I would ever see them again. But, for me, this was a much better option than to be brought up blinkered and cut off, as the majority of the white community was: the inhuman, racist apartheid system was regarded as the norm. It was dangerous to question the apartheid regime, but my parents taught me to think for myself and to question the status quo.

My parents had friends of all backgrounds; they genuinely cared about people and taught me optimism and a love of life and people. They saved me from white guilt. Being white just happened to be the colour I was born with: I was born in South Africa and therefore I was an African.

I have very similar feelings. My parents were not perfect, but I would not have changed them for anything. I was brought up to believe that, regardless of race, wealth or background, every human being was worthy of respect. They taught me that true leadership has responsibility, courage, honour and integrity. They gave me a deep understanding of the psychological and physical suffering of the poor, which led me to learn compassionate detachment rather than to become overwhelmed by pity. These are precious gifts, even though the price was high. Witnessing cruelty every day and knowing that some of our close friends were imprisoned, betrayed, tortured to death or assassinated leaves scars that will never heal. Yet I experienced – and continue to experience – true and sustained comradeship. Would I have traded the pain for a more comfortable life? Living with real and fallible but caring heroes was well worth the price.

Had it not been for my parents, I might not have understood that it is possible for one to have pride in what one does for its own sake rather than for recognition. They were very humble but also proud of what they were doing. Although life was sometimes hard for me, my inheritance of their love of the arts saved my sanity. I learnt through poetry, literature and music that human suffering was universal and that people could transcend pain through their art. It reassured me of the greatness of humanity.

Without their example and the example of other struggle leaders, I might never have been motivated to build a consultancy that helps leaders to use their power wisely. Rather than being punished for thinking independently and questioning the status quo, I now get paid for it, even though I occasionally get into trouble for speaking my truth.

In personal terms, it seems that we all feel that the benefits were greater than the costs. However, the costs – human suffering and lives that were lost – can be worthwhile only if the legacy that they left behind is valued.

For me, there is no doubt that they and their comrades left a valuable legacy. Not only did they help liberate the country from racialism, but they were an example to the younger comrades, as they set values and standards of respect, integrity and discipline. Because of this many more lives were saved. Many of the people who were educated by and who worked with Fred and Sarah would agree with Garth Strachan, who said, 'They influenced me because of their humility and quiet, calm commitment – a reward in itself which goes beyond the glamour of the limelight.'

According to Pallo Jordan, struggle veteran and Member of Parliament from 1994 to 2009, 'It would have been virtually impossible to sustain an environment of non-racism in South Africa today if there had not been a minority of whites like Fred and Sarah, who visibly diametrically opposed apartheid, who actually lived non-racism and who were persecuted for their pains. It says a great deal about tenacity, perseverance and just plain guts. That is a hell of a legacy.'

Rainbows often appear after stormy times. The end of the rainbow for me is full of treasures far beyond any crock of gold. Were it not for the 'Reds' in the Rainbow and the sacrifices a small band of white activists made to help educate, provide intellectual rigour, discuss, campaign, organise and fund-raise during those divided times, the outcome of the struggle might have been different.

My parents and their comrades come from a different generation and historical time. Although sometimes their language and thoughts seem old-fashioned, they have left us a wonderful legacy on which to build. The fundamental principles of truth and justice for all remain the same. We have our own concerns – fear of global economic collapse or crisis and the effects of human abuse of our environment. We have not yet found a way of stopping wars or a thriving arms trade. We also have to accept that millions, possibly billions, of young people all over the world, including in South

Africa, are likely never to find conventional employment. Although daunting, it also provides an opportunity to review our mindsets and look for better solutions.

South Africa is a good place to be right now. The democracy of South Africa is still very new but, amid the idealism and vision, it also has its share of greedy and corrupt individuals who are abusing their power. They make headlines, but what we don't often hear about are the millions of decent people from every race and background who are taking initiatives and building a better country at ground level. There is no comparison between the South Africa of today and the South Africa of the apartheid era: the country today is a better place.

I leave the reader with two questions. Firstly, can any oppressive regime be overthrown without suffering and self-sacrifice by those who oppose it? Secondly, what is the dream that inspires us today? Perhaps, for all South Africans, it is our time to dream again, and then to dance our dream awake – this time joyfully and in a safer environment.

Finally, I hope that, having read this book, readers will agree with the tribute that the great hero Nelson Mandela expressed in the inscription he wrote for my parents in their copy of *Long Walk to Freedom*: 'To comrades Sarah and Fred, compliments and best wishes to a dynamic couple of veterans whose names will live beyond the grave.'

Appendix: South African 'Comrades'

ONE OF THE themes that emerges in this story is the importance of comradeship. The word 'comrade' is and was used by both the SACP and the ANC to express the quality of a specific relationship between people that is much more than 'colleague' or 'friend' or even 'relative'.

When members of the Communist Party addressed each other as 'comrade', it meant that they shared the same values of Marxist/Leninist ideology and that they were committed to fighting oppression as a group. Because during apartheid South Africa this was usually dangerous and had isolating effects, it meant that comrades were not only politically close, but socially close as well.

As a child, and later as an adult, I came to understand the importance and meaning of true comradeship – not as an academic exercise, but in how the comrades lived their lives in practice.

I have tried to define what 'comrade' means to me and to others, including my mother, in the hope that the use of the term in this book is more fully understood:

A comrade is a like-minded person with whom you work closely.

A comrade has a similar philosophy, belief system and understanding of the world.

A comrade is family; a comrade is part of a close and long-standing community.

For comrades, the collective is more important than the individual.

Comrades are prepared to live and die by their principles.

Comrades are loyal to each other and will stand by each other.

A comrade will do his or her best to give support when needed.

You can trust your life with a good comrade.

A real comrade will never betray you.

During the struggle, the term had similar meaning within the SACP and the ANC. When used by the ANC, it inferred that you belonged to a liberation movement and that you were part of a 'family' that believed in and fought for freedom for your people. 'Comrade' therefore has a wider application than referring purely to members of the Communist Party, given that the ANC is a broad-based organisation spanning many different interest groups.

When I greet a person as 'comrade', I know that we share similar values and, in South Africa, a similar background. There is a feeling of recognition that that person is my brother or sister, my equal as a human being regardless of race, class, colour or creed.

Abbreviations

ANC: African National Congress
BOSS: Bureau of State Security
CID: Criminal Investigation Department
CODESA: Convention for a Democratic South Africa
COSATU: Congress of South African Trade Unions
CPSA: Communist Party of South Africa
GCE: General Certificate of Education
IDASA: Institute for a Democratic Alternative for South Africa
IFP: Inkatha Freedom Party
ILO: International Labour Organisation
MK: Umkhonto we Sizwe
NUT: National Union of Teachers
OAU: Organisation of African Unity
RDP: Reconstruction and Development Programme
SACP: South African Communist Party
SB: Special Branch
UDF: United Democratic Front

Index

The abbreviation 'FC' is used for Fred Carneson, and 'SC' is used for Sarah Carneson.

Aaron, Sam ix–x, 10, 40, 50
Abbey Life 196
Advance 123, 294
African Communist 39, 172
African National Congress *see* ANC
African Queen 129
Alexander, Dora 153
Alexander, Ray ix, 171, 172
Amnesty International 212, 218
Anatomy of a Revolution 169
ANC
    activities of 128, 206, 228–229
    assassination of Paris representative 242
    Bisho massacre 267–268
    bombings 238–239
    Carnesons' frustration with 262
    clashes with IFP 272
    and Communist Party 81
    conferences and seminars 243, 255, 260
    and COSATU 248
    headquarters of 248
    Islington office 237, 239
    and MK 167–168
    negotiations with Nationalist government 240, 252–255, 260, 267–268
    and *New Age* 146
    policy on political prisoners 240–242
    Political Prisoners' Committee 243
    Political Regional Committee 243
    unbanning of 253–254
    Youth League 81
Anti-Apartheid Movement 64, 230
Anti-Apartheid Trade Union Committee 230, 242–243
anti-communism 105, 111, 121
anti-pass demonstrations 128, 129, 133–134, 136–137, 150
    see also pass laws
anti-Semitism 75, 76, 125
apartheid 112, 122–123, 147
April Fool's Day prank on FC 231
Arenstein, Jackie 139
Arenstein, Rowley 39, 209
Argus see Cape Argus

Baker, Douglas 89
Baker, Louis 210
Bantu Authorities Act 122
Barnett, Jack 96, 260, 263, 277
Barnett, Naomi 263, 277
Barsel, Hymie 139
Battle of El Alamein 89
Battle of Monte Sole 283–284
'Bella, Ciao' 289
Ben-Uziel, David 171–172
Bernadt, Himie 9, 63–64, 131, 142, 188
Bernadt, Jean 105, 151, 153
Bernstein, Rusty 93, 139, 178–179, 283–284
Berry, Cicely 176
Berry, Joe 231, 233, 278, 280
Bethel farmers 147
Beyleveld, Piet 44
Bible, the 30–31, 156
Bien Donné prison 153, 156–157

INDEX

birthday celebrations 155, 285–286, 287, 289
Bisho massacre 267–268
Black Beauty 129
Blacks (Urban Areas) Consolidation Act 252
Bodenstein, Minnie 109
Boipatong massacre 267
Bologna, Italy 283–284
bombings 238–239
BOSS 228, 238
Botha, P.W. 252, 253
Brener, Ida (née Rubin, later Reichman) [SC's sister] 24, 28, 45, 70, 75, 78, 79, 96, 108, 109, 158, 212, 214–215, 219
Brener, Jasper 79, 108
Brener, Leo 212
Brener, Roland 108
Brener, William 212
Brener, Zoë 212
British Trade Union Movement 230
Brooks, Alan 40, 41–42
Brown, Doug ('Dougie') 146–147
bugs *see* electronic bugs
Bunting, Brian
   character 121
   friendship with FC 91, 93, 109
   political work and working life 99–100, 102, 165, 171, 172, 227, 262
   Treason Trial 139
   move abroad ix, 172
   on release of Denis Goldberg 240, 242
   attendance at social events 104, 202, 247, 289
Bunting, Sonia 139, 202, 204
Bureau of State Security *see* BOSS
Butcher, Mary *see* Turok, Mary

Cadbury, Evelyn 60–61
Caledon Square Police Station 8–9, 12, 63, 154, 156, 276
Camara, Archbishop Helder 279
Canterbury Tales 166
Cape Argus 40, 45, 273
Cape Times 114
Carneson, Adam [grandson] 234, 251, 292

Carneson, Albert [FC's brother] 82
Carneson, Alfie [FC's brother] 82
Carneson, Annie [FC's aunt] 107
Carneson, Annie [FC's mother] 83–84
Carneson, Anthony [FC's brother] 82, 83, 212
Carneson, Anthony [FC's father] 82–83, 90, 97
Carneson, Bella [FC's aunt] 107, 263
Carneson, Busisiwe ('Busi') [granddaughter] 248, 249–250, 251, 269, 280, 287, 291
Carneson, Fred
   background xv, 82–84
   description 94, 96, 121, 251
   childhood 82–85
   studies 84–85, 194, 213, 225
   first girlfriend 86
   World War II experiences 86–93, 283–284
   poetry of 89, 92, 207
   meets and marries SC 94–100
   homes 98–99, 100–101, 110, 141, 260, 282
   birth of children 96–98, 120, 127
   move to Cape Town 100–101
   leisure activities 102, 120, 145–146, 263–264, 280, 285–287
   temper of 99, 105, 107, 125–126, 165
   arguments with SC 99, 107, 165, 224–225, 282, 295–296
   extramarital affair 107–108
   reconciliations with SC 110, 225–226
   love for SC xiv–xv, 46–47, 232, 280–281, 288, 295–296
   political work and working life ix–x, 85–86, 92, 95, 99–102, 105, 112–113, 121–123, 127–129, 146–147, 163, 168–172, 180, 224, 225, 227–231, 237–240, 242–244, 246, 261–262, 265–266, 270–272, 284–285, 288, 296
   financial hardship 144, 180
   attack on 125–126
   sniper attack on Carneson family 182–184
   banning orders 127–129, 131–132, 178–180

INDEX

life in hiding 150, 152, 161–162, 180–181, 186, 188–189
arrests 3, 5, 106, 138–139, 186–189
interrogation of ix, 11–18, 20–21, 23, 27, 52–53
cracking under torture ix–x, 16–17, 20–21, 36, 44, 47–48, 52–53, 209, 275–278
trials 39–50, 139–147, 148–149
life in prison 8–9, 11–18, 20–38, 53–58, 207–220
solitary confinement 20, 22, 32, 53, 54, 57–58, 64, 221
prison letters withheld 21–22, 25–33, 34–35
visits while in prison 8–9, 27–28, 33, 140, 214–215
smoking habit 24, 209–210
on Ruth's breakdown 67–68
fellow prisoners of 47, 54, 209–210, 285
release from prison 217–222
move to England 221–223
travels to other countries 223–224, 233–234, 246, 247, 248–250, 283–284
women's liberation 205–206, 222
on release of Denis Goldberg 240–241, 242
return to South Africa 255, 259
experiences of crime in SA 266–267, 286–287
autobiography not completed 278–280
eightieth birthday party 289
on 'was it worth it?' 235–236, 296
illness and death xiii, 289–294
Carneson, Hester [FC's sister-in-law] 212, 221
Carneson, Joe [FC's brother] 82, 279
Carneson, John [son]
  birth of 120
  arrest of FC 5, 11
  visit to SC in prison 154–155
  at school in SA 174, 180
  as teenager 18–19
  memories of FC's imprisonment 37–38
  chemistry set of 173–174
  move to England 56–57, 60–63
  life in England 69, 197–199, 201, 206
  relationship with Jenny Naidoo 206
  meets and marries Ntombi Mbhele 246
  birth of children 248, 281
  in Tanzania 248–249
  return to England 251
  return to South Africa 269
  concerned about crime 286
  on 'was it worth it?' 296–297
Carneson, Lynn [daughter]
  diary entries 6–7, 175–177
  on love of literature 31
  poetry of 140, 191
  quoted 114
  birth of 98
  childhood 101, 108, 114, 115–120, 141
  at school 115, 133, 141
  visit to Tebby and Joan Sachs 147–148
  arrest of SC (1960) 151–152
  visits to FC in prison 7–9, 27–28, 140, 143, 214–216
  finding lawyers to defend FC 9–10
  on interrogation of FC 18
  surveillance by Special Branch 150–151, 154, 174
  interrogated 129–130, 154
  relationship with Peter Lawton 173
  studies 55–56, 153, 165–166, 232
  move to England 174–175
  life in England 6, 28, 40, 55–56, 175–177, 195, 229, 232, 235
  United Nations peace march 184–185
  women's liberation 204–206
  relationship with Charles McGregor x, 69, 195–197, 199, 200, 201–202, 217, 232, 235
  birth of son 231–232
  working life 28, 40, 232, 235
  visits to SA 3–10, 265–267, 286, 290–292
  general election (1994) 273
  political activities 28, 168, 173, 174, 229, 273
  correspondence with Denis Goldberg 226, 240

307

INDEX

counselling and therapy 235–236
interest in Native American
  teachings 245
relationship with Lionel Snell 245, 287–288
FC's illness and death 289–292, 293–294
on 'was it worth it?' xvi–xvii, 298–299
Carneson, Mattie [FC's brother] 82
Carneson, Ntombi (née Mbhele) [daughter-in-law] 246, 248–249, 251, 291
Carneson, Ruth [daughter]
  birth of 127
  surveillance by Special Branch 5
  SC's arrest and trial 63–64, 65–67
  memories of FC's imprisonment 37
  poems of 151–152
  at school in SA 65–66, 67, 180, 194
  as teenager 5–6, 18–19
  breakdowns 66–67, 194, 196, 203–204
  move to England 69
  life in England 194, 196, 203–204, 226, 234, 250–251
  letter to FC 199–201
  English boyfriends 226
  relationship with Ed Suleiman 234, 250
  birth of children 234
  visiting Cape Town 262–266
  on 'was it worth it?' 297–298
Carneson, Sarah (née Rubin)
  background xiv–xv, 75–78
  description 158, 237, 251
  illnesses 77, 78, 96, 98, 157, 233, 280–282
  meets and marries FC 94–100
  birth of children 96–98, 120, 127
  homes 98–99, 100–101, 102–103, 110, 141, 163, 193, 202–203, 260, 282
  arguments with FC 99, 107, 165, 224–225, 282, 295–296
  FC's affair 107–108
  reconciliations with FC 110, 225–226
  love for FC 288, 295–296
  working life 4, 41, 59, 79–81, 103, 108–109, 121, 144, 196, 201, 202–203, 231, 246

political and social work 78–81, 99, 128–129, 145, 163–164, 228–229, 231, 237–240, 243, 262, 264–266, 270–272, 284–285
financial hardship 4, 59, 144, 180, 196
on religious beliefs 148
friendship with Dora Tamana 03–104, 228
banning orders 4–5, 127–129, 131–132, 178–180
surveillance by Special Branch 5, 62, 64–65, 69, 132, 150, 179–180
arrests and imprisonment 63–65, 69–70, 151–152, 153–161, 186–188
hunger strike 157
visits to FC in prison 33, 41, 70–71
on interrogation of FC 23
on letters from FC 46–47
move to England 70–71, 193
women's liberation 204–205
travels to other countries 223–224, 233–234, 246, 247, 248–250
return to South Africa 255, 259
eightieth birthday party 285–286
experiences of crime in SA 266–267, 286–287
leisure activities 145–146, 193–194, 202–203, 263–264, 280, 285–287
after FC's death 293
on 'was it worth it?' 235–236, 296
Carneson, Sipho [grandson] 281, 287, 291
Cavendish Square, accident at 280–281
Central Committee of Communist Party 39, 105, 106, 124, 157, 167
  see also CPSA; SACP
Central School of Speech and Drama, London 3, 165–166, 175, 176
chess playing, in prison 54
Chetty family 117
Christian Action, London 10
Churchill, Winston 105
Clarion 123
Clissold Park School 40
CODESA talks 267
Cohen, Maurice 5

INDEX

Cold War 184
Comins, Hilda (née Carneson)
   [FC's sister] 82, 212, 221
Committee for the Banished 145
Commonwealth Conference 239
communism xvi, 100, 254
Communist Party of South Africa
   see CPSA
Congress Alliance 135
Congress of South African Trade Unions
   see COSATU
Congress of the People 134, 135–136
Convention for a Democratic South
   Africa see CODESA talks
Corbett, Justice Michael 50
COSATU 248
CPSA 78–79, 81, 100, 104, 114, 121
   see also SACP
Crawford, Joyce 153
crime in South Africa 266–267, 286–287
   see also violence in South Africa
Cry, the Beloved Country 85

Dadoo, Yusuf 80–81
Das Kapital 78
De Crespigny, Caroline 39, 59, 186–188
Defence and Aid 9–10
Defiance Campaign 123
Defiance Trial 144
De Klerk, F.W. 253, 267–268, 273–274
De Lange, Johnny 265
democratic election (1994) *see* general
   election (1994)
Diamond, Mike 94
Dick, Nancy 153
Die Burger 125
District Six 104
Downs, Aggie (née Carneson)
   [FC's sister] 82, 221
Duke's 10th Brigade Signal Company
   87–89
Du Preez, Barney John 197–198, 210

Eaton Square 222
Edinburgh Castle 62
Eggert, Simon x, 39

Eid 117
El Alamein, Battle of 89
election *see* general election
electronic bugs 4, 6, 59
Elk, Black 245

Fabian Society 76
Fairston, Kate ('Katie', 'Kay') (née Rubin,
   later Bergen) [SC's sister] 75, 77, 78,
   109, 165, 175, 176
Fairston, Sol 175
feminism 204–206, 222
Ferreira, Mr 12
Fighting Talk 100
First, Ruth 139, 147, 238–239
Fischer, Bram 11, 16–17, 24, 35, 39, 182,
   209–210, 216, 223
Fischer, Molly 216
Fischer, Paul 216
food in prison 30, 141, 156–157, 211, 217
Foreman, Sadie 154
Freedom Charter 128, 129, 134–137,
   243–244, 261, 271
Fučik, Julius 20, 32

Gandhi, Mohandas 106
garden metaphor 25, 26–27
general election (1966) 34–35
general election (1994) xv, 270, 272–274
General Law Amendment Act 39
Ginsberg, Allen 177
Goldberg, Alex 77, 112
Goldberg, Annie 123, 153
Goldberg, Denis
   friendship with FC 38, 67–68, 123, 209
   on attack on FC 125
   Umkhonto we Sizwe 170
   takes test tubes from chemistry set
      173–174
   Rivonia Trial 178–179
   correspondence with Lynn Carneson
      226, 240
   release of 240–242
   mentioned by Bernie Gosschalk 275
Goldberg, Esmé 193, 226, 242
Golden Grove Primary School 133

INDEX

Good Hope School 115, 180
Gordon-Fish, Zelda 275–278
Gosschalk, Bernard ('Bernie') x, 39, 51–52, 171, 275–277
Gosschalk, Ruth 52, 131–132, 145, 276
Graves, Robert 177
Great Depression 76, 85
Greenwood, Mr 124–125, 164
Greyshirts 97
Group Areas Act 122
Guardian 102, 104, 105, 106, 111, 122, 123, 259, 294

Hani, Chris ix, 171, 172, 262, 265, 269–270
Harare Declaration 253
Hardcastle, Justin 265
Hayter, Sir William 197
Hepple, Bob 178–179
Hlapane, Bartholomew 40, 44–45
Hofmeyr, Willie 265
Holloway, Major 86–89
Holmes, Mr 133
Hopkins, Gerard Manley 153
Horovitz, Crystal 151
Horovitz, Natie 151
Hughes, Lord Bob 230
Human Rights Commission 267
Huna, Mrs 60
Huna, Bernard 178
hunger strike by prisoners 157
Hutton, Anne and David 3, 10, 50

IDASA 252–253
IFP 252, 267, 272
illegal literature 127, 129–130, 163, 187
Immorality Amendment Act 122
Inkatha Freedom Party *see* IFP
Inky (pet dog) 130, 138, 139–140, 146
Institute for a Democratic Alternative for South Africa *see* IDASA
International Labour Organisation (ILO) 253
International Red Cross 208–209, 211, 212
interrogation of prisoners ix, 7, 12–18, 21, 51–53, 154, 178

Jaffe, Basil 152, 161, 259, 286
Jaffe, Norma 259, 286
Jaffer family 117
Jaffer, Kay 271
Jaffer, Mansoor 271, 286
Jewell, Gillian x, 39, 186–188
Joffe, Joel 70, 196
Johannes, George 238, 242, 255
Jordan, Pallo 169, 179, 243–244, 299
Joseph, Helen 149
Joseph, Paul 139
Juta's book shop 27

Kahn, Sam 112
Kasrils, Ronnie 267, 283–284, 285, 291, 292
Kathrada, Ahmed 149, 178–179
Kennedy, Judge Alexander 144
Kent, Lucille 133
Kerouac, Jack 177
Kessling, Mr 105
King, Dr Tracy 98
Kitson, Dave 195
Klein, Mavis 235
Klopper, General 88
Kodesh, Wolfie 93, 229, 251, 259, 283–284, 293
Kompol 217
Kompol building, Pretoria 14
Kotane, Moses 81, 101, 139, 226–227

Labour Party (SA) 77–78
Labour Party (UK) 243
La Guma, Alex ix, 39, 52, 116–117, 139, 171, 172
La Guma, Blanche 52, 116–117, 131–132, 139, 145, 193–194
Lategan, Mr 39
Lawton, Peter 173
Lazarus, Ruth 108
Learning Through Drama 235
Lee-Warden, Len 179
legislation, South Africa 39, 50, 112, 114, 121, 122–123, 182, 252, 284
Leighton Park School 69, 197, 198–199
Lenin Peace Prize 223

INDEX

Lesser, Andrew 199
letter bombs 238–239
letters
  importance of 207–208
  unsent letters from FC 21–22
  from Bernie Gosschalk about
    FC 275–277
  from Charles McGregor to
    FC (1971) 217
  from Denis Goldberg to Lynn
    Carneson (1984) 241–242
  from FC, read at wedding x, 202
  from FC to authorities 68, 182–184,
    197–198, 208
  from FC to children (1966) 36–37
  from FC to Lynn Carneson 35–36,
    43–44, 45–46, 47, 205–206, 211,
    263–264
  from FC to SC (1956) 141–143
  from FC to SC (1960) 158–159
  from FC to SC (1965) 23–24
  from FC to SC (1966) 25–26, 28–35, 42,
    46, 48, 54–55, 57, 257
  from FC to SC (1967) 195
  from FC to SC (1968) 201–202, 205
  from FC to SC (1970) 213, 215–216
  from FC to SC (1971) 216–217
  from FC to SC (1972) 218–220
  from Ivan Schermbrucker to Lynn
    Carneson (1970) 213–214
  from John Carneson to FC, returned
    to John (1967) 197–198
  from John Ounsted to FC (1967)
    198–199
  from Louis Baker to Carneson
    family 210
  from Ruth Carneson to FC (1968)
    199–200
  from SC to authorities (1967) 57–58
  from SC to children (1960) 155–156,
    160–161
  from SC to FC 55–56, 194, 202–203,
    219, 220
  from SC to Lynn Carneson 41–42, 61,
    62, 64–65, 179–180, 263–264
  from Thabo Mbeki to FC (1966) 49–50

Levy, Norman 211–212
Lewin, Hugh 38, 210
Liberal Studies Group 78
Liliesleaf farm 178
Lives of the Great Philosophers, The 85
Logue, Christopher 176–177
Loza, Elijah ix
Ludorf, Judge Joe 144
Lukhele, Nomvula 273
Lumumba, Patrice 167
Luthuli, Chief Albert 137, 139, 149

Machel, Graça 293
Macmillan, Harold 221
Macmillan family 186
MacNeice, Louis 34
Mafu, Dumisani ('Mazolo') 144,
  246–247, 269
Mafu, Nontobeko ('Bongi') 229,
  246–247, 262, 269
Magennis, Father 67, 70, 195
Malan, D.F. 111
Malindi, Lettie 60
Malindi, Zolli 39, 124, 136, 150
Mandela, Nelson
  Umkhonto we Sizwe 167–168
  Treason Trial 139, 143, 149
  Rivonia Trial 178–179
  negotiations with Nationalist
    government 240, 252, 253–254,
    267–268
  at first legal ANC conference 260
  public appeal for stability 270
  becomes first black president of SA xv,
    273–274
  inscription written for FC and SC 300
  telephone conversation with FC 291
  condolences to FC's family 293
Mandela, Winnie 255
'Man with the Silver Belly
  Button, The' 181
Maritzburg College 84–85
Mbeki, Govan 178–179, 260
Mbeki, Thabo 49–50, 252–253, 255, 260
McGregor, Charles x, 69, 195–197, 199,
  200, 201, 217, 232, 235

INDEX

McGregor, Dorothy 196
McGregor, Kenneth 195–196
McGregor, Lee 77
McGregor, Simon 231–232, 235, 240, 292
meeting places, secret ix, 161, 170–171, 180, 186
Mhlaba, Raymond 178–179
Miller, Charlie 289–290, 291
miners' strikes 78, 105–106
Mini, Vuyisile 174
Ministry of Justice 217–218
Minna [Lynn Carneson's nanny] 115–116, 118–120, 128
MK *see* Umkhonto we Sizwe
Mkwayi, Wilton 293–294
Modern Youth Society 124
Mongolian ambassador 230
Monte Sole, Battle of 283–284
Morley-Turner, John 163–164
Morning Star 201, 231, 246, 279
Moscow News 94
Motsoaledi, Elias 170, 178–179
Mount Pleasant 4, 110, 133, 138, 153, 163, 180
Mphuma, Josie 79
Msimang, Mendi 239, 247
Mtshali, Oswald Joseph 20
mushroom picking 59, 145, 161, 195

Naidoo, Dr Goonam 94, 98
Naidoo, H.A. 80, 112, 128, 288
Naidoo, Jenny 206
Naidoo, Karen 112
Naidoo, Pauline 96, 112, 128, 206, 288
Naidoo, Sandra 112, 128
National Party 100, 105, 109, 111, 112, 128, 240, 252, 267–268, 270
National Union of Distributive Workers 80
National Union of Teachers 225, 246, 293
Native American teachings 245
Native Representative Council 111, 122
Nazi movement, South African 97
Neame, Sylvia 39
New Age 52, 60, 123, 124, 127, 139, 146, 147, 163, 169, 179, 259, 288, 294

news, prisoners' lack of 211–212
New Year's Eve parties 104–105
Ngudle, Looksmart ix, 12, 164, 169, 178, 275–276, 277
nightmares 5, 19, 155
Nokwe, Duma 39
Notes from the Gallows 20
NUT *see* National Union of Teachers

OAU 253
Old Fort prison, Johannesburg 139, 143
Opie, Lionel 7
Organisation of African Unity *see* OAU
Osman, Achmat 171
Ounsted, John 198–199

Pan Africanist Congress 167
pass laws 122–123
    see also anti-pass demonstrations
People's Book Shop 94, 95
People's World 294
Pillay, Vella 230
police force strike (1939) 81
Political Prisoners' Committee 243
Pollsmoor Prison, Cape Town 21, 40, 53, 54, 58
Population Registration Act 122
poverty 76, 79, 80, 85, 86, 261, 298
Pretoria Central Prison 23, 57, 179
prison letters *see* letters
prisons *see* food in prison; warders; Bien Donné prison; Caledon Square Police Station; Old Fort prison, Johannesburg; Pollsmoor Prison, Cape Town; Pretoria Central Prison; Robben Island; Roeland Street Prison
Prohibition of Mixed Marriages Act 112

Quakers 60

Radcliffe-Maud, Lord 197
radio, threat to national security 132
Railway and Harbour Workers' Union 79–80, 103
Ramsden, Pamela 245

Reconstruction and Development
    Programme (RDP) 270
Record of Understanding 268
Red Cross 208–209, 211, 212
'Red Flag, The' xvi
Redgrave, Vanessa 177
Reichman, Manny 108
Reitstein, Amy *see* Thornton, Amy
Rhodes Memorial, visit to 115–116
Richman, Michael 64
Richman family 286
Rivonia Trial 167, 178–179, 182, 196
Robben Island 4, 62, 71, 179, 279–280
Roeland Street Prison 52, 140, 152, 153, 156
Roll, Sir Eric 197, 218
Romania, visit to 233–234
Rommel, Erwin 87
Rosenberg, Celia 153
Rousseau, Major 11–12, 15, 183
Ruben, Harold 161, 162
Ruben, Lisa 161
Rubin, Anna [SC's mother] 70, 75–77, 97, 108, 110, 117–118, 132–133, 140, 146, 157, 171–172
Rubin, Eli [SC's uncle] 75, 165
Rubin, Ida *see* Brener, Ida
Rubin, Kate *see* Fairston, Kate
Rubin, Omer 212–213
Rubin, Ralph 171, 212
Rubin, Sarah *see* Carneson, Sarah
Rubin, Solly [SC's brother] 75, 77, 212
Rubin, Zelic [SC's father] 75–78, 108, 110, 117–119
Rumpff, Judge Frans 144
Ryan, Tommy 79–80

Sabotage Act 39, 284
Sachs, Albie
    description of 124
    attendance at social events 202, 288
    underground work 162, 170–171, 172
    interrogation of ix, 39, 51, 52–53, 276
    on FC's interrogation 52–53
    on death of Ruth First 239
    wounded by bombing 253
    on FC and SC ix–xi, 172
Sachs, Joan 147–148, 154
Sachs, Tebby 147, 154
SACP 121, 147, 167–168, 204, 227, 253, 254, 265
    see also CPSA
Sato, Reverend 184–185
Schermbrucker, Ivan 90, 93, 141, 213–214
Schools Council Drama Project 232
Schoon, Marius 38, 250
Sebokeng massacre 255
Sechaba 229, 255
sedition trial 111
Senn, Mr 208–209
September, Dulcie 242
September, Reggie ix, 171, 172, 265
Shakespeare, William (quoted by FC) 26
Shan-Min, Ch'ên 22
Sharpeville massacre 150
Shchedrin, Joan 66, 153
Sibeko, Archie ix, 171, 172, 193
Sibyak (boat) 91
Simons, Professor Jack ix, 172
Sisulu, Albertina 255
Sisulu, Walter 39, 144, 149, 164–165, 178–179, 252, 260
sleep deprivation practices ix, 13–17, 21, 52–53, 276
sleeping on floor 21, 34, 40, 42, 156–157
Slovo, Joe 139, 238–239, 254
Smith, Ian Douglas 35
smoked fish 137
smoking habit of FC 24, 99, 102, 136, 209–210
Smuts, Jan 102, 105–106
Snell, Lionel 245, 286, 287–288
sniper attack on Carneson family 82–184
Socialist Party 124
solitary confinement
    Bernie Gosschalk 51
    FC 20, 22, 53, 57–58, 64, 221, 223, 285
    Rivonia Trial prisoners 178

INDEX

Solomon Mahlangu Freedom College 246, 248–249
songs of prisoners 36, 47
South African Communist Party *see* SACP
South African Congress of Trade Unions 229
South African Railway and Harbour Workers' Union 79–80, 103
Soviet Union 92, 100, 233, 254
Soweto uprising 228
Spark 123, 179, 180
Springbok Legion 90, 99–100, 169
St Alfred's School, Hampstead 194
Stalin, Joseph 97, 100, 296
Stanley, Errol 243
state of emergency (1960) 151, 163
Stephens, Miss 145
Steyn, Dr Colin 127
Strachan, Garth 285, 292–293, 299
sugar-cane workers 80
suicides in prison 7
Suleiman, Ed 234, 250
Suleiman, Julie 234
Suleiman, Omri [grandson] 234, 292
'Sunday Morning' (poem) 34
Suppression of Communism Act 39, 50, 114, 121, 122, 182
surveillance by Special Branch 5, 62, 64–65, 67, 69, 129–130, 132, 150–151, 171, 179–180
Swanepoel, Theuns 12–14, 51
Swart, Minister C.R. 115
Swersky, Mr 29, 34
Swiftdeer, Diane 245
Swiftdeer, Harvey 245

Tabakin family 151, 152
Tale of Two Cities, A 140
Tamana, Dora 103–104, 136, 139, 228
Tambo, Adelaide 247
Tambo, Oliver 149
Taylor, Mr 141, 153
telephones, tapped 6, 10, 163, 179
Terry, Mike 230
Thorn, Athol 259, 260, 286

Thorn, Bubbles 259, 260, 286
Thornton, Amy (née Reitstein) x, 39, 52, 158, 186–188, 260
Tobacco Workers' Union 80
Tobruk 87–88
torture *see* interrogation of prisoners
townships 79, 103–104, 117, 163–164
trade unions 242–243
Treason Trial 43, 138–149
Tshabalala-Msimang, Manto 247
Tsolekile family 259
Turnbull, Dick (FC's alias) 180, 186
Turok, Ben 124, 142, 143, 222, 227
Turok, Mary (née Butcher) 123–124, 204, 224, 227

UDF 267
Ulysses 187
Umkhonto we Sizwe 26, 39, 167–172, 173, 178, 206, 228, 229, 283
Unemployment Amendment Act 112
United Democratic Front *see* UDF
United Nations 70, 108, 184–185, 253
United Party 105, 106, 111
University of Cape Town 166, 169–170, 269

Van Wyk, Mr 7, 61, 64, 69–70, 138
Van Zyl, Dr 66–67
Van Zyl Slabbert, Frederik 252–253
Vaughan, Miss 115
violence in England 238–239
violence in South Africa 147, 150, 228, 255, 267–270
   see also crime in South Africa
Vrygrond 103–104, 136

Wannenberg, Alf 147
warders 30, 41, 45, 46, 187, 197, 198, 210
Warr, Edith 86
Weinberg, Eli 154
Westerford High School 65–66, 141, 153
Western Cape Council 102, 112
Whitman, Walt 95, 158
Wiener family 150, 164

INDEX

women's liberation 204–206, 222
Women's March 136–137
World War I, effect on FC's father 83, 90
World War II 81, 86–93, 99, 283–284
World War 2: People's War 89

Xtumi, story of 118–119

Yengeni family 259

Zulu soldiers, World War II 87
Zuma, Jacob 255

Do you have any comments, suggestions or
feedback about this book or any other Zebra Press titles?
Contact us at **talkback@zebrapress.co.za**